BENJAMIN HAWKINS: INDIAN AGENT

Benjamin Hawkins

Benjamin Hawkins
—Indian Agent

BY

MERRITT B. POUND
HEAD OF THE POLITICAL SCIENCE DEPARTMENT
UNIVERSITY OF GEORGIA

THE UNIVERSITY OF GEORGIA PRESS
ATHENS

Copyright 1951
The University of Georgia Press

Printed in the United States of America

To the memory of my father
Jere Madison Pound (1864-1935)
and of my sister
Ida Elizabeth Pound (1903-1938)
without whose encouragement
this book never would have been written

Contents

Preface _____ ix

I   Early Life_____ I

II   In Continental Congress_____ 13

III   United States Commissioner for Indian Affairs___ 35

IV   In the United States Senate_____ 61

V   The Treaty of Coleraine_____ 81

VI   A Journey Through the Creek Country_____ 99

VII   Tracing Boundary Lines_____ 118

VIII   Life on the Agency_____ 138

IX   Control of the Indians_____ 155

X   Treaties: Negotiations and Enforcement_____ 174

XI   Diplomacy and Commerce_____ 190

XII   Prophets and Propaganda Among the Creeks_____ 211

XIII   The Red Sticks on the War Path_____ 223

XIV   Conclusion _____ 241

Bibliography _____ 251

Index _____ 261

Preface

BENJAMIN Hawkins, more than any other, was responsible for whatever national policy of Indian relations evolved between the Treaty of Paris of 1783 and the end of the War of 1812. Possibly had he lived longer our subsequent treatment of the Southern Indians would have reflected greater credit upon our national character.

My father, a serious student of the Southern Indian, collected a sizeable library of Indian history and lore. Though he never found time for writing during a busy life as school and college administrator, his interest in Hawkins whetted mine and his many notes aided me materially in my early research.

Several sketches have been written of Hawkins and he is referred to in numerous published works but this is, I believe, the first attempt to tell in detail the story of his life or to trace his relations with the Southern Indian tribes. I have endeavored to confine my research as far as possible to primary materials. Official records and correspondence, both published and in manuscript, have been consulted extensively. Many interesting events which have been published by others have been omitted because I have been unable to authenticate them with sources. If the story has thereby lost something in human interest, I can only hope that this loss may have been somewhat compensated for in historical accuracy.

Adequate acknowledgements to the many who have aided my study would extend this introduction to an extreme length. I trust the warmth and sincerity of my personal thanks to each of them will excuse the omission of their names here. However, it would be unpardonable should I not express gratitude to Dean George H. Boyd of the Graduate School of the University of Georgia for making research funds available for publication.

M. B. P.

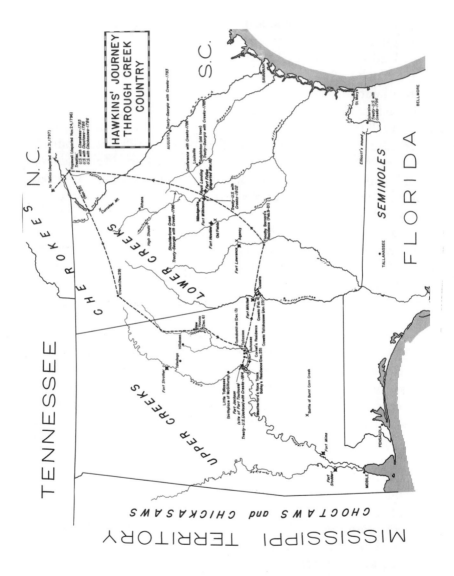

HAWKINS' JOURNEY
THROUGH CREEK
COUNTRY

CHAPTER I

Early Life

IN 1737 Philemon Hawkins, twenty-year-old Virginian, moved with his sixteen-year-old bride into North Carolina and settled on Six Pound Creek in Bute County. There the young couple established a home and founded a family destined to play an important role in the history of North Carolina.

Hawkins was born September 28, 1717, on the Chickahominy River near Todd's bridge in Charles City County, Virginia.[1] His background gave him every assurance of an established place in his community; but, motivated by the pioneer spirit, he chose to seek his fortune on the frontier. One of the first settlers on Six Pound Creek, he was energetic and ambitious and, in the words of the family Bible, "The great Creator blessed him with a great share of health and wealth. . . ."[2] Delia, his wife, was a daughter of Zachariah Martin, also a Virginian of planter stock.

Among their early enterprises was the building of a grist mill, for years the only one in the sparsely settled community. Both were generous and neighborly, Mrs. Hawkins, especially, being kind to the poor and a benefactor to her less fortunate neighbors. When the poorest of the settlers came to the mill with their scanty yield of corn, instead of taking toll from them, she added to their supply from her husband's

---

1. John D. Hawkins, *Oration Commemorative of Col. Philemon Hawkins;* John H. Wheeler, *Historical Sketches of North Carolina*, 426. Wheeler says Hawkins was born in Gloucester County.
2. From an entry in the Hawkins family Bible. A copy of the entries from which this is taken is in North Carolina Historical Commission Library, Raleigh.

cribs and ground all into meal without charge. Despite such unbusinesslike conduct, "the great Creator of us all blessed her with a great share of health and wealth and she lived [until August 20, 1794] to be 73 years of age."[3]

Elkanah Watson has left an interesting account of this unusual woman. Journeying to Warrenton in 1786 he was introduced to Benjamin Hawkins and invited to Pleasant Hill where the latter lived with his parents. Shortly before the introduction Watson had his attention called to a very obese but extremely active woman working at the election polls, though the identity of the lady had not been revealed to him. Later, in amusement, he called Hawkins's attention to her with subsequent embarrassing results. He tells of his arrival at Pleasant Hill:

> Col. H. met me cordially, and I was immediately intro-duced to the lady as his mother. My embarrassment and mortification was evident: but I was most relieved by her kindness and affability from my awkward position. I at once formed one of the members of the family and passed in it several of the most agreeable days. I never met a more sensible, spirited old lady. She was a great politician, and I was assured she had more political influence, and exerted it with greater effect than any man in the county.[4]

William E. Dodd wrote of Philemon Hawkins and his neighbors: "They were good, loyal subjects of King George, rather disposed to follow his Majesty's governors than the eastern oligarchy then so potent in North Carolina affairs. Hawkins actually rose to some rank as an official under Tryon, the best hated of all our English governors."[5] He bore the military title of Colonel, probably as a result of his acting as chief aide to Governor Tryon in the Battle of Alamance.[6]

---

3. *Ibid.*
4. Winslow C. Watson, editor, *Men and Times of the Revolution, or Memoirs of Elkanah Watson*, 251.
5. William E. Dodd, *The Life of Nathaniel Macon*, 10.
6. Wheeler, *Sketches*, 426.

Colonel and Mrs. Hawkins were the parents of four sons and two daughters: Colonel Joseph Hawkins, an officer in the Continental service, who died in 1783; Colonel John Hawkins, the father of five sons, two of whom became generals in the militia, four of whom served in the North Carolina Assembly, and one who served for many years in Congress; Colonel Philemon Hawkins, Jr., father of seven sons, six of whom graduated from the University of North Carolina, and five daughters; Colonel Benjamin Hawkins, the subject of this work; Delia, who married L. Bullock; and Ann, who became Mrs. Macajah Thomas.

So respected was the memory of the father of this large and prominent family that on the 112th anniversary of his birth, twenty-eight years after his death, memorial services were held in his honor at the homeplace in Warren (formerly a part of Bute) County. Colonel John D. Hawkins, son of Philemon Hawkins, Jr., delivered the oration. He paid his tribute to the home life of his grandparents as follows:

> . . . and as they travelled on through life, increasing in wealth, they also increased in respectability and refinement, till at length their house—this house—was the resort of the fashionable and the gay, the men of business and the literati of the country. All found here a plentiful and elegant, and a sumptuous repast. Although Colonel Philemon Hawkins was not himself a man of science, his sons Benjamin and Joseph were, and they lived there with their parents, and added zest to all that was agreeable. The style and fashion of the place was noted and exemplary, and the resort to it from many parts of the world considerable. During the French Revolution in 1793, there were many men of note from France, who resorted here to enjoy the great pleasure of conversing in their own language, which Col. Benjamin Hawkins, from his classical knowledge of it, was able to afford them.[7]

Other witnesses support this account, which might otherwise be thought exaggerated. Elkanah Watson in recounting

7. John D. Hawkins, loc. cit., 9.

his pleasant visit in this house spoke of "social convivialities," deer hunting and other amusements.[8]

Benjamin Hawkins was born on August 15, 1754, in the old home on the north side of the highway about three miles from the Bute County courthouse.[9] Nearly five miles on the opposite side of the courthouse lived Gideon Macon, father of Nathaniel Macon.[10] By the time of the birth of Benjamin, his father, like Gideon Macon and the other planters, was growing tobacco with some success. A road had been opened for the purpose of carrying this staple to market at Petersburg, Virginia, and once a year the Bute County tobacco crop was transported to the marketplace. The journey to Petersburg afforded the Hawkins brothers and their friends, John and Nathaniel Macon, an occasional adventure and fired their ambition to see more of the world.

Gideon Macon and Philemon Hawkins were the two leading citizens of the section. The home of the former was the first in the county to have glass windows instead of heavy wooden shutters, but Hawkins seems to have been the wealthier of the two neighbors, though even his wealth was relatively small in comparison to that of the not-too-distant Virginia planters. As late as 1760 the leading families in Bute owned less than a thousand acres of land and few had more than twenty slaves.[11] Nevertheless, as their holdings increased they became conscious of the defects of frontier life and were concerned lest their sons be deprived of the advantages which they, but not the frontier, could afford. Consequently, in 1766, when Benjamin Hawkins was twelve years of age, his father and the widow of Gideon Macon induced Charles Pettigrew to open a school at the courthouse, nearly equidistant between the two estates. This young pedagogue, later to become a bishop in the Protestant Episcopal Church of

8. Watson, *op. cit.*, 251.
9. The name of the county was changed to Warren in 1779.
10. Joseph Blount Cheshire, *Sketches of Church History in North Carolina*, 228; Dodd, *op. cit.*, 2.
11. Dodd, *op. cit.*, 3.

North Carolina, had a great influence on at least four of his pupils, leading them to seek further knowledge at the College of New Jersey at Princeton. Pettigrew boarded with the Hawkins family and many years later in a letter to Benjamin Hawkins, then an Indian agent on the Georgia frontier, spoke of the pleasant evenings in this hospitable home and of the walks to school with Benjamin and his brother Joseph.[12]

When this first school had suspended, Benjamin and Joseph went with John and Nathaniel Macon to Princeton. Here the Hawkins brothers were in the final year when the American Revolution brought an end to the work of the college. Dr. James Witherspoon, famous and beloved president of the college at the time, tells of the termination of Benjamin's academic career. As the British advanced, students and faculty fled the town. On January 8, 1777, Dr. Witherspoon wrote to his son, David, about the flight. "We carried nothing away of all our effects, but what could be carried upon one team. Benjamin Hawkins drove your mother in the old chair, and I rode the sorrel mare and made John Graham drive the four young colts."[13] The fact that Dr. Witherspoon had confidence in Benjamin and the many references to his ability to read French with ease argue that he was a diligent and accomplished student who profited by his educational experiences.

There is a persistent belief, stated in practically every sketch of Benjamin Hawkins, that he and Joseph entered the Continental forces as soon as they left the classroom. Equally persistent is the opinion that because of Benjamin's proficiency in French he was recommended by Dr. Witherspoon to General Washington and was added to the staff of the Commander-in-Chief as an interpreter.[14] Authentic records are silent, but the persistence of the latter belief in the minds of writers, coupled with the fact that Dr. Witherspoon

12. Cheshire, *op. cit.*, 227-228.
13. *The Christian Advocate*, II (1824), 443; *Journal of American History*, V, 51 note.
14. Dodd, *op. cit.*, 10; Wheeler, *Sketches*, 427.

advised his son David to be diligent in the study of French so that he might aid the American cause by reading letters from and conversing with French officers, makes it the more probable.[15]

John Macon, who had left Princeton for Continental service, returned from Valley Forge in 1778 because of a superabundance of officers. "Benjamin Hawkins, too, was living quietly at home since March or April 1778—more than likely he had returned with John Macon and for similar reasons."[16]

Though the Hawkins family was never strongly democratic, having adopted an aristocratic political philosophy in spite of a frontier abode, its members were extremely loyal to the interests of North Carolina and the other states when the break with England came. This was especially true of Benjamin. Whatever the character of his Continental service and whatever the cause of his return home might have been, he did not long remain idle when work in behalf of his state was to be done. Only twenty-four years of age, with no public record behind him, Hawkins's patriotism and ability were recognized when the Assembly of North Carolina in 1778 named him one of the commissioners to receive, sign, and pay to the public treasurers eight hundred and fifty thousand pounds in bills of credit "for discharging the debts incurred by this state in raising men to Reinforce the Battalions belonging to this state in the Continental Army. . . ."[17]

The service of Hawkins in this capacity was satisfactory and he was subsequently named Commercial Agent for the

---

15. *The Christian Advocate*, II, 443.
16. Dodd, *op. cit.*, 22; cf. Wheeler, *Sketches*, 427, who says Benjamin Hawkins was with Washington at Monmouth, June 28, 1778, and after that time. Practically no letters written by Hawkins before 1780 have been found. The perusal of several hundred written to and by him after that date has failed to reveal any mention of his services in the Continental forces in any capacity. On the other hand, the cordial relationship between him and General Washington is difficult to explain in any other way.
17. *North Carolina State Records*, XXIV, 184. Hereafter to be cited as *N.C.S.R.*

state.[18] In this new position he was instructed to purchase two hundred hogsheads of good tobacco to be shipped abroad, and to proceed as early as possible to France, Spain, Holland, or any other foreign port to purchase supplies of war.

In September, 1779, Governor Caswell laid before the Council of State a letter from Hawkins informing the executive that the Commercial Agent was about to depart for the West Indies and that he "desired to know" what he might barter for salt and to what extent he might pledge the faith and credit of the state.[19] He was authorized to barter one thousand barrels of pork and to borrow 20,000 pounds.[20]

Upon receipt of this authorization Hawkins acted with energy. He purchased on behalf of North Carolina 200,000 pounds of tobacco and chartered a vessel to transport 80,000 pounds to the island of St. Eustatius. Unable to secure vessels for the remainder he was empowered in November to dispose of the surplus at his discretion and to contract in any foreign port for pork not exceeding one thousand barrels.[21]

Sometime within the next three months Hawkins made the trip to the West Indies and informed Governor Caswell from Bath in February, 1780, of his return and the results of his foreign journey as Commercial Agent. Contrary to expectations, he found it impossible to barter tobacco and pork for salt except at severe losses, as the West Indian merchants, realizing the need for salt on the continent, were attempting to profiteer in this commodity. Extensive shipping of tobacco had glutted the market in this staple and, to make matters worse, he could not procure anything on the faith of the state. The price of tobacco was so low in the West Indies that Hawkins reshipped his cargo to Europe in Dutch bottoms and secured an advance payment with which he purchased six hundred stand of arms. On his per-

18. *Ibid.*, XIII, 605-606.
19. *Ibid.*, XXII, 910.
20. *Ibid.*, XIV, 204.
21. *Ibid.*, XIII, 889.

sonal credit he bought eight hundred and seventy-eight other muskets and loaded them at Edenton and Washington, North Carolina. The arms were of good quality and Hawkins arranged to purchase three thousand more and one thousand suits of clothing provided North Carolina could manage to pay for them. He also suggested that state-owned ships would be cheaper for transporting these supplies and munitions because of the exorbitant prevailing war rates, and he asked for authority to draw on the state for the purchase of vessels.[22]

As indicated by this report, the first official duties of Benjamin Hawkins were performed with efficiency and with some degree of success. The failure to carry out his mission to complete success was due to the unstable finances of North Carolina rather than to any lack of initiative on his part.

While performing his duties as Commercial Agent, young Hawkins had opportunity to acquaint himself with the events of the war. In a letter written to Governor Caswell on his return from St. Eustatius, he reported the seizure of a Continental brigantine at Saley, discussed the probable whereabouts of Count D'Estaing, the exploits of John Paul Jones, the possibility of the Dutch joining the English, and the promise of mediation on the part of the King of Prussia and the Empress of Russia. He apologized for the imperfections of his letter, but it showed a grasp of the situation and an ability for analysis and interpretation unusual in one of his years, and extraordinary under the existing conditions of communication.[23]

In 1780 a Board of Commissioners composed of Richard Caswell, Robert Bignall, and Benjamin Hawkins was appointed to carry on trade. This board was empowered to purchase, build, or charter vessels for procuring military stores for the state.[24] Hawkins continued, however, to act on his own initiative and with the same freedom as under his former

---

22. *Ibid.*, XV, 337-339.
23. *Ibid.*
24. *Ibid.*, XXIV, 322; see page 8, note 22, for probable origin of this idea.

commission. The other members of the Board seemed willing to permit him to perform the duties in his own way.

Hawkins made no further voyages to foreign ports but continued to collect supplies in North Carolina. Governor Nash, who had succeeded Caswell, depended on him in addition for military information.[25] In June, 1780, he reported to Nash the condition of the troops in the Wilmington region, the seizure of arms there on his own responsibility, and his orders commandeering supplies, wagons, and livestock. Several officers mentioned in this letter as taking orders from Hawkins were of the rank of colonel.[26]

While acting in his capacity as a commissioner of the Board of Trade, Hawkins was bonded at one million pounds, and by July, 1780, had obtained warrants on the state treasury to the amount of 600,000 pounds.[27]

Next to munitions, salt continued to be the principal commodity Hawkins was ordered to procure. In November he reported that there were one thousand bushels of salt at Wilmington, but he ordered in addition two hundred bushels of "good alum salt" to be delivered there.[28] A month later the Board of War instructed him to concentrate his efforts on securing more to fill a need for four thousand bushels. He was authorized at that time to appoint agents, to seize salt if necessary, and to arrest all persons found speculating in this much needed commodity.[29]

Considerable sums of money continued to pass through his hands, and transactions involving large amounts were often closed simply on his orders, or even upon his personal

25. Wheeler, *Sketches*, 427, says he was aide-de-camp to the Governor. This seems entirely probable and it is possible that he secured the title "Colonel," which he bore the remainder of his life, in this manner rather than from any war service in the Continental forces.
26. *N.C.S.R.*, XIV, 839-840.
27. Governors' Papers, State Series VI, North Carolina Historical Commission Library.
28. *N.C.S.R.*, XV, 374.
29. *Ibid.*, XIV, 476.

credit. He wrote to Thomas Burke in November that he had paid out $27,573 two days before and had procured $6,000 for Burke. He also reported sending horses to Virginia.[30] In June, 1780, James Speed of Edenton district was commissioned to buy corn on Hawkins's order.[31] In August, Henry Young accounted to Governor Nash for the expenditure of 20,000 pounds advanced him by Hawkins for public use.[32] The next month Colonel Joseph Leach reported receipt of 700,000 pounds for one of Hawkins's warrants.[33] Even under inflationary conditions these were considerable sums for a young man of twenty-six to be negotiating, often on his personal responsibility.

When the news of the defeat of the American forces at Camden reached Hawkins he was convalescing from an illness; nevertheless, he took a census of all the wagons in his county and requested each of the principal farmers to furnish teams and vehicles to replace the baggage trains lost in the battle. "I believe we are all Whigs, and I hope we shall not complain at complying with any such requisition for the good of our country should it be greatly more than our proportion. I am impatient to be well, and anxious for to be doing what I can for the common good."[34]

The year of Hawkins's greatest contribution to the winning of independence and his greatest activity as Commercial Agent was 1780; however, in November, 1781, he was buying tobacco in order to pay for cannon he had previously purchased.

Despite large expenditures and the impossibility, under the conditions, of keeping accurate records and correct accounts, no question was raised officially as to the honesty

30. *Ibid.*, XV, 374.
31. *Ibid.*, XIV, 863.
32. *Ibid.*, XV, 23.
33. *Ibid.*, 67. These sums were unquestionably in depreciated Continental or state currency.
34. *Ibid.*, 63-64, letters to Governor Nash, August 24, 1780. This is the first mention in Hawkins's letters of the ill health which continued to plague him at intervals until his death.

of the young agent or the faithful execution of his trust. However, in 1790, the executor of the estate of John Wright Stanly entered suit against Hawkins personally for losses sustained as a result of public purchases from Stanly in June, 1780. The defendant was found by the court not to be personally liable for contracts entered into in his official capacity and no further litigation ensued.[35]

In the midst of official duties Hawkins found time to attend to some of the private interests of his friend, Governor Nash. He wrote the Governor in June, 1780: "Application has been made to me to load your schooner with provisions and send her to Hispaniola. The owners are desirous of doing it as being most advantageous to them. If I bargain with them, I shall bargain for you in the same manner as tho' I was the owner."[36] A short time later he informed Nash that he had collected his deeds to some Roanoke lands.[37]

The training of Benjamin Hawkins, his ability, and the prominence of his family in the northern part of the state, all tended to draw him into politics. It was, however, the manner in which he had executed his trust during the Revolution that inspired in his neighbors a confidence which led them to select him for important local and state offices with no solicitation on his part, despite frequent absences from his county and state as a delegate to Congress.

By an Act of the Legislature of 1784 he was commissioned to sell all public granaries in Warren County which cessation of hostilities had made useless.[38] In the same year by "An Act for Extending the Navigation of the Roanoke River" he was named one of the trustees for clearing those portions of the Roanoke and Don rivers within North Carolina.[39] Upon his return from Congress in 1784 he was elected to represent

35. Martin, et. al., editors, North Carolina Reports, I, 52-53.
36. N.C.S.R., XIV, 863-864.
37. Ibid., XV, 64.
38. Ibid., XXIV, 626.
39. Ibid., 600.

his county in the Assembly,[40] and was elected again in 1788 after further service in Congress.[41]

An activity which engaged Hawkins often in his later life was that of running boundary lines. His first experience in this work came when he was named a commissioner to run the line when a part of Granville County was annexed to Warren in 1787.[42]

Following the war there were signs of an educational renaissance in North Carolina and an insistence by public spirited citizens on better educational facilities for the state. "The men who insisted on this increase in the facilities for education were the graduates of the good old Presbyterian College of New Jersey . . . . "[43] When an act was passed in 1786 to erect an academy in Warrenton, Benjamin Hawkins, several of his kinsmen, and Nathaniel Macon were made members of the Board of Trustees.[44] The greatest recognition of, and testimonial to, the interest of Hawkins in education came when by an act passed in 1789 he was named one of the original trustees of the proposed University of North Carolina.[45] Prior to this honor at the age of thirty-five, he had served his state long and well as a delegate to Congress and the United States with distinction as a member of Indian treaty commissions. A useful public life among friends and equals, a life of comfort and culture, seemed his for the choosing.

40. Madison Papers, V, 22. Library of Congress.
41. N.C.S.R. XII, 655.
42. Ibid., 866.
43. Dodd, op. cit., 53.
44. N.C.S.R., XXIV, 863.
45. Ibid., XXV, 22.

CHAPTER II

In Continental Congress

HAWKINS'S success as Commercial Agent attracted favorable attention from the General Assembly. In July, 1781, as the war was drawing to a close, he was elected to serve as a delegate to Congress. He was subsequently re-elected for a total of five terms and attended four sessions, having declined to serve in 1788 and retiring the following year in favor of his friend Hugh Williamson.

William E. Dodd said of his first election: "Benjamin Hawkins, who was leaning more and more toward the Conservatives, was . . . chosen a delegate to Congress. This indicates the change of sentiment which began [in North Carolina] about this time."[1] He was elected by a large majority of the votes of both Houses of the General Assembly, and Samuel Johnston, William Sharpe, and Ephraim Brevard were chosen as his colleagues.[2]

The North Carolina delegation reached Philadelphia in October, 1781, and Hawkins remained until late April or May, 1782. A part of this time he attended alone. In December, 1781, Governor Martin addressed the Council of State: "The representation of this State in Congress is an object of the first consequence at this crisis, which at present it is deprived of by the death of Mr. Brevard and the resignation of Messrs. Johnston and Sharpe, Mr. Hawkins attending alone without an assistant."[3]

Throughout his first term Hawkins served his state faith-

---

1. Dodd, *op. cit.*, 35.
2. *N.C.S.R.*, XVII, 975.
3. *Ibid.*, XIX, 876.

fully and creditably but without outstanding distinction. He was four times a member of the committee of the week and once chairman of that body. Shortly after his arrival he received his first appointment to a special committee to examine the report of the Board of Treasury. In February, 1782, he became a member of the committee on finance for the settlement of public accounts. The report of this committee recommending measures for paying the war expense obligations was approved.[4]

The committee of states, of which he had become a member, resolved in February, 1782, "That Congress approve the establishment of a mint . . . . "[5] He was also on the committee which in March reported favorably on the admission of Vermont as a state.[6] When this report had been voted down, Hawkins voted against a resolution to send a commissioner to "enforce upon the inhabitants . . . the necessity of their . . . submitting themselves to the jurisdiction of the States of New Hampshire and New York . . . . "[7]

The committee record of Hawkins in his first session is not enlightening. The same may be said of his voting. His first recorded vote, twelve days after his arrival at Philadelphia, seems to have been entirely sectional as North Carolina, South Carolina, Georgia, and Virginia voted down a resolution to hear claims of land companies adverse to the claims of certain states.[8] Later in the session he voted with the same Southern states, plus Maryland, to confiscate all British goods within twelve leagues of the coast. This motion was lost.[9]

North Carolina was frequently deprived of a vote during the 1781-82 session because Hawkins alone represented the state, but he did not neglect her interests. In November, 1781,

4. *Journals of the Continental Congress, 1774-1789*, XXII, 83.
5. *Ibid.*, 87.
6. *Ibid.*, 105.
7. *Ibid.*, 113-114.
8. *Ibid.*, 1058.
9. *Ibid.*, 1148.

he introduced a resolution for the Board of War to deliver 1,000 muskets, 2,000 cartridge boxes, 20,000 cartridges, 6,000 gun flints, and 1,000 musket balls from the stores lately taken from the enemy in Virginia to the delegates of North Carolina.[10] The success of this resolution is attested to in a letter to Abner Nash written two weeks later.

> I have obtained from Congress for our State one thousand stand of arms, in addition to the thousand furnished by the commander in chief, to be delivered immediately to our [or]der at Richmond with Cartridge boxes, Flints, Cartridges, powder & musket Ball, in proportion to the muskets, tho I hope by this [time] you do not need them, as I expect the post at Wilmington will be this month reduced or evacuated, and the enemy be pent up at Charleston . . . until we shall be able to reduce them.[11]

Although his work in Congress was obviously not without success, Hawkins wished to return home. He requested Nash to come to Congress so that he might leave, though he was drawing his monthly pay of $150.00 with regularity and continued to do so through March, in contrast to later periods of service when he was often reduced to want because of failure to receive his pay.

The exact date of his return from this session is unknown. Since he was consulted by Robert Morris, Superintendent of Finance, late in April and was placed on a committee on April 28, his re-election evidently took place while he was en route as, on May 3, Abner Nash, Hugh Williamson, Benjamin Hawkins, and William Blount were elected to Congress for a year.[12]

After a stay of several months at home, Hawkins returned to Philadelphia in December, 1782, and remained there continuously in attendance on Congress for a year, having been

10. *Ibid.*, 1126.
11. Edmund C. Burnett, editor, *Letters of Members of the Continental Congress*, XXIV, 37-38.
12. *N.C.S.R.*, XVI, 95; *Journals of Continental Congress*, XXIV, 37-38.

elected for the third time in the spring.[13] After taking his seat he showed independence by occasionally voting in opposition to his colleagues Williamson and Blount.

William Blount's stay in Congress at this time was very brief. He returned home and resigned. Abner Nash and Richard Dobbs Spaight were elected in April, 1783, to serve with Hawkins and Williamson,[14] but they did not attend. North Carolina was represented throughout the year by only Williamson and Hawkins, and they, disagreeing often, nullified the vote of the state by dividing it.

Hawkins remained in Philadelphia through a sense of duty and at some sacrifice, often completely without funds. He wrote for money in June, 1783,[15] and again in September he addressed Governor Martin:

> I observed to you that I should have no objections to be put in the present delegation & to continue at Congress till the Gentlemen appointed [Nash and Spaight] should be able to come forward with conveniency to themselves. I did not then expect that I should be obliged to continue so long as I must necessarily be, and above all, without any support from the State.
>
> I have for sometime been absolutely without as much money as will support me one day except what I can borrow and perhaps not be able to repay. Surely it can never comport with the dignity of a sovereign State, to let their delegates depend on such humiliating & precarious means for support. How long we could be supported in our own State on a resolution allowing us two hundred dollars p. month, without the money I know not; but of this we are certain no money can be raised here on such security.[16]

No immediate relief came through and in October the two delegates in a joint letter to the governor complained:

> Our situation begins to be very disagreeable; we are now and have been for some time without one shilling of money,

---

13. *N.C.S.R.*, XVI, 783.
14. *Ibid.*, XIX, 269.
15. *Ibid.*, XVI, 837; Burnett, *op. cit.*, VII, 198.
16. *N.C.S.R.*, XVI, 894. Hawkins to Martin, Sept. 27, 1783.

and the prospects formerly held out to us have vanished; our colleagues are not yet arrived, and we know not when to expect them. The Treasurers of all the States in the Union except North Carolina regularly send forward monthly the Salary of their Delegates; we depend on borrowing for our decent support, and fear very shortly that our credit will be like our remittance from our State. How far this will comport with the dignity of a Sovereign State we leave the Chief Magistrate to judge.[17]

The inadequacy of the records of the Continental Congress and the absence of recorded debates make inferences as to a delegate's service, and generalizations thereon, of doubtful validity. However, certain glimmers of light may be revealed by a study of committee assignments, reports, and votes on the commitment of resolutions.

During his second term, Hawkins served more frequently on committees and, in general, on more important ones. He was a member of a grand committee appointed in January, 1783, to devise and report the most effective method of estimating the value of lands in the United States for determining the quotas of the states.[18] In August a committee report in Hawkins's handwriting recommended that Thomas Paine be appointed "Historiographer of the United States."[19]

Perhaps his most important assignment was to the committee which reported on July 28. The legislature of Maryland had directed the Intendant of Revenue to give five months' pay to the soldiers of that state in the army of the United States without the sanction of any act of Congress. In so doing Maryland had revoked an act appropriating the revenue of a particular tax levied to pay requisitions of Congress. The Superintendent of Finances of the United States had remonstrated at the tendency of the act to "subvert the foundations of the public credit." The committee appointed to consider the case was composed of Hawkins, James Duane, and

17. *Ibid.*, 905.
18. *Journals of Continental Congress*, XXIV, 114 note.
19. *Ibid.*, XXIV, 512.

James Madison as chairman. Its report, written by Hawkins, follows in part:

> If acts of Congress most essential to the common interest
> . . . may be defeated by the interference of individual legis-
> lature; if actual grants and appropriations as the Quota due
> from a State towards the pressing burthens of the public may
> be revoked . . . . vain must be every attempt to maintain a
> national character or national credit. . . .
>
> Resolve, That the legislature of the State of Maryland be
> called upon to take into their serious consideration the per-
> nicious tendency of the measure complained of by the Super-
> intendent of Finances.
>
> That the State of Maryland be therefore earnestly required
> to pay into the public treasury the Quota so appropriated
> for the use of the United States by their Legislature. . . .[20]

The wording of this resolution shows definitely that as early as 1783 Hawkins was conscious of the defects of the Articles of Confederation as a constitution and presages his attitude toward the Constitution of 1787.

During this period he was frequently placed on committees dealing with Indian affairs and the West, and he demonstrated the ability and qualifications which led to his later choice for a life of service among the red tribes on the Georgia frontier.

Throughout the year 1783 he and Williamson worked together cordially, but a study of the votes cast indicates that each voted his own convictions. In February Hawkins's vote of "no" nullified Williamson's vote, and that of North Carolina, on a resolution which carried by the affirmative vote of seven states to none. The resolution, prepared by James Madison, provided:

> That it is the opinion of Congress that the establishment of
> permanent and adequate funds on taxes or duties, which
> shall operate generally throughout the United States are in
> dispensably necessary towards doing complete justice to the

---

20. *Ibid.*, 454-455.

public creditors, for restoring public credit and for providing for the future exigencies of war.[21]

Hawkins's vote on this resolution would seem to deny his conservatism and is inconsistent with former votes. In April, however, he voted with the affirmative majority on a resolution recommending to the states that Congress be empowered to levy a tariff on imported goods "as indispensably necessary to the restoration of public credit, and to the punctual and honorable discharge of the public debts . . . ."[22] It is of interest to note that only Rhode Island voted against this early attempt to levy a tariff in Congress, though the vote of New York was nullified by the negative vote of Alexander Hamilton.

On a resolution introduced by James Wilson, of Pennsylvania, and seconded by Alexander Hamilton, to open the doors of Congress during debate, Hawkins voted negatively. His conservatism and respect for authority seemed to commit him to a denial of the principle of freedom of the press when he and Hugh Williamson voted affirmatively with Jacob Read of South Carolina, who introduced the motion to require David C. Claypole, printer of the *Philadelphia Packet*, to reveal by what means a copy of a letter signed by Sir Guy Carleton directed to Elias Boudinot came into his possession. Only two votes were cast in the affirmative, those of North Carolina and Virginia.[23]

When the question of a permanent capital came up for consideration in Congress, the delegation of North Carolina, like those of other states, voted first for the interest of its state and then for sectional compromise. In separate resolutions every state was voted on. Hawkins and Williamson voted "aye" only for North Carolina and Maryland. The attempt to agree upon a state by this method failed, as was expected. On the compromise motion to locate on the Delaware or

---

21. *Ibid.*, 127.
22. *Ibid.*, 261.
23. *Ibid.*, XXV, 540.

the Potomac both North Carolinians voted "aye," but they split on the addition of the Hudson, Hawkins voting negatively. Both opposed elimination of the Potomac, but agreed later to another substitute calling for two capitals, one at or near Georgetown, the other at or near Annapolis.[24]

In October it was finally agreed to move the capital to the lower falls of the Potomac, and Hawkins was appointed chairman of a committee to visit the location and report the proper district for erecting public buildings.[25] A few days after this agreement the North Carolina delegates in a joint letter to Governor Martin explained their votes on the location of the capital and frankly admitted they were influenced by sectional interests.*

> You will readily believe that we contended with zeal for fixing Congress on the waters of Chesapeak Bay. . . . We urged that the center of the United States, if length be considered, is as far South as Georgetown, but when the breadth is considered, the center is 100 miles to the Southward of Georgetown. That a wise government should look forward to the numerous States that are fast rising out of the Western Territory. . . . That our dignity and duration would depend on our regard to Justice and equality. . . . We need hardly inform you that our zeal on this occasion was excited by additional arguments which we did not detail viz, the honor and prosperity of the Southern States.[26]

After the mutiny of the soldiers in Philadelphia in the summer of 1783, Hawkins and Williamson explained in another long letter to Governor Martin their agreement to the removal of the capital to Princeton:

> On the whole we flatter ourselves your Excellency will think with us, that the respect we owe to the Sovereign State we have the honor to represent, required that we should

*The location of the capital came up again when Hawkins was a member of the Senate. For his votes on this matter in 1790 see chapter IV.
24. *Ibid.*, 649-654, 670.
25. *Ibid.*, 770.
26. Burnett, *op. cit.*, VII, 354; *N.C.S.R.*, XVI, 908.

leave a city in which protection was expressly refused us, even though there had not been other motives more closely connected with the public safety.[27]

Both delegates placed the blame for the difficulties of Congress squarely on the states and used the removal to Princeton as argument for a stronger central government and an adequate public treasury as the means toward restoring national honor and safety.

> From your general acquaintance with Civil History you must have observed that the cases are numerous in which armies have overturned the liberties of a nation whom they had been hired to defend. More than half of the Empires now on the face of the Earth have been formed, not like ours by the choice of the people, but by the swords of a mutinous or victorious army. We have nothing to fear from the disposition of our army, provided they could have been paid; but we believe there never was an instance of an army being kept together who were so ill paid as ours, much less of their being disbanded without pay.[28]

Naturally a matter of first importance during the session of 1783 was the ratification and execution of the Treaty of Paris as the definitive end of the Revolution. When the committee on the treaty reported in May it resolved that the several states be required to remove all obstacles to the execution of articles four and six (providing respectively for the recognition of bona fide debts, and no future confiscation and prosecutions on account of war participation), and seriously to consider conformity to article five (restoration of confiscated property). Every state voted unanimously in support of the resolution with the exception of New York, in which delegation Alexander Hamilton cast the only negative vote.[29] Hawkins favored ratification of the treaty, interested himself in foreign affairs and, with an insight into

---

27. *N.C.S.R.*, XVI, 852-855.
28. *Ibid.;* Burnett, *op. cit.*, VII, 246-248.
29. *Journals of Continental Congress*, XXIV, 372.

the international situation, corresponded throughout the summer and fall with James Madison, Governor Martin, Henry Knox, and others. He and Williamson were the authors of a memorial to Congress complaining of the seizure by the British ship *Cormorant* of the *Endeavour* in 1781 while the latter was sailing with permission under a flag of truce with supplies for North Carolina prisoners in Charleston. This memorial was addressed to the General and Admiral at New York and finally forwarded by Sir Guy Carleton to England for adjustment.[30]

The *Journals of the Continental Congress* record that on January 14, 1784, Thomas Jefferson, Elbridge Gerry, William Ellery, Jacob Reade, and Benjamin Hawkins were named as a committee to consider the definitive treaty of 1783 and the joint letter concerning it from John Adams, Benjamin Franklin, and John Jay.[31] Although Hawkins had been elected in May, 1783, to serve as a North Carolina delegate for another year, he had departed for home in December after a full year of service and thus did not participate in the deliberations of this distinguished committee.

After Hawkins's departure Hugh Williamson paid tribute to his service:

> For the general detail of occurences during the last year . . . . I shall now take the liberty of referring you to my worthy friend & honorable colleague Mr. Hawkins who has served during the whole of the last year with so much reputation to himself and advantage to the nation.

Complaining of the number of states not represented and the difficulties resulting therefrom, Williamson concluded:

> I flatter myself that any national misfortunes will never pass to the acct. of the Delegates from our State. Whether we have suffered any personal inconveniences from our attendance during the last 12 months is a question that Mr.

---

30. *N.C.S.R.*, XVI, 823-824.
31. *Journals of Continental Congress*, XXVI, 22.

Hawkins will be able to explain. If several gentlemen had not shrank from such inconvenience we should have had a larger representation for the last eight months and our business might now have been finished, by which means our finances would have been greatly improved and our national honor placed in a favorable point of light.[32]

Upon his departure from Congress in 1783, Hawkins was ineligible for further membership for a period of three years.[33] The interval was by no means spent in idleness and his talents were utilized by the country in an important manner.[34] As soon as the period of his ineligibility ended he was elected twice in three days' time. On December 16, 1786, he was elected for the 1787 session and two days later was chosen to fill the unexpired term of his deceased friend, ex-Governor Abner Nash.[35] His colleagues selected for the regular term were James White, Alexander Martin, John B. Ashe, Timothy Bloodworth, and Thomas Polk.[36]

The session of 1787 was rendered impotent by lack of a quorum more often than earlier sessions. Not until January 17 were seven states represented.[37] After a disagreeable journey Hawkins arrived in Philadelphia and took his seat on February 13. Between the opening of the session and October 27, there were 112 days on which business was transacted. North Carolina, with six delegates, in contrast to some of its former records and those of many states, was represented 104 days by two or more delegates and was surpassed in attendance only by New York and Virginia.

When news of Hawkins's election for the unexpired term of Nash reached Philadelphia, William Blount, formerly a colleague and longtime friend but recently a severe critic, expressed pleasure at the choice. It was confidently expected

---

32. *N.C.S.R.*, XVII, 27.
33. *Articles of Confederation*, Article V.
34. See Chapter III.
35. Burnett, *op. cit.*, VIII, xciii.
36. *N.C.S.R.*, XVIII, 106.
37. *Journals of Continental Congress*, XXXII, vii.

that he would look out for sectional interests, and Blount explained that the arrival of Hawkins and James Madison would make the Southern delegation complete and "the Southern interests will be strong."[38]

The choice of Hawkins to represent his state again indicates that he was still politically strong, but for the first time his record was under attack. His popularity had diminished and bitter political opposition had developed. As United States treaty commissioner to the Southern Indians his actions had antagonized many North Carolinians. Governor Caswell intimated as much to William Blount:

> Mr. Hawkins you informed me has arrived, I was really glad to hear he was so; I have, and always since I knew him, had a warm affection for him and notwithstanding the opinion that some hold respecting his conduct as a Commissioner under the authority of Congress, in the late Indian treaties as Delegate of No. Carolina, I am sure he will discharge his duty to his country in a becoming manner.[39]

Committee assignments for Hawkins during 1787 were generally for the consideration of Indian affairs and frontier conditions, though he served on one or two other committees of importance. In March he was appointed as one of three to whom voluminous papers from Governor Bowdoin and the Massachusetts legislature on Shays' Rebellion were submitted.[40] He also was of the committee which recommended provision by contract for carrying the mails from Portland, Massachusetts, to Savannah by stage.[41]

Hawkins was ever a man of modesty, even to the point of timidity in public. Always a poor speaker, he expressed himself best in private conversation and in letters. His correspondence shows little evidence of vanity or aggressiveness in the interest of personal fame. The frequency with which

38. Burnett, *op. cit.*, VIII, 533. Blount to Caswell.
39. *N.C.S.R.*, XX, 630. Caswell to Blount, May 1, 1787.
40. *Journals of Continental Congress*, XXXII, 105 note.
41. *Ibid.*, XXXIII, 401.

he was appointed to committees dealing with Indians and frontier problems indicates that his colleagues held his opinions on such matters in high regard. He was friend, colleague, and confidant of Thomas Jefferson, and there is some evidence for claiming for him a share of the credit for influencing the form of the Northwest Ordinance. In October, 1783, a committee of which he was a member reported:

> That it will be wise and necessary . . . to erect a district of the western territory into a distinct government . . . that a committee be appointed to report a plan, consistent with the principles of the Confederation, for connecting with the Union by a temporary government, the purchasers and inhabitants of said district, until their numbers . . . shall entitle them to form a constitution for themselves, and as citizens of a free, sovereign and independent state, to be admitted to representation in the Union; provided always that such constitution shall not be incompatible with the republican principles which are the basis of the Constitutions of the respective States in the Union.[42]

This resolution, anticipating to a remarkable degree the Northwest Ordinance, was referred to another committee of which Jefferson was chairman, and which reported the Ordinance in 1784.

When the Northwest Ordinance finally came up for passage, Hawkins had the pleasure of voting for its adoption, and it was passed by the affirmative vote of the eight states in attendance on July 13, 1787. The four Southern seaboard states and Massachusetts, New York, New Jersey, and Delaware were represented in the vote. Yates of New York, who in the same summer played an obstructionist role in the Constitutional Convention, cast the only negative vote.[43]

Prior to the passage of this ordinance Hawkins served on a committee which criticised and recommended changes in the ordinance for surveying and selling the western terri-

---

42. *Ibid.*, XXV, 694.
43. *Ibid.*, XXXII, 343.

tory. In a report submitted to Congress in April, the committee found fault with the methods used because they were too slow and expensive, pointing out that although the Ordinance of 1785 had been in operation for more than two years little more than half of the land had been surveyed because of Indian hostility. It advocated that western lands be sold at a profit for public use and that a public geographer should be appointed for each district to sell direct to individuals and to survey at a nominal fee the lands sold.[44]

Hawkins violently opposed the sale of western lands to speculators or land companies. In July, 1787, it was proposed to sell lands to the Ohio Company by a contract with Samuel Parsons. John Kean of South Carolina moved an amendment, seconded by Hawkins, to advertise the land for three months and then to contract with any persons desiring to buy the lands for personal use.[45] The amendment was lost, and three days later Hawkins and Blount cast the only negative state vote against the sale to Parsons.[46] This was one of the few times that Benjamin Hawkins and William Blount saw eye-to-eye on any question involving western lands. There is no evidence that Hawkins was ever a land speculator. Blount, on the other hand, was probably at the moment an investor and his speculations became greater later on. Because of his insatiate desire for land, when Blount became Governor of the Tennessee Territory he was known to the Creek Indians as The Dirt King (Tucke-mico) and to the Cherokees as The Dirt Captain.

It would be natural to suppose that the man who had represented his state in Congress most frequently under the Articles of Confederation, and who was later to become a first Senator from his state, would have been selected as a delegate to the Constitutional Convention. Although he was in New York when the selection of delegates took place, this

44. *Ibid.*, 167.
45. *Ibid.*, 346.
46. *Ibid.*, 351.

would not have disqualified him, as Blount, who was also in Congress, was appointed by the Governor to fill a vacancy in the delegation.[47] Even Hawkins's reputed disposition to align himself with the conservative element, later to be called Federalists, did not disqualify him. Although the majority of his fellow citizens soon demonstrated a hostility to a change in government, the legislature by manipulation chose a conservative delegation. Hawkins's participation (with the Cherokee Indians) in the unpopular Treaty of Hopewell was probably the real reason he was not selected.

Hawkins, with the majority in Congress, voted against the New York delegation's resolution to call a convention to revise the Articles of Confederation in conformity to the action of the Annapolis Convention of 1786. He favored the substitute Congressional resolution which set the convention for the second Monday in May in Philadelphia "for the sole and express purpose of revising the Articles of Confederation and reporting such alterations as shall . . . render the federal Constitution adequate to the exigencies of government and the preservation of the Union."[48]

On June 18, 1787, Hawkins left New York for Philadelphia in company with William Pierce of Georgia and William Blount, the latter two to take their seats belatedly in the convention hall and the former en route home. The departure of the North Carolinians left their state unrepresented in Congress and, after an absence of only a few days, both were importuned to return to New York, which they did. A long letter from Hawkins to Governor Caswell, written from New York, explained in detail his absence from and return to Congress.

I wrote your Excellency in June and informed you of my intention to return to North Carolina immediately on the arrival of Mr. Burton, and accordingly I set out as early as

47. D. H. Gilpatrick, *Jeffersonian Democracy in North Carolina, 1789-1816*, 30.
48. *Journals of Continental Congress*, XXXII, 72-74.

practicable by way of Philadelphia. Mr. Burton & Mr. Ashe having thought proper to return to North Carolina for reasons which they did assign to you, the State for a short period was unrepresented.

It being of great importance to the Union at this time particularly, that Congress should be and continue in session, His Excellency Richard Caswell, the Members present and the Secretary wrote after me and Mr. Blount & requested our return[.] The letters reached me on the eve of my departure for Virginia, and altho' I had scanty means of support, having not drawn on the public resources and my own being nearly exhausted, yet I determined to return, induced thereto in a great measure from a hope of being able to procure some aid from the Union towards the protection of our Western citizens and of securing and preserving our right to the free and common use of the navigation of the Mississippi.

The first we find impracticable for the want of information, and our having but seven States represented in Congress. But the latter which is very interesting to the Western citizens of the Southern States as it regards their peace and welfare, has at length from a variety of circumstances unnecessary, as well perhaps as improper to relate, been put to a better situation than heretofore. As soon as another state shall arrive and in expectation of the return of Mr. Ashe and Mr. Burton agreeable with their promise, I shall set out again for North Carolina & Mr. Blount to the Convention in Philadelphia . . . . it is indisputably necessary for the well being of the Southern States that they should keep up respectable representatives in Congress until their Rights are perfectly secured.[49]

Hawkins and Blount remained in New York for a month before they had the assurance that their places would be filled. On August 14 Hawkins wrote from Philadelphia:

I shall sail this day for North Carolina. I arrived here a few days past, having had a fever for some days, with Mr. Blount, he continues in Convention. We have rec'd a Letter from Mr. Ashe informing us of his sailing on the 4th Instant from our Country for New York. We do not know who is to be

---

49. *N.C.S.R.*, XX, 735-736; Burnett, *op. cit.*, VIII, 618.

his Colleague. I would return to New York with pleasure if my want of money was not an indispensable object. It is of the first importance that our State be represented when the Convention make their report to Congress and I believe Mr. Burton and Mr. Ashe promised each other to be there then. But if any unforseen accident should frustrate their intention it follows that some others of the Delegation must attend, and I shall put myself in readiness as soon as possible Provided it is necessary for me to return. Since writing the foregoing Mr. Blount has a letter from Colo. Ashe of the 12th from New York, informing that Col. Burton was come by land. . . .[50]

Hawkins proceeded to North Carolina as planned and, though elected to Congress again in September, the third choice in a list of six (only three to serve), he declined in favor of Hugh Williamson who was further down the list but already in New York.[51] His service for his state had never been greatly remunerative and his public duties had prevented the building of a private estate. He reached home, therefore, in need of funds and again addressed the governor from his home in Warren County requesting a warrant on the treasury for six months back pay plus two months pay in lieu of travel allowance.[52]

During the intervals between Hawkins's service in Congress he was frequently in correspondence with prominent citizens and officials. Washington, Jefferson and Madison, among others, sought his opinion as to conditions in North Carolina and the West. Some of this correspondence is of major importance for an understanding of his political beliefs.

In 1784 he had written a long letter to General Washington pointing out a disposition on the part of the North Carolina legislature, in which he was serving at the time as a member of the House, to comply with the views of Congress and to grant it such "powers as may render the Confederation

50. *N.C.S.R.*, XX, 761; Burnett, *op. cit.*, VIII, 639, Hawkins to Caswell.
51. *N.C.S.R.*, XXI, 500.
52. *Ibid.*, XX, 775; Burnett, *op. cit.*, VIII, 645.

more competent to purposes of the Union." He felt that the act for levying North Carolina's proportion of a requisition of one and a half millions would not raise the amount but might lead to showing the states the necessity of their taking effectual measures to enable Congress to meet its obligations. North Carolina had purposely not voted the entire sum requested because of the recent cessions of the western lands of New York, Virginia, and her own. The representatives of the people felt that the state had done its share and that the profits from these lands should be used for governmental expenses. Washington was informed of the contest over the cession of North Carolina's western territory and the passage of the act of cession in the House by the close vote of 53 to 41. He was also told that the recommendations of Congress regarding Article Five of the Treaty of Paris were not being complied with and that some men were "forming the passions of the common people against the refugees." Other citizens were charging speculation and embezzlement to government officials, and criticising the Cincinnati. All of these things Hawkins deplored as disgraceful, but admitted that a little reflection had stopped charges against the soldiers. He personally felt that suspicion ought to rest on those who had "screened themselves in the hour of danger," and not upon the defenders of their liberties.[53]

This correspondence again lends credence to the belief in Hawkins's war service, else how did he become so well acquainted with General Washington by 1784? There is also a persistent belief that he held membership in the Cincinnati. His defense of this society seems to point to the truth of this belief.

A few months later Hawkins wrote James Madison a similar letter concerning local conditions:

53. Jared Sparks, editor, *Correspondence of the American Revolution*, IV, 69-71; Elizabeth G. McPherson, editor, "Unpublished Letters from North Carolinians to Washington," *North Carolina Historical Review*, XII, 159-160.

The cession of the western territory was long debated and opposed by a party powerful in number in the house of Commons but was carried by fifty-three against forty-one. Some of those of the minority have been illiberal in attributing the conduct of some of the advocates for it to improper motives and representing them in their counties as unfit for members of the legislature. A friend informs me that I was accused (as he calls it) at our election in August by a man of much influence tho' of infamous character of being sent to Congress to negotiate the cession, that I was to receive if I succeeded ample compensation by an agency for the disposal of it. The report had such an effect on the electors that I was not elected for the ensuing year.[54]

This was the first political defeat of Hawkins and the first public attack on his integrity and character.

In 1785, while engaged as one of the commissioners of the United States to treat with the Southern Indians, Hawkins had made some statements to the settlers in the West, assuring them, in order to allay their fears, that they would secure fair treatment from Spain and that navigation of the Mississippi would be opened to them. William Blount had issued similar assurances. When Hawkins left Congress in the winter of 1786 a letter was addressed to him and Blount jointly by a representative from Davidson County in the General Assembly: "You told us and particularly Col. Hawkins while he was negotiating with the Southern Indians that everything would go well within the present year, as the Spanish minister was now with Congress to settle any differences that might subsist between them." The writer then complained of the difficulties being encountered with the Spanish on the Mississippi and added as a postscript:

We have received Col. H's letter of the 27th from Warren respecting the giving of the navigation of the Mississippi to Spain is very pleasing to us ... you may depend on our exertions to keep all things quiet, and we agree entirely with

---

54. Madison Papers, V, 22, in Library of Congress.

you, that if our people are once let loose there will be no
stopping of them. . . .[55]

This letter and papers respecting the seizure of the goods
of one Thomas Amis by the Spanish at Natchez were presented to Congress and resulted in a long report by the Secretary of the United States for the Department of Foreign
Affairs, on April 12, 1787. The Secretary stated that it was
well known that Spain would not permit navigation of the
river and that citizens attempting it should take the consequences. He was convinced that, though the United States
had the right of navigation, three alternatives were presented:
a treaty with Spain, preparations for war, or giving up of
navigation. Madison moved and Hawkins, who had again
taken his seat in Congress, seconded that this report be referred to a committee, but the motion was killed by the negative votes of Massachusetts, New York, and Connecticut.[56]

The sympathies of Hawkins and Madison were with the
western citizens and their actions were directed in their behalf. Hawkins, however, was made to bear the brunt of the
criticism of the westerners and their supporters in his home
state. The two men who had served most frequently and inti-
mately with him in Congress were the perpetrators of an
interesting hoax against him. An open letter was addressed
to the "Hon. B.H.," dated Nashville in Davidson County,
May 1, 1787, and printed in the New York Journal and
Weekly Register on July 19. It stated that there were rumors
to the effect that Spain not only claimed sole navigation rights
on the Mississipppi but most of the western territory of the
United States as well. "Their perseverance in such claims
does not well accord with the flattering hopes you gave us
last summer, when you said all would go well in the course
of a year." The writer demanded an explanation of Spain's
actions and denied her claims by quoting the Carolina charter

---

55. *Journals of Continental Congress*, XXXII, 202.
56. *Ibid.*, 189-204.

of 1662, article 27 of the Peace of Paris of 1763, the ninth article of the Treaty of 1783, and the fifth article of the Treaty of Versailles of that year. He further stated that Spain's only title was the "longest sword," and demanded that the West be not sacrificed to the interests of the Atlantic seaboard. The letter concluded with an expression of surprise "That she [Spain] would forfeit the reputation of good faith, and hazard other things that are more substantial, for the mere pleasure of distressing a few honest planters, who are only desirous to paddle their canoes up and down the river Mississippi."

The authorship of this open letter is divulged in a message of William Blount to John Gray written from New York the day it appeared in print.

> Herewith I forward to your address the Papers of today in one of which is contained a letter dated at Nashville May 1st, addressed to the Honorable B. H. You will readily conjecture it was fabricated by a person better informed that [sic] any inhabitant of Davidson County can be and it only remains for me to tell you it has been written on my motion in the first Inst and by my friend H. W. It has been here much applauded as well written and it certainly is well timed. He is not suspected of being the Author. It has been translated into french [sic] and will be published in Paris and London.
>
> I arrived here on the 3rd July from Philadelphia accompanied by Mr. Hawkins.[57]

Whether the embarrassment of Hawkins was a primary object or that this means was used simply to get the attitude of the West across to the Spanish, the records do not divulge. Hawkins seems never to have mentioned this letter in writing.

Whatever the object of the letter, Hawkins, despite his support of the cession of western lands, was sincerely concerned with the interests of the citizens of the West who were

---

57. Burnett, *op. cit.*, VII, 623. H. W. referred to as the author of the letter could have been no other than Hugh Williamson.

not on lands reserved to the Indians by treaty agreement. In March, 1787, he had written to Thomas Jefferson in France expressing the opinion that Spain would be the first state to strengthen "our bonds of union" by her friendly attitude, and mentioning sympathetically the protests of North Carolina, Virginia, and New Jersey over the seizure of boats and the closing of the Mississippi. He criticised Jay's attitude toward the closing of the river as likely to cause difficulties in the West. "Probably our western citizens might skirmish for some years without bringing about an open rupture and within eight or ten we would be able to support our right whatever be done. You may eventually be able to do something." He suggested that France in control of the Floridas, with an entrepot at New Orleans, might stimulate a mutually beneficial trade between that country and the United States, but that even then something might be done with Spain if the United States had a competent man in Madrid. Gardoqui, in his opinion, was not noble enough to acknowledge the errors he had made.[58]

On December 15, 1787, Hawkins, Robert Burton and William Blount, recent delegates in Congress, were requested to attend the Assembly at Tarborough to discuss "the present state and circumstances of the Union." Hawkins addressed the Assembly in the name of the three and made particular reference to the navigation of the Mississippi. North Carolina had already shown its opposition to any treaty with Spain which would give up the use of the river and, in December, a joint resolution demanded full rights of navigation and instructed delegates in Congress for a full declaration.[59]

---

58. McPherson, "Unpublished Letters of North Carolinians to Jefferson," *North Carolina Historical Review*, XII, 254-256. That portion of this letter in which foreign relations were discussed was written in a code used by James Madison and to which Jefferson had a code key.
59. Louise Irby Trenholme, *The Ratification of the Federal Constitution in North Carolina*, 105-106.

CHAPTER III

United States Commissioner
for Indian Affairs

For some time after the treaty of 1783 had recognized the independence of the United States, relations with the Indians were in a condition far from satisfactory. Animosities kindled in the war were not yet quieted. A firm and consistent policy was required, and this was impossible. Even if the individual states had not insisted upon the right of dealing independently with the Indians, Congress was hardly competent to handle the question . . . in the South the states were handling the question according to local interests and prejudices. In consequence the Indian policy was characterized by a greater uncertainty than had prevailed before 1760.[1]

DURING the 1783 session of Congress Hawkins served on committees dealing with Indian problems with increasing frequency. The committee on Indian affairs, composed of James Duane, Richard Peters, Charles Carroll, Benjamin Hawkins, and Arthur Lee, reported on October 15, 1783. In a long series of recommendations, parts of which suggested a government of the western territory, control of the Indian received extended treatment. Congress was cautioned against the dangers of Indian wars and the unfortunate results of attempting to drive the red men out by force. At the same time the committee recognized the necessity of clearing parts of the West in order to carry out pledges as to bounties. It was, therefore, "Resolved, That a Convention be held with the Indians residing in the Northern and Middle

---

1. Max Farrand, "The Indian Boundary Line," *American Historical Review*, X, 789.

departments . . ." to attain the following objects: surrendering of all prisoners by the Indians; informing them of territory ceded by Britain; reminding them that a less generous government might require them to leave its territory because they had sided with England, but that the United States intended to adopt an attitude of friendliness, simply drawing lines beyond which neither the Indians, on the one hand, nor the whites on the other, would be allowed to go; making known to all of the Northwest Indians that the United States would treat collectively with them; and assuring the Oneidas and Tuscaroras, who had remained friendly, of American goodwill and that they would be confirmed in their lands. The committee also suggested that the French inhabitants be assured of friendship and protection but that to all Americans living in the Northwest without authorization Congressional displeasure be made known. It was further recommended that trade with the Indians be strictly regulated "so that violence fraud and injustice toward the Indians may be guarded against and prevented, and the honor of the federal government, and the public tranquility, be thereby promoted."[2]

Hawkins's part in the preparation of this report is a matter of conjecture. However, the plan of Indian control advocated was in keeping with his later actions. He either influenced the committee or was influenced by its report and conformed to the expressed principles in his many dealings with the Indians.

Two months later Hawkins, who had served his constitutional three years, retired from Congress until his eligibility should be restored. During this interval he first represented Congress on diplomatic missions to the Indians.

In 1784 Alexander McGillivray, educated chief of the Creeks, who despite the fact that he was half Scotch, a quarter French and only a quarter Creek was a power among the

2. *Journals of Continental Congress*, XXV, 681-694.

Southern Indians, had written Governor O'Neill of Florida proposing an Indian alliance with Spain. This threat led Congress to appoint a commission to negotiate treaties with the Southern tribes.

John Sitgreaves, delegate from North Carolina, wrote William Blount in March, 1785, that Congress was debating the appointment of commissioners to conclude "lasting peace with the Indians in the Southern Department" and that he desired to nominate either Blount or Hawkins.[3] Benjamin Hawkins, Daniel Carroll, and William Perry were elected. Two additional members, Andrew Pickens and Joseph Martin, were subsequently added to the committee, and any three members were to constitute a quorum.[4] Whether Blount wanted this assignment, or was nominated, is not revealed; but six days after the election Richard Dobbs Spaight, another North Carolina delegate, wrote that Hawkins was favored by eleven of the twelve states voting:

> . . . the jealousy of the circumscribed States, who thought that under the Idea of making peace with the Indians we had some underhand designs, which might be fatal to their claim of equal partition of unlocated western territory among the Members of the Union, occasioned a Mr. Danl. Carrol and a Mr. Perry to be elected his Colleagues, the first from Maryland and the other from Delaware State. They thought that these two persons would be a check upon any designs that the Southern States might have. This of course gave very great dissatisfaction to the Southern States, and occasioned a motion to be brought forward, for the appointment of two additional commissioners, as neither Virginia, So. Carolina or Georgia had one, which after considerable opposition was at last agreed to—the persons elected were Genl. Pickens of So. Carolina and Col. Joseph Martin of our State, he being nominated by the State of Virginia.[5]

---

3. Burnett, *Letters*, VIII, 61; John Gray Blount Papers, North Carolina Historical Commission Library.
4. *N.C.S.R.*, XVII, 431; *Journals*, XXVIII, 183.
5. Burnett, *Letters*, VIII, 75.

Blount, representing North Carolina at the treaty grounds, was the most severe critic of the United States Commission, particularly of his former friend and colleague, Hawkins. Neither Carroll nor Perry appeared at the conference, but the fears of the Northern states concerning the designs of the South were not realized, and it was the Southern states, especially North Carolina and Georgia, who felt themselves aggrieved.

As soon as it was evident that independence from England would be secured, the Southern states became interested in opening up their western lands for the benefit of their citizens. Georgia and North Carolina were determined to eliminate Indian claims. These two states, particularly Georgia, had been unwilling to recognize the exclusive right of Congress to treat with Indians within the boundaries of the states and neither was willing to abide by Article IX of the Articles of Confederation. Accordingly, Georgia had signed a treaty with the Creeks at Augusta in 1783, which the Creeks later repudiated. McGillivray, bitter opponent of Georgia policy, stirred up discontent among the Indians and proclaimed the Treaty of Augusta void. He maintained that the treaty had been signed by the chiefs of only two towns, both of whom were friendly to Georgia and had been in Augusta simply on a visit and not for the purpose of signing a treaty. Despite their friendship they had refused to grant the concessions demanded until they were threatened and coerced by armed Georgians.[6] When the other towns learned of this treaty, the chiefs of a majority of them immediately protested and declared the Nation could not be bound by the unauthorized action of only two towns. Georgia, on the other hand, maintained that the treaty was perfectly valid and determined to enforce it and clear the lands of Indians. Settlers moved in, relations became increasingly strained, and conflicts inevi-

---

6. *American State Papers, Indian Affairs*, I, 19-20, letter to Gov. Thomas Pinckney, Feb. 26, 1789; *ibid.*, 18-19, letter to James White, April 8, 1787.

tably resulted. North Carolina, similarly, wished to move the Cherokees farther west. It was under such conditions that Congress appointed commissioners to treat with the Southern tribes.

Some weeks after Hawkins's appointment he was visited by General Nathanael Greene at his home in Warren County. General Greene invited Hawkins to accompany him to the South where he was going to select a home. The invitation was accepted and after reaching Savannah they set out again to visit his Excellency Don Vincent Emanuel de Zespedes, the Governor of East Florida at St. Augustine. Zespedes entertained them lavishly and heaped honors on General Greene.[7] Upon their return Hawkins stopped in Charleston and began to make plans to carry out his duties as treaty commissioner.

Congress had instructed its commissioners to notify the governors of the interested states of the time and place of holding treaty conferences in order that each state executive might appoint representatives to attend. General Pickens and Joseph Martin had joined Hawkins in Charleston, and in June they notified Governor Caswell of their plans to meet the Creeks at Galphinton, a famous trading post on the Ogeechee River in Georgia, on the third Monday in September, and the Cherokees, Choctaws and Chickasaws "at or near where Fort Rutledge stood on the Keowee" in South Carolina on the second Monday in October. They also informed the governor that Congress had authorized them to call on the states of Georgia, North Carolina, South Carolina and Virginia for a sum not to exceed $13,000 for expenses and presents to the Indians. South Carolina had been able to contribute scarcely enough to pay for immediate expenses and notification of the Indians. Since they felt they would need a guard of one hundred men as a protection the commissioners stated that it would be impossible to carry on

7. George Washington Greene, *Life of Nathanael Greene*, III, 530.

negotiations without the financial support of North Carolina. They, therefore, requested Governor Caswell to provide them with one third of the total amount authorized not later than the second Monday in October.

The commissioners promised to keep all interested states constantly notified of developments but warned Caswell that the Creeks and Cherokees would jointly repel any attempts on the part of disorderly elements to seize their property. They also informed him that certain disorderly whites had stirred up the Indians to a point where they were willing to commence hostilities.[8]

Scarcely had this letter been posted when the commissioners decided the original dates set for the treaties were too early. The following day a letter was addressed to the "Kings, Headmen, and the Warriors of the Creeks," announcing the end of the war, the appointment of commissioners, and a meeting at Galphinton on October 24th.

From Charleston the commissioners went to Savannah seeking unsuccessfully to raise funds. While in Savannah they got in touch with Lachlan McIntosh who had been named to serve with them when William Perry and Daniel Carroll declined.[9]

Governor Caswell made sincere efforts to comply with the requests of the commissioners and, though North Carolina's treasury was practically empty, he tried by every legitimate means to raise funds to further the negotiations.[10] Virginia, likewise, honored the drafts of the commissioners but did not see fit to send an agent of the state in contrast to Georgia which furnished a guard and was otherwise well represented by agents and commissioners but contributed no funds.[11]

As soon as it was known that Congress would negotiate with the Southern Indians, North Carolina selected William

---

8. *N.C.S.R.*, XVII, 473-475.
9. Burnett, *Letters*, VIII, 152 note.
10. *N.C.S.R.*, XVII, 493-494.
11. *Ibid.*, 514-515.

Blount to attend the talks. Blount and Joseph Martin, who was also serving as United States commissioner, were authorized to treat independently with the Cherokees on behalf of North Carolina in the event the congressional commissioners failed to reach an agreement.

On August 24th, the governor transmitted to Blount warrants for one thousand pounds and instructed him to purchase, among other things, six hogsheads of West India rum for the Indians, all goods to be transported to the Keowee River in time for the treaty. North Carolina was determined to secure a treaty with the Cherokees, regardless of the outcome of the negotiations between them and the agents of Congress.[12]

Hawkins wrote Governor Caswell expressing pleasure that William Blount would be present to look out for the interests of North Carolina and pledging himself to make his "situation as agreeable as possible."[13]

Although the difficulty of securing funds and transporting goods had caused postponement of the negotiations by more than a month, Hawkins was optimistic of success, feeling that the Indians would be anxious for peace because of the withdrawal of the British. Congress was not so confident but transmitted to the commissioners copies of the treaties of Fort Stanwix and Fort McIntosh to be shown to the Southern Indians as evidence that the Northern tribes were committed to peace and that a general confederation of the Indians had no hope of success.[14]

The fate of negotiations with the Creeks rested with the capable but unpredictable Chief Alexander McGillivray. He had written General Pickens expressing pleasure at the invitation to attend the treaty conference and also belief that through efforts of the United States commissioners differences would be settled equitably. He had been waiting since

12. *Ibid.*, 510-511.
13. *Ibid.*, 514-515.
14. Burnett, *Letters*, VIII, 224-225.

1783 for such action. McGillivray was harsh in his criticism of Georgia. "Their talks breathed nothing but vengeance . . . ." Despairing of fair treatment at the hands of Georgians, he had signed treaties of friendship and alliance with Spain. He further informed the commissioners that the Creeks were a free nation, knew their own hunting grounds, and would not abide by any boundaries set by the Americans and British, regardless of whatever agreement the United States reached with Spain. Such attitudes, McGillivray continued, had been adopted from necessity. The Indians wanted only justice, their hunting grounds, and the cessation of hostilities. However, he agreed to restrain all predatory parties until after the meeting with the commissioners.[15]

This letter and the determination it revealed boded little success for the negotiations at Galphinton. McGillivray unquestionably kept the Indians away but later blamed the treaty's failure on the neglect of the commissioners, Hawkins in particular, to notify the Indians when and where to come.[16]

One recent writer says of McGillivray:

In 1785 his heart was light and his disappointments were concealed in the glorious mist of the future. Flattered by the consideration with which the Spanish officials treated him and heartened by the supply of munitions that Panton had brought to Pensacola, he gave a cold reception to the peace overtures of the Commissioners of Congress in the fall of 1785.[17]

Before Congress had made any definite plans for treaties with the Southern Indians or had appointed its commissioners, the legislature of Georgia, on February 22, 1785, determined if possible to secure additional lands from the Creeks and to "ascertain and define the line" agreed upon at Augusta in 1783. General Lachlan McIntosh, Colonel

---

15. *American State Papers, Indian Affairs*, I, 17-18.
16. *Ibid.*, 19-20.
17. Arthur Preston Whitaker, "Alexander McGillivray, 1783-1789," *North Carolina Historical Review*, V, 194.

Elijah Clarke, and Colonel Benjamin Hawkins were named as agents for the state to treat with the Indians. Why Hawkins, a North Carolinian, with no previous association with either Georgia or the Creeks should have been chosen is difficult to imagine, though he was requested by Governor Elbert to act for Georgia even after his appointment as a commissioner for the United States was known. Neither private nor official correspondence throws light on his selection and some writers have erroneously assumed from this fact that Hawkins was a Georgian.[18] Both Hawkins and McIntosh declined to serve on two commissions and each accepted the appointment from Congress. John Twiggs was appointed by Georgia in Hawkins's place, and he and Elijah Clarke were the only Georgia commissioners.

When it became known in Georgia that the United States was contemplating a treaty with the Creeks, every effort was made to have the state commission negotiate with the Indians first. Governor Elbert had written the Georgia delegation in Congress protesting the proposed congressional action as disregarding the interests of Georgia and an insult to the state since no Georgian was on the United States commission. It was first decided to meet the Indians at Beard's Bluff, then Savannah, but the plans did not materialize, though Governor Elbert had informed Clarke and Twiggs in June: "It is a business of first consequence to the State, and should not be delayed, especially as the commissioners from Congress will shortly be on the same errand, and if we get thro' with this before they commence, it may be a capital point gained."[19]

Though a conference between Georgia's commission and the Creeks at a different time and place could not be worked out, Georgia planned to have some of her citizens present when the Indians sat down in council with the congressional

---

18. James R. Gilmore, *John Sevier as a Commonwealth Builder,* 61.
19. *Georgia Historical Collections,* V, Part II, 207, Gov. Samuel Elbert to Elijah Clarke, June 9, 1785.

representatives. Accordingly, in addition to Clarke and Twiggs, Edward Telfair, William Few, and James Jackson were appointed to attend the conference "with instructions to aid and assist the commissioners in forwarding this business as far as they are authorized by the Confederation to go; and they are further instructed to protest against any measures which they may adopt contrary to the Articles of Confederation and the Constitution and Laws of the State."[20]

Georgia, accustomed to handling its own Indian affairs, and denying the right of interference of Congress, was not openly defiant, but was determined to be adequately represented when the Indians gathered. Perhaps all prominent Georgians did not accept the official view that the state should continue to treat with the Indians without outside interference. At any rate, William Few and James Jackson refused to attend the conference and were replaced on the "advisory" committee by John King and Thomas Glascock.

When the United States commissioners called upon Governor Samuel Elbert for two thousand dollars expense money he informed them he could not comply but would put their request before the legislature when it next met.[21] He did, however, agree to supply a guard of one hundred men, twenty of them mounted, and this guard was on hand when the conference assembled.

On October 24, 1785, the date set for the beginning of negotiations, the commissioners arrived at Galphinton.[22] After waiting five days they were joined by the chiefs of only two towns and about sixty warriors, though they were assured that the Creeks were well pleased and would eventually arrive. This was evidently a ruse on the part of the Indians

20. *Ibid.*, 220-221, Elbert to William Houstoun, John Habersham and Abraham Baldwin, delegates to Congress, Sept. 14, 1785.
21. *Ibid.*, 212, Elbert to Hawkins, Pickens, and Martin, July 20, 1785.
22. Galphinton, later called Old Town, was located about twelve miles below the present town of Louisville, Georgia. It was then in Indian country but in 1795 Louisville was made the capital of the state.

to secure gifts from the commissioners through professions of friendship. While waiting for the Indians the commissioners showed the agents of Georgia and North Carolina the treaty they wished to propose. The Georgia agents made a copy of it and later entered a formal protest on the grounds that it tended to deprive Georgia of part of its soil and its sovereignty. To this protest the commissioners replied that treaties with Indian tribes were the sole right of Congress.[23]

When more than two weeks had passed and still the expected Indians had not arrived, the commissioners of Congress, explaining that they could not treat with so few chiefs, distributed presents and departed. Clarke and Twiggs, representing Georgia, were frankly pleased at their withdrawal. They had no compunction against negotiating with the small number of Indians present, and the day following the departure of the congressional commission signed a treaty with the Creeks. By its terms Georgia was to secure all lands east of a line running southwest from the junction of the Ocmulgee and Oconee rivers to the St. Marys, and confirmation of the Treaty of Augusta of 1783. Georgians generally applauded this action.[24]

When Hawkins, Pickens, and Martin left Galphinton they set out to meet the Cherokees who had been asked to assemble at Hopewell on the Keowee River on November 15. William Blount accompanied them as the agent of North Carolina, and Edward Telfair, John King and Thomas Glascock went along to protect Georgia's interests. Arriving at the appointed place they found neither money, supplies, nor Indians in sufficient numbers, and another delay was necessary. The Cherokees came slowly but in much greater numbers than had been expected. North Carolina's goods were on the way but money to meet obligations the commissioners had assumed was still being sought even after the treaties were signed. Because of this shortage of funds the commis-

23. N.C.S.R., XVII, 566-567, Blount to Caswell, Nov. 11, 1785.
24. American State Papers, Indian Affairs, I, 16.

sioners were forced to dismiss their guard before the middle of December, though negotiations with the Choctaws and Chickasaws continued into January.[25]

On November 18, five hundred Indians met with the commissioners with information that the representation of the tribe was not yet complete and more were on the way. Negotiations were consequently postponed.[26] In the meantime, a large bower of pine trees was erected and plans were completed for the treaty. Three days later the headmen of the Cherokees gathered and were informed that negotiations would begin on the morrow.

On November 22, 1785, nine hundred and eighteen Indians, men, women, and children, assembled. Only the headmen had been invited but, professing fear of the disorderly elements in North Carolina's western territories, they brought along their families and younger warriors.[27] Probably the real reason was the expectation of government supplies and presents.

Before the negotiations began William Blount presented to the commissioners of Congress a letter outlining North Carolina's claims and prepared the way for a subsequent protest.[28]

Hawkins acted as chairman of the commission and wrote most of the correspondence regarding its work. Published explanations of the conference records were signed "B.H.," and the treaty itself and every communication about it show Hawkins's signature first.[29]

---

25. *Ibid.*, 49.
26. *Ibid.*, 40.
27. *Ibid.*, 38.
28. *N.C.S.R.*, XVII, 578-579.
29. *American State Papers, Indian Affairs*, I, 41. Trenholme, *Ratification of the Federal Constitution in North Carolina*, 58, says, "The negotiations were left largely to Martin. . . ." There seems little evidence to support this opinion though the Cherokees knew Colonel Martin from former contacts and referred to him frequently in their talks. After the treaty had been signed the Indians, even while in conference with Martin, looked to Hawkins for its enforcement and the relief of their grievances.

The negotiations began with an address to the Indians expressing the good will of the United States, despite the fact that the Cherokees had generally supported England in the recent war. The Indians were told that Congress disclaimed any desire for their lands and wished only peace and friendship. They were then invited to retire and to return on the morrow for the purpose of submitting their grievances.

On the second day the venerable Chief Tassell of Chota, followed by the old War-Woman of the same town, pledged the friendship of the Indians but complained of encroachments by North Carolina and Virginia in violation of treaty obligations. The meetings continued for a week with the Indians doing most of the talking. At the end of the session on November 28, the treaty was read, explained in detail, and signed.[30]

This first Treaty of Hopewell contained thirteen articles. Twelve were articles of friendship, calling for mutual restoration of prisoners, regulation of trade, and respect for laws and boundaries. Article IV described explicitly boundaries between Cherokees and whites and repudiated the treaty signed in June, 1785, on Dumplin Creek between these Indians and John Sevier for the newly-organized and short-lived State of Franklin.[31]

During the negotiations the Cherokees had demanded the removal of all whites within the Indian lands, particularly the three thousand settlers between the forks of the French Broad and the Holston rivers. William Blount, on the other hand, protested the encroachment upon lands claimed by North Carolina and the removal of any settlers whatsoever from those lands who were there by the consent or knowledge of the state.[32] The commissioners would not agree to trouble settlers between the Holston and the French Broad

30. *Ibid.*, I, 42-43.
31. Charles J. Kappler, editor, *Indian Affairs, Laws and Treaties*, II, 8-11; *N.C.S.R.*, XVII, 582-586; *Journals*, XXX, 187-190.
32. *N.C.S.R.*, XVII, 579-580.

but promised that others would be removed. As soon as the treaty had been read to the Indians and before it was signed Blount presented to the commissioners a formal protest in writing:

> The underwritten Agent on the part of the State of North Carolina protests the treaty at this instant about to be signed and entered into between Benjamin Hawkins, Andrew Pickens, Joseph Martin and Lachlan McIntosh Commissioners on the part of the United States of America and the Cherokee Indians on the other part as containing several stipulations that infringe and violate the Legislative rights of that State.[33]

The commissioners invited Blount's cooperation in carrying out the terms of the treaty, but declared unequivocally:

> We are certain that a steady adherence to the treaty alone, can insure confidence in the justice of Congress, and remove all causes for future Contention or quarrels. The local policy of some States is certainly much opposed to federal measures, which can only, in our opinion, make us respectable abroad and happy at home.[34]

Though all the commissioners were Southerners, two of them North Carolinians and one a Georgian, protests continued from North Carolina and Georgia. Georgia was primarily interested for the future as there was relatively little contact with the Cherokees at the time. Probably the complaints of North Carolina were motivated in part by personal interests of William Blount, his brothers, and Governor Caswell, all of whom were in possession of titles from North Carolina to lands included in the hunting grounds relinquished to the Cherokees.[35]

Immediately upon receiving news of the signing of the treaty Governor Caswell, supported by his Council of State, instructed the North Carolina delegates in Congress that they should not assent to it.[36] James White, a new member of Con-

---

33. *Ibid.*, 580.
34. *American State Papers, Indian Affairs*, I, 44.
35. H. M. Wagstaff, editor, *Steele Papers*, I, 21 note; Trenholme, *Ratifiscation of the Federal Constitution in North Carolina*, 58.
36. Trenholme, *op. cit.*, 59; *N.C.S.R.*, XVIII, 599.

gress, replied that he and his colleague, Timothy Bloodworth, had reached Congress too late to oppose the treaty and that it had already been ratified. He promised, however, that "If anything can be done, at this time, to counteract the evil we have to complain of in the indian treaty, and you will please suggest it, our duty will be to comply with it."[37]

North Carolina had suffered an initial defeat at the hands of Congress. Her protests, however, did not cease. She continued to invoke her rights as a sovereign state with power to treat with the Indians. In January, 1787, the General Assembly instructed the North Carolina delegation in Congress to renew the protest of the state, and in April, Ashe and William Blount, again a delegate to Congress, introduced a resolution to disavow all treaties so far as they allotted hunting grounds to the Indians within North Carolina other than those allotted them by state laws.[38] Needless to say, this resolution failed of passage.

Perseverance in promoting personal interests was a character trait William Blount did not lack. In November, 1788, three years after the Treaty of Hopewell, as a member of the North Carolina Senate, he introduced the following resolution:

> Resolved, That all treaties made with any tribes or nation of Indians whereby lands allotted to them for hunting grounds within the chartered limits of this State other than those allotted by the law of the State heretofore made are a violation of the Constitution and not warranted by the Confederation of the United States.
>
> Resolved, That all and every person holding land under grants legally obtained from this State shall be protected in the possession of the same, any Treaty made by the commissioners appointed by the United States with any tribe or nation of Indians to the contrary notwithstanding.[39]

With the adoption of this resolution by the Senate and

---

37. Burnett, *Letters*, VIII, 385; *N.C.S.R.*, XVIII, 648.
38. *Journals*, XXXII, 237-238.
39. Wagstaff, *Steele Papers*, I, 21-22.

concurrence by the House, North Carolina officially declared the work of the commissioners at Hopewell null and void insofar as it applied to that state.

While by no means as seriously affected by the treaties as North Carolina, Georgia had preceded the neighboring state in official protest. In February, 1786, the General Assembly of Georgia resolved that certain commissioners of the United States had attempted at Galphinton to negotiate and at Hopewell had entered into "pretended treaties" which "are a manifest and direct attempt to violate the retained sovereignty and legislative right of this State, and repugnant to the principles and harmony of the Federal Union; inasmuch as the aforesaid commissioners did attempt to exercise powers that are not delegated by the respective States to the United States. . . ." It was therefore recommended that Georgia delegates attempt to have the commissioners immediately dismissed on the grounds that their continuance in office would weaken confidence in the wisdom and justice of Congress; that copies of the commissioners' instructions be sent to Georgia that steps might be taken to protect the state; and that the acts of the commissioners be declared null and void. These resolutions were the result of reports to the General Assembly by Edward Telfair, John King, and Thomas Glascock.[40]

Lachlan McIntosh returned to his home in Georgia after the treaty with the Cherokees. The remaining three commissioners signed additional treaties with the Choctaws on January 3, 1786, and with the Chickasaws a week later. Hawkins wrote an interesting account of the conditions under which the treaty with the Choctaws was signed:

> The 4th instant, the Commissioners agreed to adjourn, and report their proceedings; and Joseph Martin and Laughlin McIntosh set out for their respective homes, leaving Mr. Pickens and myself to discharge the Indians, to wind up

---

40. *American State Papers, Indian Affairs,* I, 17.

everything, and close the report. The ninth, we received advice from Captain Woods, that the chiefs of the Choctaws were on the way, and would be here this month. Mr. Martin hearing about it, returned on the 27th; but Mr. McIntosh was so far on his way home as to prevent his having advice in time, although I wrote for him immediately on the receipt of the information. The Choctaws arrived on the 26th, after a fatiguing journey of seventy-seven days, the whole of them almost naked. The Creeks endeavoured all they could to prevent their coming, by false information, stealing horses &c; but they have a particular aversion to the Spaniards and the Creeks and are determined to put themselves under the protection of the United States.[41]

The Choctaws were so ragged that it was necessary for the commissioners to clothe them in discarded army coats before they were presentable for a conference.

Except for the article respecting boundary lines the treaties with the Choctaws and Chickasaws were identical to the Cherokee treaty. The later conferences were attended by fewer chiefs. Thirty-seven chiefs signed for the Cherokees, thirty-one for the Choctaws, and only three for the Chickasaws. William Blount continued in attendance and signed each of the three treaties as a witness, though he again wrote a protest against the treaty with the Chickasaws.[42]

Hawkins, through his prominence in the negotiations, incurred the displeasure of influential citizens in both North Carolina and Georgia. Political opposition to him developed in his own state and Georgians never entirely forgave him for what was done at Galphinton and Hopewell. His efforts were not entirely unappreciated, however, and the secretary of Congress in acknowledging receipt of the treaties wrote, "I have no doubt your conduct will meet the approbation of Congress."[43]

A few months after the signing of the treaties Hawkins wrote to Thomas Jefferson:

41. *Ibid.*, 49.
42. *N.C.S.R.*, XVIII, 490, 491.
43. Burnett, *Letters*, VIII, 341.

You will see by the Treaties which I enclose how attentive I have been to the rights of these people; and I can assure you there is nothing I have more at heart than the preservation of them. It is a melancholy reflection that the rulers of America in rendering an account to Heaven of the aborigines thereof, will have lost everything but the name. The interposition of Congress without the cooperation of the Southern States is ineffectual, and Georgia and North Carolina have refused by protesting against their authority. The former will not allow that the Indians can be viewed in any other light than as members thereby, and the latter allows a right of regulatory trade only without the fixing of any boundary between the Indians & Citizens, as they claim all the land Westward according to their bill of rights and that the Indians are only tenants at will.[44]

Jefferson answered from Paris:

The attention which you pay to their rights also does you great honor, as the want of that is a principal source of dishonor to the American character, the two principles on which our Conduct towards the Indians should be founded, are justice and fear. After the injuries we have done them they cannot love us, which leaves us no alternative but that of fear to keep them from attacking us, but justice is what we should never lose sight of & in time it may recover their esteem.[45]

After the conferences the other commissioners had departed, leaving Hawkins to bear the brunt of dissatisfaction by those who had furnished goods on the commissioners' drafts but who had not been paid. The funds were not forthcoming, and not until June, 1788, did Congress consider Hawkins's request to know the pleasure of that body respecting the unpaid balances, and then only to refer it to the Board of Treasury where the matter became a part of the great financial chaos of the period.[46]

---

44. McPherson, "Letters of North Carolinians to Jefferson," *North Carolina Historical Review*, XII, 252-254.
45. Jefferson Papers, XXIII, 3995, Library of Congress.
46. *Journals*, XXX, 339.

Despite treaties of friendship signed with three of the Southern nations the Indian problem continued to plague Congress. Not only had the commissioners refused to treat with the Creeks, the strongest and most warlike of the Southern Indians, who were consequently threatening war, but also those tribes which had signed were restless and constantly reported grievances and trespasses.

Congress, confronted with almost insuperable problems of the post-war period, considered amity with the Indians imperative. Accordingly, on August 7, 1786, an ordinance for the regulation of Indian affairs was passed. For the benefit of such states as Georgia and North Carolina, the sole and exclusive right of Congress under the Articles of Confederation to deal with the Indian tribes was reasserted. Two districts were set up with a superintendent for each. The superintendent, not the governor of any state, was the highest administrative authority in the Indian country. He would regulate trade and travel, enforce the law on whites and Indians, report rumored hostilities, and handle the Indians as his personal wards.[47] Under this ordinance James White became the first superintendent of the Southern District.

The Cherokees in the spring of 1787 were again complaining of the violation of treaty agreements by North Carolina. Hawkins had returned to Congress, but the Indians still looked to him for relief. In March, Joseph Martin, agent for North Carolina, met the Cherokees at Chota where Chief Hanging Maw said to him: "When you went away you told us you expected Colo. Hawkins from Congress Every Day; that he was a good man and would do something for us. But we have heard nothing from him yet. We now hope you can tell us Some thing about him." Continuing with an assertion that, though past treaties had always been violated, the Indians expected a treaty with Congress to be carried

47. *American State Papers, Indian Affairs,* I, 14.

out in the interest of justice, he warned of meddling among the tribes by "people a great way off."[48]

Old Corn Tassel then took up the conversation:

> . . . the Franklin people are settling all our Lands; but you inform us that Congress have not gone fully into our business yet, which we are Very Sorry to hear. You tell us you saw Colo. Hawkins and that he has gone Back to Congress; that you Expect he will do Something for us. We hope he will, as we all look on him to be a good man . . . . We therefore hope you will write to Colo. Hawkins and all the Beloved men of Congress and let them know how we are used.

He also stated that French, Spanish, and English agents were among the Indians and that a confederation of the Northern Indians and Creeks was planning to strike later in the spring. Corn Tassel claimed he had persuaded the Cherokees to hold off, but he had not been able to prevent some of his tribesmen from going out to take vengeance on the Kentucky people for the killing of Indians. "I want to sett still till I hear from Congress, and as you tell us not to go to the Spaniards, we will not go, though they have sent several asking of Beeds."[49]

Hawkins did not get back among the Cherokees for many years and the relief requested by the Indians was not forthcoming. Border clashes continued with increasing bitterness. Ignoring the ordinance of 1786 for the regulation of Indian affairs, as it had consistently ignored Article IX of the Articles of Confederation, Georgia had signed with the Creeks the Treaty of Shoulderbone on November 3, 1786. Again only a small body of Creeks pretending to speak for the nation signed and gave up the Indian claims to all lands in Georgia east of the Oconee River.[50]

---

48. *N.C.S.R.*, XXII, 492-493.
49. *Ibid.*, 493-494.
50. Lucian Lamar Knight, *Georgia and Georgians*, I, 338; Marbury and Crawford, *Digest of the Laws of Georgia*, 619-621.

On the frontier conditions were serious. Alexander McGillivray, who had refused to attend the conferences at Galphinton and Shoulderbone, repudiated those treaties, as he had the one signed in Augusta in 1783. Frequent border conflicts led to complaints by both Georgia and the Indians and threatened an early outbreak of a general war.

James White, superintendent for the Southern District, hurried into Creek country in the spring of 1787 to attempt pacification.[51] An extensive correspondence developed between him and McGillivray. White was confident that if each side would "condescend" a little and McGillivray would use his influence, differences could be reconciled.[52] In April White held a conference with the Lower Creeks, attempting to get concessions for Georgia, but the Creeks returned unfavorable replies. Again war was impending. In the meantime, both Congress and Georgia had become alarmed over conditions and were making plans for hostilities.[53]

Under such conditions Congress appointed a commission composed of Richard Winn, Andrew Pickens, and George Mathews to treat with the Creeks and issued instructions to them in October. Before the commission could begin its work the Creeks attacked and burned the town of Greensboro, Georgia, and a few weeks later Governor George Mathews announced the raising of three thousand troops for the war which seemed inevitable. War did not begin immediately, however, and McGillivray agreed to a conference to be held in September, 1788; but Governor George Handley, who had succeeded Governor Mathews, arranged for a postponement on account of Georgia's financial difficulties. A proposed treaty with the Cherokees also failed to materialize.[54]

When the commissions of Winn, Pickens, and Mathews

51. *American State Papers, Indian Affairs*, I, 20.
52. *Ibid.*, 21-22.
53. *Ibid.*, 22-23, 25.
54. *Ibid.*, 23, 26, 28-29, 34.

had expired, Pickens was reappointed with Henry Osborne as his colleague. Plans for a conference with the Creeks on the Tugalo River were changed and the meeting was set for Rock Landing on the Oconee River in June, 1789. McGillivray opposed these plans and the conference was again postponed.[55] A new Federal commission was appointed composed of Benjamin Lincoln, late general in the Continental service and more recently lieutenant-governor of Massachusetts; Colonel David Humphreys, formerly aide-de-camp to Washington; and Cyrus Griffin, last president of the Continental Congress and a Federal judge. They arrived at Rock Landing on September 20, 1789, unopposed by any Georgians except a few land jobbers, and welcomed by McGillivray who seemed earnestly desirous of peace.[56]

Despite such favorable signs McGillivray withdrew the Indians across the river on September 25, presumably for a conference, and the following day they disappeared without so much as an adieu. The commissioners blamed the failure of the conference on McGillivray's desire to retain an alliance with Spain, especially since the Indians had recently received from Florida a large quantity of arms and ammunition. Such an explanation may have been well founded, but Humphreys, at least, conducted himself with little tact and gave McGillivray an excuse for departure by suggesting to him that there was some doubt whether McGillivray and the Indians present could speak for the nation.[57]

Nearly five years of attempted negotiation had thus broken down. Bad blood, border warfare, depredations, and massacres continued. The new national government was faced with the necessity of proving its ability to cope with the Indian problem.

In 1790 Hawkins took his seat in the United States Senate.

55. *Ibid.*, 34-35.
56. Frank Landon Humphreys, *Life and Times of David Humphreys*, II, 3, 5.
57. *Ibid.*, 9-13.

President Washington and Secretary of War Knox decided to make use of his experience in Indian affairs and his acquaintance with McGillivray in an effort to induce this powerful chief to come to New York for negotiations.[58] Hawkins had never seen McGillivray but had carried on a correspondence with him since 1785 and there had grown up mutual respect between them. It was not the desire of the President either to send Hawkins to Georgia or to have him invite McGillivray to New York by letter. He was to be used to prepare the way for a personal representative of President Washington.

Colonel Marinus Willett was chosen for the mission. Washington's plans for him, and the part Hawkins played, are best expressed in a notation in Washington's *Diary*:

> Exercised on horseback between 9 and 11 o'clock. On my return had a long conversation with Colo. Willet, who was engaged to go as a private agent, but for public purposes, to Mr. McGillivray, principal Chief of the Creek Nation. In this conversation he was impressed with the critical situation of our affairs with that Nation-the importance of getting him and some other Chiefs to this City- with such lures as respected McGillivray personally, and might be held out to him. His [Colo. Willet's] going was not to have the appearance of a governmental act- he, and the business he went upon, would be introduced to McGillivray by Colo. Hawkins, of the Senate, [from North Carolina] who was a correspondent of McGillivray's - but he would be provided with a passport for him and other Indian Chiefs, if they inclined to make use of it; but not to part with it if they did not. The letter from Colo. Hawkins to McGillivray was calculated to bring to his and the view of the Creek Nation the direful consequences of a rupture with the United States. The disposition of the general government to deal justly and honorably by them- and the means by which they, the Creeks, may avert the calamities of war, which must be brought on by the disorderly people of both Nations, if a

58. John C. Fitzpatrick, editor, *The Diaries of George Washington*, IV, 90; Washington Letter Books, Correspondence with the War Department, I, Library of Congress.

treaty is not made and observed. His instructions relative to the principal points to be negotiated would be given to Colo. Willet, in writing by the Secretary of War.[59]

When Colonel Willett left New York he carried with him a letter from Hawkins to McGillivray warning of the "dreadful consequences" which might result from failure to agree to Willett's proposals.[60] Upon entering the Indian country Willett was met by McGillivray and conducted to Hickory Ground, McGillivray's home in Alabama near the junction of the Tallapoosa and Coosa rivers, where he remained for about a week.[61] For two weeks thereafter Willett and McGillivray visited Creek towns and secured approval for treaty negotiations in New York. Accompanied by McGillivray, his nephew, and eight warriors, Willett began his return journey on June 1 and was joined by other Indians en route through the Creek country.[62]

On August 7, McGillivray and twenty-three other Creek chiefs signed the Treaty of New York with General Knox, sole United States commissioner. On the same day President Washington laid it before the Senate, calling attention to the fact that while the Creeks had ceded lands between the Ogeechee and Oconee rivers they denied Georgia's claims under the Treaty of Galphinton to lands "eastward of a new temporary line from the forks of the Oconee and Oakmulgee, in a southwest direction, to the St. Mary's. . . ." The President hoped, however, that Georgia would be satisfied with the Oconee grant, particularly since the lands the Creeks refused to give up were "barren, sunken and unfit for cultivation," and valuable only for timber and as winter hunting grounds for the Indians.[63]

59. *Diaries*, IV, 95-96.
60. Whitaker, "Alexander McGillivray," *North Carolina Historical Review*, V, 296.
61. William M. Willett, *A Narative of the Military Actions of Colonel Marinus Willett*, 103.
62. *Ibid.*, 110.
63. *Annals of Congress*, I, 1068.

Shortly after the treaty was signed, General Knox wrote the Governor of Georgia a letter in explanation of his failure to secure all Georgia had demanded.

> It would have been a desirable circumstance to have obtained an entire confirmation of all the territory claimed by Georgia, and every argument was used to effect this object. But the chiefs who were present decidedly refused, at the hazard of all events, any confirmation of the land lying eastward of the temporary line mentioned in the treaty of Galphinton . . . .[64]

Hawkins served the commissioner of the United States in an advisory capacity. He also voted with the Senate majority for ratification on August 12. It is significant that both Georgia Senators and one from South Carolina were among the four voting in the negative.[65]

Thus the first treaty between the United States and the Creek Indians was signed. Since the Creeks under Alexander McGillivray had given more trouble than any of the other Southern tribes it was confidently believed that a new era in Indian relations had been established, especially since McGillivray, whose great influence had been responsible for previous failures, was the first chief to sign the treaty. Georgia, however, was far from satisfied and McGillivray, despite stipends, annuities, and a commission as brigadier general, continued to oppose Georgia until his death in 1793.

With the Creek problem apparently solved, President Washington wished to pacify the entire Southern frontier. The day before the Treaty of New York was ratified he sent a message to the Senate calling attention to the violation of both the Treaty of Hopewell of 1785, and the Act of Congress of September 1, 1788, by the settlement of five hundred families on Cherokee lands on the French Broad and Holston rivers. He asked for approval of administrative efforts to enforce existing treaties and to make new ones. The

---

64. *American State Papers, Indian Affairs*, I, 561, Aug. 20, 1790.
65. *Abridgement of Debates of Congress*, I, 174.

Senate, which had only to ratify the Treaty of New York before adjourning gave the President a free hand.[66]

When in March, 1790, North Carolina ceded her western territory to the United States, William Blount became the first Governor of the Territory South of the River Ohio, and also Superintendent of Indian Affairs in the Southern District. In the latter capacity he was commissioned to treat with the Cherokees in 1791 and made certain suggestions to the President concerning a treaty about which Washington consulted General Knox. Knox reported that Governor Blount's suggestions were contrary to instructions and that his recommendations to disregard the Treaty of Hopewell "would have pernicious effects" because of unrest in the Indian country caused by the recent organization of land speculation companies in Georgia. Knox further advised President Washington that " . . . as Mr. Hawkins is about going out of town, and is well acquainted with this important subject, I submit the propriety of your consulting him on the subject."[67]

The objectionable plans of Blount were not carried out, but on July 2, 1792, he, as sole commissioner, signed the Treaty of Holston with forty-one Cherokee chiefs.[68] In October, Washington presented this treaty to the Senate and Hawkins, chairman of the committee to which it was referred, recommended its ratification.[69] Hawkins also was consulted about appointment of commissioners to run the line agreeable to the treaty.[70]

By the end of 1792 the United States had entered into one or more treaties with each of the Southern tribes within its territories. The Indians were being pacified with stipends and annuities. Optimism prevailed; only Georgia was greatly perturbed.

66. *Annals of Congress*, I, 1072.
67. Clarence Edwin Carter, *The Territorial Papers of the United States*, IV, 50-52.
68. *American State Papers, Indian Affairs*, I, 124-125.
69. *Ibid.*, 135.
70. Carter, *op. cit.*, IV, 104.

CHAPTER IV

In the United States Senate

H AWKINS, though not a member of the Constitutional Convention of 1787, had been present at the Congress which called it, and voted for the call. In New York as a member of the North Carolina delegation when the Convention assembled in Philadelphia he wrote Thomas Jefferson ". . . every citizen of the United States is looking up with eager anxious hopes to the Convention for an efficient government."[1]

Twice in Philadelphia when the deliberations were going on, Hawkins seemed especially concerned that Congress have a full attendance with North Carolina adequately represented when the Convention reported to it. Although he had reached Philadelphia en route home, he returned to New York to represent North Carolina.

The North Carolina delegation in the Convention, while not outstanding, was reputable and of average ability. It was composed of men well known to Hawkins and with whom he had been associated in various public affairs. Alexander Martin, considered a radical, was perhaps more nearly a moderate; the remaining four, William R. Davie, Richard Dobbs Spaight, Hugh Williamson, and William Blount, were conservatives.[2] The last three named signed for North Carolina.

After the adoption of the Constitution by the Convention, Hawkins, although not playing a leading role, favored ratification and took part in an active campaign to this end. He corresponded with James Madison and used his influence to

---

1. Burnett, *Letters*, VIII, 608.
2. H. M. Wagstaff, *Federalism in North Carolina*, James Sprunt Historical Publications, IX, 8.

create a favorable opinion in Warren County. Writing Madison from Warrenton in February, 1788, of his efforts to counteract Richard Henry Lee's attacks, being circulated in North Carolina, he reported plans for the ratifying convention and concluded:

> I believe the Constitution is daily gaining friends, as far as I have been able to know, it is certain that the honest part of the community whether merchants or planters are for it. People in debt and of dishonesty and cunning in their transactions are against it, this will apply universally to those of this class who have been members of the legislature. If you or our friend Mr. Jefferson should publish any thing upon it, I wish you would send it to me . . . .[3]

The North Carolina convention at Hillsborough July 21, 1788, failed to ratify the Constitution. The year went by, and only North Carolina and Rhode Island refused to join their sister states in the new government. When, in the spring of 1789, the first Congress under the Constitution assembled in New York with North Carolina unrepresented, Hawkins, Davie, Spaight, James Iredell, William Blount, Hugh Williamson, and other prominent North Carolinians continued to hope for the accession of the state. James Madison was in the House of Representatives from Virginia and Hawkins praised him for his work in Congress: "Go on as you have begun and all things will come right." He had particular reference to Madison's support of the tariff and his proposals of amendments, the latter having contradicted and confounded the enemies of the Constitution and created a more friendly attitude toward it in North Carolina. Hawkins also expressed great pleasure that General Washington had departed from the determination never to serve in public capacity again. He prophesied North Carolina's eventual adherence: ". . . we certainly are more friendly than we were at the meeting of our Convention, several counties who were so much opposed to it, are now decidedly

---

3. Madison Papers, VIII, 109, Library of Congress.

very friendly, and I count on its being adopted at our next Convention."[4]

A month later, after a tour of five counties, he reported an increased sentiment favoring ratification. Asking Madison for information on his attempts to add amendments, Hawkins expressed the hope that if difficulties were being met with, the whole matter might be dropped until after the second North Carolina convention, as "The opponents here will, I expect, avail themselves of anything to strengthen their party."[5] Again in August he reported growing Federal leanings, the calling of a convention at Fayetteville for November 16, 1789, his election to the convention by a large majority, and Colonel Davie's election as a delegate from Halifax.[6]

Upon Hawkins's arrival at the Fayetteville convention he, Davie, and Blount were named on a committee of five to draw up rules of order,[7] and he had the pleasure of voting for ratification on November 21.[8] The contest for ratification had been won before the Fayetteville convention met and the 118 majority made it unnecessary for the advocates of the Constitution to wage a bitter fight.[9]

Prior to the entrance of North Carolina into the Union, Benjamin Hawkins was a Federalist as Thomas Jefferson and James Madison were Federalists, in opposing the anti-Federalists and favoring ratification. Afterward, when that term was applied to the political party supporting Hamilton and the administration, Hawkins is more difficult to classify, though by contemporaries and most historians he has been placed in the party of Hamilton. A recent writer explains North Carolina Federalism of the Hawkins type as follows:

> On the whole, these men were not unaffected by the ideas of political liberalism which prevailed during the Revolutionary

---

4. *Ibid.*, XI, 74.
5. *Ibid.*
6. *Ibid.*, XII, 20.
7. *N.C.S.R.*, XXII, 39-40.
8. *Ibid.*, 48.
9. D. H. Gilpatrick, *Jeffersonian Democracy in North Carolina*, 35-36.

period, but they opposed the more advanced forms of Democracy. Their Conservatism has been overstressed. In many ways they were more liberal than those who posed as the particular friends of the people. This is especially true of some of the younger men, Benjamin Hawkins being a conspicuous example.[10]

At the time Hawkins was elected to the convention his friend, John Macon, was elected to the state Senate, and his brother, Philemon, and a nephew, Wyat Hawkins, were elected to the House of Commons.[11] Three days after ratification the House nominated for the United States Senate Samuel Johnston, Benjamin Hawkins, William Blount, William Lenoir, and eight others.[12] On November 27, Samuel Johnston was elected on the first ballot and Lenoir, Blount, and Hawkins were renominated.[13] Eventually Hawkins was elected.

The election for the second senatorial seat was hotly contested. Professor Abernathy says of it:

> Blount was anxious to represent his state in the Federal Senate. He had worked as hard as any man for the adoption of the Constitution, but, unfortunately for him, his motives were understood and he was not admired by the regular conservatives.[14]

Both Blount and Hawkins had brothers in the General Assembly, and at least one writer feels that Philemon Hawkins turned the election. Benjamin, according to this account, was not inclined to push his candidacy because of the unpleasantness he felt it would produce. Indeed, the election did cause a breach between the Hawkins and Blount families which never entirely healed.[15]

---

10. Thomas Perkins Abernethy, *From Frontier to Plantation in Tennessee*, 45-46.
11. *State Gazette of North Carolina*, September 24, 1789.
12. *N.C.S.R.*, XXI, 253. The other nominees were: James White, Joseph McDowell, Timothy Bloodworth, Thomas Person, John Williams, John Stokes, Richard Dobbs Spaight, and William Folk.
13. *Ibid.*, iv, 282.
14. Abernethy, *op. cit.*, 114.
15. Wheeler, *Sketches*, 427-428.

Although it is probable that the radicals, or anti-Federalists, were still in the majority in 1789, the Constitution was ratified because the Federalists were better organized and had superior leadership. The fact that eleven states had ratified also produced some doubt as to the wisdom of North Carolina's remaining out of the Union. Both Senators and three of the five original Representatives were conservatives.[16]

Senator Hawkins arrived in New York on January 13, 1790, and, taking the oath administered by Vice-President John Adams, was seated on that day. Always punctual and diligent in carrying out public obligations in spite of rather frequent illness and a constitution far from robust, his service in the Senate was no exception. During his entire tenure Hawkins was generally the first North Carolina Senator to appear and the last to leave. In his last session, when he was a "lame duck," he was on hand a week in advance of his colleague, Alexander Martin, and attended each roll call for two weeks before a quorum arrived.[17] Samuel Johnston did not arrive for the 1790 session until January 29, and it was on this day that he and Hawkins drew lots for terms. Johnston drew the term ending in 1793 while Hawkins's lasted two years longer.[18]

As a member of the Continental Congress Hawkins had favored secret sessions. As a Senator he voted five times between 1791 and 1794 with the minority for opening the Senate doors during legislative session, often in opposition to his colleague. Finally, on February 20, 1794, the majority voted with him and the Senate doors were opened and the debates published.[19] Meanwhile, he cast his vote with the majority against the motion to allow a dissenting member of the Senate the right to enter his reasons for dissent on the *Journal*. Hawkins also reported to President Washington in January, 1792, that he had called the attention of the

---

16. *North Carolina Manual* (1913), 911.
17. *Annals of Congress*, IV, 785.
18. *Ibid.*, I, 978.
19. *Ibid.*, IV, 47.

Senate to the impropriety of publishing its executive proceedings for the perusal of foreign "public characters," and as a result the Senate decided to present one copy of the Executive Journal to the President and to publish no part of it.[20]

The frequency with which Hawkins dined in the Presidential residence is indicative of the cordial relationship that existed between him and Washington. Eight days after his arrival in New York he was the guest of the President. Almost monthly thereafter he was invited to Washington's table.[21] As a result he became acquainted with all of the cabinet members, Justices of the Supreme Court, and other prominent officials. In one letter to Washington, Hawkins referred to his "long acquaintance with and attachments to" the President, which he judged would make a letter from him not "unacceptable," and asked that his cordial regards be conveyed to Mrs. Washington.[22]

In January, 1790, Hawkins was made chairman of a special committee to consider a bill with "several acts therein mentioned, in respect to the State of North Carolina."[23] This bill, called "The Carolina Bill," was concerned with the problem presented by that state's belated entrance into the Union. One of the early acts of the First Congress was a tariff which applied to North Carolina and Rhode Island as well as foreign countries. On February 1, Hawkins reported for the committee thirteen amendments relieving his home state of economic penalties. The amendments were adopted and the bill was accepted by the House substantially as passed in the Senate.[24]

20. McPherson, "Letters from North Carolinians to Washington," *North Carolina Historical Review*, XII, 162. Hawkins to Washington, January 27, 1792.
21. John C. Fitzpatrick, editor, *The Diaries of George Washington*, IV, 72.
22. McPherson, Letters of North Carolinians to Washington," *North Carolina Historical Review*, XII, 162. Hawkins to Washington, May 28, 1795.
23. *Annals of Congress*, I, 977.
24. *Ibid.*, 978.

On the same day the committee reported these amendments, Johnston and Hawkins laid before the Senate the act of cession by North Carolina of her western lands, and on February 25, they executed a deed of cession to the United States.[25] The act of Congress accepting the cession was signed by President Washington on April 2, and what was later to be Tennessee became United States territory.

A Jefferson memorandum records that when the government of the Territory south of the River Ohio was being considered, Benjamin Hawkins joined other North Carolinians in recommending William Blount for the governorship. Hawkins suggested another North Carolinian, Daniel Smith, as secretary. Both were appointed.[26]

His sponsorship of Blount was typical. There is no indication that he was ever vengeful or harbored grudges. His various clashes with Blount may have caused a coolness, even bitterness, between the families, but he seems never to have been a party to this ill-feeling. In writing to Daniel Smith he commended to him his newly-acquired superior.[27]

Blount, on the other hand, did not take his politics equally impersonally. On July 6, 1790, he received his commission. The following day he referred to Hawkins and Williamson, to whom he was indebted for his new appointment, in terms of slight respect. "I hope it will not injure the feelings of yourself nor others that I have givern [sic] this Business into the hands of these two old politicians."[28]

Hawkins had been interested in the welfare of North Carolina citizens in the West since the first settlers crossed the mountains into the valleys of the French Broad, the Holston, and the Cumberland, but his desire and determination to see justice done to the Indians caused, at times, a

25. Carter, *Territorial Papers*, IV, 9-13; James Phelan, *History of Tennessee*, 147; J. G. M. Ramsey, *The Annals of Tennessee to the End of the Eighteenth Century*, 522.
26. Carter, *Territorial Papers*, IV, 23.
27. *Ibid.*, IV, 26. Hawkins to Smith, June 10, 1790.
28. *Ibid.*, 30-31. Blount to John Steele, July 7, 1790.

distrust of him and he was never popular over the mountains after the Treaties of Hopewell. He wrote Daniel Smith:

> You may rest assured that although you are no longer a part of the State of North Carolina yet I shall not cease my endeavours to contribute my mite to the prosperity of your country. I had an abundant share of odium for my disposition evidenced to be serviceable to them at Hillsborough in 1784 and I believe I was the only one perfectly disinterested in my endeavours, as well as entirely regardless of what was said of me.[29]

After the western territory of North Carolina had become Federal, Hawkins continued to figure in the details of the transfer. He was consulted by Secretary Knox before commissioners were appointed to run the Cherokee line in conformity to the Treaty of Holston;[30] and in January, 1793, he was chairman of the Senate committee to which was referred "An act for determining the Northern boundary of the territory ceded to the United States by the State of North Carolina."[31] A month later he wrote to Jefferson that he thought the people of the territory ought to run this line themselves and save the United States the expense and possibility of being charged with interference.[32]

By all accounts, Senator Hawkins was not a talented speaker. In fact, there is evidence that he spoke with exceptional difficulty and lack of effectiveness. William Maclay, the democratic Senator from Pennsylvania, wrote of him two weeks after he took his seat:

> Hawkins, the new member from North Carolina, rose . . . . He was not very clear. I, however, rose—really from motives of friendship. I will not say compassion, for a stranger. I stated that, as far as I could collect the sentiments of the honorable gentlemen, he was opposed to our copying the law language of Great Britain . . . .[33]

---

29. Carter, *op. cit.*, IV, 26.
30. *Ibid.*, 104.
31. *Ibid.*, III, 631.
32. McPherson, "Unpublished Letters from North Carolinians to Jefferson," *North Carolina Historical Review*, XII, 266.
33. Edgar S. Maclay, *The Journal of William Maclay*, 182-183.

He spoke at infrequent intervals but was often chairman of committees, frequently wrote and read committee reports, and seems to have been very effective in such work.

Two days after taking his seat Hawkins was appointed to a committee to consider a bill in addition to "An Act to establish the Judicial Courts of the United States."[34] Less than two weeks later this committee reported a bill defining crimes and punishments under the Federal law. It was passed on January 28, 1790, and became an important supplement to the Judiciary Act of 1789.[35] Other important committees upon which he served in the Senate were: to consider setting up the first census; to regulate trade with countries and settlements of European powers in America; to consider the message of the President relative to the petition of Vermont for statehood; and to consider the House bill to establish the post office and post roads.[36]

A better criterion of his Senate activities is his record of voting in that body. In May, 1790, he voted with the minority opposing the bill to prevent trade with Rhode Island. Elected as a Federalist, his vote on this measure might be explained as sympathy for Rhode Island resulting from North Carolina's similar relationship to the Union in the previous year. His colleague, Johnston, however, voted with the majority.[37]

In April, 1792, both North Carolina Senators opposed the House bill to sell one hundred thousand acres of land in the Northwest Territory to the Ohio Company of Rufus Putnam, Manassah Cutler, Robert Oliver, and Griffin Greene. The Senate divided equally on this bill and it was passed by the vote of Vice-President John Adams.[38] After its passage Hawkins and Johnston voted in the minority with Aaron

34. *Abridgement of the Debates of Congress from 1789 to 1856*, I, 170.
35. *Annals of Congress*, I, 976.
36. *Ibid.*, passim. The meagerness of the records makes it impossible to judge Hawkins's influence on these committees. The fact that he served on so many which reported important bills would seem to indicate some influence in the organization of the Federal government.
37. *Ibid.*, I, 112.
38. *Ibid.*, III, 124.

Burr and James Monroe to add to this bill a provision offering the same terms to John Cleves Symmes for his purchase.[39]

Hawkins kept himself informed of the history and contemporary conditions in North Carolina even when engaged in national affairs as Senator. He wrote Jefferson in 1792, asking for a copy of Ramsey's *History of South Carolina*.[40] Some weeks later, Jefferson addressed letters to Hawkins, Nathaniel Macon, William B. Grove, and John Steele, all of whom were in the North Carolina delegation in Congress, asking information about the case of *Bayard* vs. *Singleton* (1787), which had arisen from the confiscation of Tory property in the state. None of them was able to give him the complete information desired, but Hawkins's answer was much more specific in detail than any of the others and showed a better knowledge of contemporary happenings.[41]

As a member of the Senate Hawkins was thoroughly convinced that that body had no right to hold up Presidential appointments except on the grounds of unfitness for office. He was confused, however, as to whether the Senate had the right to refuse requested appropriations to pay the expenses of ministers to foreign courts after confirming their appointments,[42] and he voted against the confirmation of John Jay as Envoy Extraordinary to Great Britain.[43]

When objection was raised to Washington's nomination of Henry Lee to lead the campaign against the Northwest Indians on the ground that his rank did not qualify him for the command, Hawkins argued "that the President had the exclusive right to nominate, and the fitness of the character, not the rank of the man, was the only inquiry to be made in

39. *Ibid.*, 125.
40. McPherson, "Letters of North Carolinians to Jefferson," *North Carolina Historical Review*, XII, 259. Hawkins to Jefferson March 26, 1792.
41. *Ibid.*, 260. For case cited see Hugh T. Leffler, *North Carolina History Told by Contemporaries*, 125-129.
42. *Ibid.*, 258-259.
43. *North Carolina Journal* (Halifax), May 7, 1794.

the Senate. . . ."[44] He thus raised early in our national history the controversial question as to the criteria of senatorial confirmation or rejection of presidential appointments. It has often been argued that "the fitness of the character" should be the sole inquiry of the Senate; otherwise it assumes power and responsibility practically equal to that of the President in the matter of appointments. Did the framers of the Constitution so intend, or was the right to confirm appointments granted to the Senate to insure that only "fit" characters take office?

In March, 1792, Hawkins wrote the President:

As I make it a rule to give my assent to all military nominations without inquiry, and I shall continue to do so, so long as a military Judge shall be President of the United States. I hope it will not be deemed indelicate in me to offer the opinion of an individual, which has resulted from reflections on the conversation which I had last evening with you.

Colo. Lee as a Military man certainly possesses a degree of enterprise caution and foresight not excelled by any of his contemporaries of equal rank. He has a comprehensive mind, he has gained experience in a sort of partisan warfare the best of all others for qualifying a man to command against Indians.[45]

Hawkins suggested John Steele, North Carolina member of Congress and a former agent of his state to the Cherokee Indians, for membership on a treaty commission under interesting circumstances. In February, 1793, in a letter to Washington concerning Indian affairs he wrote:

It is well known that Mr. Steel [sic] is one of the warmest and most decided opponents of many of the measures heretofore adopted, and if he should by the Executive be enabled to have an agency in the treaty I am of opinion it would have the effect contemplated. He will not be a member of the ensuing Congress.[46]

---

44. McPherson, "Letters of North Carolinians to Washington," *North Carolina Historical Review*, XII, 165-166. After much deliberation Washington nominated his second choice, "Mad Anthony" Wayne.
45. *Ibid.*, Hawkins to Washington, March 16, 1792.
46. Carter, *Territorial Papers*, II, 439.

Hawkins took an active role in the location of the permanent capital. In 1784, while a member of the Continental Congress, he had been chairman of a committee to select a site on the Potomac, but New York continued as the seat of government after the ratification of the Constitution. On May 24, 1790, a resolution was introduced to hold the next session of Congress in Philadelphia. Great excitement prevailed. "The Senate soon adjourned, and now Izard, Butler, Dr. Johnson, Schuyler, and King flew about. The people they most attacked were Governor Johnston, Hawkins, and Gunn."[47] According to William Maclay the New Yorkers were, the next day, "busy in the scheme of bargaining with the Virginians, offering the permanent seat on the Potomac for the temporary one in New York. Butler is the chief agent in this business."[48] Evidently the work of the New York supporters was well done for on May 26 action on the Philadelphia resolution was postponed by a vote of thirteen to eleven, with Hawkins and Johnston voting in the affirmative. On subsequent polls Hawkins voted for Baltimore; against Baltimore; for the Potomac; for Philadelphia from 1792 to 1800; and, finally, for the Potomac again. There is some evidence that he was a party to the bargain to vote for assumption of state debts by the Federal government in return for a capital on the Potomac, as he voted for the latter and changed from opposition to assumption to casting an affirmative vote for its passage.

No Federalist leader in North Carolina, in public or in private life, gave Hamilton's extreme nationalistic program his unreserved approval, while many of them came out in opposition. Senator Johnston wrote privately against assumption . . . yet at the last both he and Hawkins voted with their party in favor of the measure, while Williamson and his two Federalist colleagues in the House were in opposition.[49]

---

47. Maclay, op. cit., 265. James Gunn was a Senator from Georgia.
48. Ibid., 266.
49. R. D. W. Connor, History of North Carolina, I, 427.

North Carolina's Senators reached New York too late to
vote on the tariff bill of 1789, but voted for the excise contrary to instructions. Almost immediately after ratification,
the radicals in the state regretted their selection of Federalists
to Congress and a reaction set in. Any Federalist leaning was
distasteful to the majority of the legislative members and in
November, 1790, a resolution was passed:

> Whereas, when the General Assembly of the State of North
> Carolina in the session of 1789, did nominate and appoint
> Samuel Johnston and Benjamin Hawkins, Esquires, to repre-
> sent the said State in the Senate of the United States, every
> expectation that had confidence in their integrity, opinion
> of their abilities, or certainty of their industry, in discharg-
> ing the trust reposed with them was entertained. — With re-
> gret do we add, that our constituents and ourselves too sen-
> sibly experience the evils arising from a want of that ex-
> ercion [sic] in them, which if duly made, could not have
> failed of being highly beneficial to this State, and might have.
> rendered a government adopted under many doubts and with
> much difficulty, better adapted to the dispositions of free
> men.[50]

This resolution, adopted as a compromise between the two
chambers of the General Assembly, called upon the Senators of North Carolina to support public sessions of the
Senate; to correspond regularly with the legislature and,
during its recesses, with the governor; to report the Senate
Journal to the governor each month; to support economy,
especially regarding "monstrous salaries given to public officers and others"; and, to oppose excise and direct taxes.

Neither Hawkins nor Johnston paid much attention to
these instructions and both neglected to appear before the
General Assembly to give accounts of their stewardships.
This further increased opposition to them.[51] James Iredell,
influential North Carolina jurist, however, defended the Senators' votes on excises as being "from motives of duty."[52]

50. *N.C.S.R.*, XXI, 961-962.
51. Wagstaff, *op. cit.*, 21; Dodd, *Macon*, 68-69; Connor, *North Carolina*,
    I, 428.
52. G. J. McRee, *Life and Correspondence of James Iredell*, I, 329-330.

Hawkins consistently sided with the minority in opposition to the Bank of the United States. On January 20, 1791, he voted to limit its charter to ten years. On this ballot the six affirmative votes were: one from Virginia, one from North Carolina (Johnston not voting), and two each from South Carolina and Georgia.[53] On the same day Hawkins voted to expunge a section providing that no other bank should be chartered, and on February 5 he cast a vote, again with the minority, to add to the bank act an amendment to the effect that it might be abolished after March 4, 1802.[54] On February 19, he stood with the minority of nine against the majority of nineteen which authorized the President to borrow $800,000 from the bank.[55]

Despite such a record, Hawkins was suspected of weakening by the opponents of the bank and in May, 1793, John Taylor wrote a letter from Caroline County, Virginia, to James Madison urging Madison to "fix" Hawkins against the bank and Washington.

Hawkins was here a day or two, with Macon and Giles. He appeared to try to arrange himself right. A gentleman who knew him better than I do, informed me, that the most likely thing to fix him, would be a letter from you. Something of a kind of friendly stile. And having three or four pointed sentences against the bank law, and expressing a necessity for its repeal. His situation in his state is a little awkward, & he will probably strive to put it to rights. To help him along, he would show your letter, and if you make a Carthago est deleta business of the bank law, he would get so far enlisted in the idea, among his countrymen, that he could not retract. When your letter was seen, the reader would take up the idea, and gore Hawkins upon the subject. I cannot say more here, and perhaps I ought to apologize for having said so much on such a subject.[56]

---

53. *Annals of Congress*, II, 1748.
54. *Ibid.*
55. *Ibid.*, III, 651. Hawkins's letters fail to explain why he opposed the bank but his votes indicate forcefully that he did.
56. *Branch Historical Papers*, II (June, 1908), 253.

It cannot be said that John Taylor and James Madison converted Hawkins to their way of thinking in regard to the Bank of the United States. His entire Senatorial record is conclusive proof that he was not friendly to this financial institution. If there were some uncertainty in his mind in 1793, as Taylor seemed to fear, he rallied staunchly to the opposition again in 1794. On January 16 of that year he cast two of his most significant votes when he sided with the minority (12-13) in favor of a constitutional amendment to prevent any officer of the bank from holding membership in either house of Congress. Later, by an identical vote, a bill for the severance of the government's connection with the bank was defeated.[57]

The alignment on that day was typical of the entire session. The minority voting aye on the two resolutions was composed of Brown and Edwards of Kentucky, Monroe and Taylor of Virginia, Bradley and Robinson of Vermont, Jackson of Georgia, Butler of South Carolina, Burr of New York, Gallatin of Pennsylvania, and the two North Carolina Senators (Johnston had been replaced by Alexander Martin, an anti-Federalist). The successful and negative majority was made up of Bradford and Foster of Rhode Island, Ellsworth and Mitchell of Connecticut, Cabot and Strong of Massachusetts, Langdon and Livermore of New Hampshire, King of New York, Morris of Pennsylvania, Frelinghuysen of New Jersey, Vining of Delaware, and the lone Southerner, Izard of South Carolina, a strong Federalist and conservative.[58] A study of this vote might lead one to conclude that it was more a sectional than a party division. Even so, in line with the later party allegiances, it is sufficient evidence to cast a doubt upon Hawkins's Federalism.

Hawkins voted with a minority of six in March, 1794, for the appointment of a committee to examine into the principles upon which the accounts of the states with the United States

57. *Annals of Congress*, IV, 32-33.
58. *Ibid.*

had been settled.[59] However, the tendency to line up with the Republicans against the Federalists in the Senate did not prevent an occasional show of independence and a vote with the other side of the chamber. In May, 1792, as chairman of the committee to consider the House bill, "An Act concerning duties on spirits distilled within the United States," he reported amendments to which the Senate agreed and thus was to some extent responsible for the Hamiltonian excise tax which led to the Whiskey Rebellion.[60] He also voted for "An Act laying duties upon carriages" in 1794.[61] A year later, however, he voted with the great majority to repeal both of these taxes, James Jackson of Georgia casting the only negative vote.

Perhaps the most important Federalist vote cast by Hawkins while in the Senate was on February 28, 1794, against the seating of Albert Gallatin as a Senator from Pennsylvania. Gallatin was refused his seat by the close division of fourteen to twelve.[62] It is interesting and significant to note that every vote except that of Hawkins was entirely regular, consistent, and expected. Of the fourteen opposing Gallatin, twelve had voted on January 16 against the constitutional amendment to restrict the bank. Hawkins alone of all the Senate had voted in opposition to both the bank and Albert Gallatin. James Monroe in a letter to Jefferson in March, 1794, commented:

> On Friday last the Senate, 14 to 12, declared that Mr. Gallatin had not been 9 years a citizen of the U. States when elected & that his seat was vacant. Upon this occasion Mr. H. from N. C. left us wch. prevented a division & decision from the chair; we have reason to believe that a decision wod. have been with us, from what has since transpired, upon the principle, his vote should not displace the sitting member.[63]

---

59. *Ibid.*, 73.
60. *Ibid.*, III, 133.
61. *Ibid.*, IV, 119.
62. *Ibid.*, 57.
63. Stanilaus M. Hamilton, editor, *The Writings of James Monroe*, I, 282-283. Monroe to Jefferson, March 3, 1794.

On the other hand, Hawkins a month later also voted against seating Kensey Johns of New Jersey, a Federalist, who had been elected to fill the unexpired term of George Read.[64] He and his colleague Johnston cast half of the negative votes against passing to the third reading "An Act to establish the Post Office and Post Roads within the United States."[65] He favored a bill calling for non-importation from England in 1794;[66] and opposed authorization of the President to build and equip vessels.

As political rivalry developed between Thomas Jefferson, Secretary of State, and Alexander Hamilton, Secretary of the Treasury, Hawkins sided with Jefferson and sometimes went on confidential missions for him.[67] He showed sympathy for the French and a growing antagonism to the English, and, according to his statement to Jefferson, spent the summer of 1793 "wishing success to French Democracy and ruin to the combination of Kings and priests."[68] On March 28, 1795, he wrote an open letter to the citizens of North Carolina signed by every member of the North Carolina delegation in Congress except Nathaniel Macon. The letter expressed the feeling of obligation to acquaint North Carolinians with conditions as they were. In spite of the Neutrality Proclamation of President Washington, England continued to interfere with American shipping.

We yet hope that a temperately firm remonstrance on the part of our government may be listened to, as our republican allies have by their successful efforts since the issuing of the nefarious orders against our lawful commerce proved them-

---

64. *Annals of Congress*, IV, 73.
65. *Ibid.*, III, 65.
66. *Ibid.*, IV, 89.
67. McPherson, "Letters from North Carolinians to Jefferson," *North Carolina Historical Review*, XII, 259. Hawkins to Jefferson, March 26, 1792. It is evident from the tone of this letter that Jefferson was using Hawkins and Senator Dickinson of New York as under-cover men to force British officials to a commitment on British policy.
68. *Ibid.*, 266-268. Hawkins to Jefferson from Warren County, October 28, 1793.

selves worthy of being styled the asserters and defenders of the rights of man in Europe.[69]

North Carolinians were urged to plant cotton, hemp, and flax in abundance in preparation for war.

William B. Groves, an ardent Federalist member of the House, penned a garrulous letter to John Steele in which he said:

> I signed a paper a few days ago drawn up by Hawkins, addressed to the people of the State. 'tis to be in Hodges paper— I dont know that it can do any harm, but on reflection I wish I had not put my name to it—Macon was the only one who did not sign it.[70]

North Carolina received Hawkins's letter with more enthusiasm than Groves exhibited. At mass meetings in Fayetteville on April 17 and 18, the delegation was thanked for its endeavors in general and the letter in particular. Resolutions adopted expressed impatience with England and sympathy for France and ended: "Called on by the present appearance of affairs, to anticipate war as the event, we are happy to declare, We Will Unanimously Consider that War as Just and Necessary."[71]

Federalism and Benjamin Hawkins are frequently linked and most writers agree that he was a follower of that political faith. In North Carolina, however, Federalism was not clearly defined and a Federalist there was not necessarily a blind partisan of Alexander Hamilton.[72] "Indeed, it began to appear that in North Carolina 'Federalism' meant Federation only, an end already achieved."[73]

Hawkins, though unreliable as a party man, on the whole

---

69. *North Carolina Journal*, April 9, 1794.
70. *Steele Papers*, I, 114. Hodges was editor of the *North Carolina Journal* (Halifax). Macon was a Republican but was able to keep in the graces of the Federalists better than almost any other follower of Jefferson.
71. *North Carolina Journal*, April 30, 1794.
72. Connor, *History of North Carolina*, I, 427.
73. Wagstaff, *Federalism in North Carolina*, 21.

seemed more liberal than conservative. When North Carolina became increasingly Republican and the radical element regained its lost ascendancy, a reaction set in which cost Hawkins his senatorial seat. In the election of 1794, Timothy Bloodworth, ex-blacksmith and anti-Washington leader, was chosen to succeed him. By 1797 both Senators and ten of the eleven House members from North Carolina were Republicans; eleven electoral votes of the state were for Jefferson and only one for Adams, the successful candidate.[74]

Hawkins probably was never consciously disloyal to Washington in his leanings toward Jefferson and away from Hamilton, and after his defeat for re-election to the Senate, continued to write to the President. In May, 1795, he addressed him from Warrenton expressing great respect for him and Mrs. Washington and observing that there seemed a growing friendliness in North Carolina toward the administration.[75] His respect for President Washington, however, was not as compelling as a sincere affection for Thomas Jefferson. Hawkins was ever a nationalist, never a states' rights man, and in spite of his denial of certain basic tenets of the Hamiltonian creed, apparently considered himself a Federalist until after the election of Jefferson, though he later denied allegiance to this party. In 1811 in a letter to President Madison, for whom his only son was named, Hawkins spoke of telling Governor George Mathews of Georgia that "he was about as much a Federalist as we were."[76]

With the ending of the Third Congress in March, 1795, the legislative career of Benjamin Hawkins came to an end and he never again held elective office. On March 3, Senator Hawkins took his seat for the last time. On this day he proposed a resolution: an amendment to a bill to authorize the President to obtain Georgia's western lands. After the North

---

74. *Ibid.*, 28.
75. McPherson, "Letters of North Carolinians to Washington," *North Carolina Historical Review*, XII, 166-167.
76. Madison Papers, (Library of Congress), XLIV, 38. Hawkins to Madison, March 11, 1811.

Carolina cession Georgia alone claimed western territory. Had the amendment been adopted, Hawkins's career among the Creeks might have been greatly changed, but it bogged down in the last hours of the session when Senator James Jackson of Georgia refused unanimous consent to dispense with the rules and read the bill a third time.[77] As a result of this failure Georgia retained her claims until six years after Hawkins had moved into the Indian country.

An analysis of Hawkins's senatorial career reveals many contradictions. He was a nationalist, but voted Southern sectional interests consistently. He favored the excise, but opposed the Bank of the United States. He opposed England and sympathised with the French Revolutionists. He was interested in the welfare of the West, was critical of Spain in its attempts to close the Mississippi, but was adverse to speculation, too-liberal land policy, and the establishment of post roads and the Post Office. He staunchly supported the Indians in their claims to lands until such claims had been extinguished by valid treaty agreements to which the United States was a party. He was instrumental in depriving the Republican Gallatin of his seat in the Senate,[78] but voted against the confirmation of John Jay as Envoy to Great Britain. He voted for assumption as part of the compromise to locate the capital on the Potomac. He was loyal to Washington personally but did not care for Hamilton and drew closer to Jefferson and Madison. He resented the attempts of the North Carolina General Assembly to direct his action in the Senate and opposed the states, even his own, in their attempts to interfere in Indian relations. He was personally democratic and counted as friends many of lowly station.

---

77. *Annals of Congress*, IV, 852.
78. Hamilton, *Writings of Monroe*, I, 282-283. Monroe to Jefferson, March 3, 1794.

CHAPTER V

The Treaty of Coleraine

GEORGIA was unwilling to accept the Treaty of New York which was considered a violation of the rights of the state. The two most unacceptable features of the treaty were its failure to confirm the land cessions of Galphinton and Shoulderbone, and the implied permanency of the Indian title in the expressed purpose of the United States to furnish the Creeks with free domestic animals and tools to convert them to the white man's way of life.

> This treaty shocked the Georgians into a daze, out of which they finally emerged only to enter a rage. It was unthinkable to them that a Government of civilized white people would definitely hand over to the savages for permanent occupation all of Georgia excepting a small eastern strip, and, to fix their minds against ever being induced to move, would attach them to the land as farmers. This treaty marked the entry into the heart of Georgia of a gall-like bitterness against the United States government which tinctured her relations with the Federal government in a deep and lasting way.[1]

McGillivray, who had constantly refused to treat with Georgia, was more than ever determined to make no concessions. Border clashes occurred; trespasses were mutually committed; threats and intimidation on the part of the whites, even to the point of open war, and intrigue on the part of the Indians, prevailed. William Augustus Bowles, native Marylander and former British soldier, claiming to represent England, attempted to arouse the Creeks in 1791 against

---

1. E. Merton Coulter, *A Short History of Georgia*, 170.

both the United States and Spain. For a time he almost wrested the leadership of the Indians from McGillivray.

With the Spanish in Florida encouraging the Creeks to violate treaty obligations and pressing for a revision of the treaty of 1783 and rectification of boundaries, peace rested ever on a precarious footing. With the additional excitement produced by the organization under Georgia laws of the Yazoo land speculation companies, the wonder is that the Southern borders were not constantly the theaters of general and bloody racial warfare.

Under the new Constitution the United States had formulated certain principles upon which Indian supervision should be carried out. President Washington, especially apprehensive of the relationship between the states and the Indian tribes, devoted much of his message to Congress to this subject. William Blount, Governor of the Southwest Territory and Superintendent of Indian Affairs for the Southern District, was not trusted by the Indians. James Seagrove, agent for the Creeks, resided at Coleraine near the Georgia coast on the St. Marys River. He feared his charges and consequently was unwilling to move his residence into the Indian country proper. The Creeks had little affection and less respect for him. Despite the President's personal interest the United States government, busy with other domestic and foreign problems, adopted a policy of "watchful waiting." Georgia, likewise, after a threat of armed reprisal in 1793, was unwilling to force the issue. McGillivray died in that year and the Indians were bereft of his aggressive leadership.

In December, 1794, the General Assembly of Georgia appropriated certain lands within the territorial boundaries of the state for the payment of state troops. Under this act lands were claimed on the basis of treaties between Georgia and the Indians contrary to the terms of the Treaty of New York. Should the Indians refuse to admit the claims of Georgia, the act called upon the United States to negotiate another treaty with the Creeks, the state to be represented at the conference by three commissioners.[2] Georgia claimed the lands between the Altamaha and St. Marys rivers, called Tallassee, under the terms of the Treaty of Shoulderbone which the Creeks at New York had refused to recognize and had repudiated.

In January, 1795, a supplementary Georgia act was passed conferring upon speculation companies—the Georgia Company, the Georgia-Mississippi Company, the Upper Mississippi Company, and the Tennessee Company—millions of acres of land claimed by the state in the Mississippi region. This was the so-called "Yazoo Fraud." Georgia's action was based on the presumption of full territorial jurisdiction within the limits of its western lands with the sole right of preemption.[3]

United States Senator James Gunn and Congressman Thomas P. Carnes, both personally interested in the speculation and participants in the fraud, were designated to request the President's appointment of a commission to clear immediately the lands which Georgia contemplated occupying under the act of December.

In March the request for the treaty reached President Washington. The action of Georgia being to him a source of no little embarrassment, he delayed a decision. Timothy Pickering, Secretary of War, was instructed to inform the Governor of Georgia that the matter would be laid before the Senate when it assembled in June.[4] On June 25, in a letter to the Senate explaining the actions and request of Georgia, Washington nominated Benjamin Hawkins, George Clymer of Pennsylvania, and General Andrew Pickens of

2. *American State Papers, Indian Affairs*, I, 551-552.
3. *Ibid.*, 552-555; see also Shaw Livermore, *Early American Land Companies. Their Influence on Corporate Development*, 156. This writer, quoting M. C. Klingelsmith, "James Wilson and the So-called Yazoo Fraud," *Pennsylvania Law Review*, January, 1908, adopts the revisionist attitude that there was no more fraud than in any other state speculation but that Georgians raised the cry for political purposes and Georgia historians have since popularized the idea of fraud. Though Klingelsmith's article was published in 1908 most Georgia writers still maintain the sale was fraudulent.
4. *American State Papers, Indian Affairs*, I, 561.

South Carolina to treat with the Creeks.[5] In the meantime, Congress was investigating Georgia's right to sell the Mississippi lands.

The treaty conference was set for May, 1796, at Coleraine on the St. Marys River where Spanish Florida, Creek Tallassee country, and Georgia lands already cleared of Indian titles joined. Hawkins, with his usual punctuality, arrived on May 12 and remained for more than six weeks before the negotiations were concluded.[6]

Coleraine was sixty miles by the tortuous St. Marys River, and thirty miles overland, from the town of St. Marys at the river's mouth. In addition to the residence of Creek agent James Seagrove, there was also at Coleraine a recently established United States factory with Edward Price as factor, and a garrison of Federal troops under the command of Lieutenant Colonel Henry Gaither. Both Seagrove and Gaither were in St. Marys but hurried to their posts when informed of Hawkins's arrival, each assuring him of intentions to aid the United States commissioners in bringing negotiations to a successful conclusion.

The other two commissioners were late in reaching Coleraine due to the delayed arrival of instructions, General Pickens not having received his until May 2. Seagrove's orders from the War Department reached him on April 6.

---

5. *Ibid.*, 560.
6. *Ibid.*, 587. In justification of the inclusion of an entire chapter on the Treaty of Coleraine in this work the following facts seem pertinent. Perhaps no single event of Hawkins's career was as consequential as his participation in the negotiations of this treaty. It played no small part in his appointment as Agent. James Jackson, the most severe critic of the United States commissioners was soon to become Governor of Georgia in which position he was to have frequent official relations with Hawkins. Because Hawkins had been at Coleraine the Creeks received him cordially as their Agent. Georgians bitterly resented the treaty, on the other hand, and Hawkins was destined to reside in the state for twenty years. During this entire period many Georgians never forgot, nor forgave, the fact of his presence there.

He then dispatched a single messenger with the following invitation to each chief throughout the Creek Nation:[7]

> By desire of our great and good friend and father the President of the United States, I now call on my friends the Chiefs of the Creek land to a great and General Treaty, to be held at Coleraine, on the River St. Mary's, to commence at the middle of the next moon.[8]

On May 16 twenty Indians arrived with cattle to sell. From them Hawkins learned that it would be some time before the chiefs came, if they decided to come at all. Rumors were circulated in the Nation by the Spanish and the agents of Panton, Leslie and Company, an English trading firm operating extensively in Creek and Cherokee country out of Pensacola and Mobile, that the Creeks would be met by armed Georgians and coerced into ceding their lands.[9]

On May 21 Seagrove's messenger returned with information that the Indian delegation would probably be at Coleraine by June 10. News was also received that George Clymer had reached Savannah and was en route to St. Marys, whereupon Hawkins ordered Seagrove to report to the Governor of Georgia the probable date negotiations would begin.

When Clymer reached St. Marys on May 22 he was met by Hawkins, but was so worn out with his journey that the departure for Coleraine was delayed for several days. Even so, upon the arrival of the commissioners at Coleraine, they found no Indians and no representative of Georgia. Preparatory work had to be done, however, and Hawkins and Clymer selected Ensign Samuel Allison from the garrison to receive and issue provisions for the Indians. Of a more important nature, and fraught with serious consequences, was

---

7. *Ibid.*, 588.
8. *Augusta Chronicle*, May 21, 1796. There are at least three variations of the spelling of Coleraine, i. e., Colerain, Colrain, Coleraine. The form used in this chapter seems the most common.
9. *American State Papers, Indian Affairs*, I, 588. In the meantime Hawkins was visited by a Captain Atkinson, a former acquaintance in the Spanish service and he accompanied his guest to St. Marys.

the posting on the garrison gates of regulations to be observed throughout the conference.

According to these regulations, the Indians would encamp above the garrison with the agent among them, but no other white man should camp there. White men might not enter the camp under arms nor converse with the Indians except by permission of a United States commissioner. Only the garrison could bear arms in the vicinity, and trading with the Indians, particularly in spirituous liquors, was forbidden. Colonel Gaither gave his complete approval to the actions of the commissioners and promised full compliance with their orders. He also prepared a camp with tents and other necessary articles for their use.[10]

In the meantime, the schooner *William* reached Coleraine with stores, unloaded, and dropped back down the river en route to Philadelphia. On May 28, General Pickens and the Georgia commissioners arrived and two hundred Indians, under Chief Big Warrior and the half-breed Alexander Cornells, were reported to be within ten miles of the post, their fears abated somewhat by supplies they had received.

The Georgia commission, composed of James Hendricks as chairman, James Jackson, and James Simms,[11] held that Georgia's claim to the region between the Altamaha and St. Marys rivers was not subject to negotiation since an act had already been passed by the General Assembly for occupation of this territory. A desire to prevent bloodshed and to have her claims recognized by the Indians and the United States, however, led the state to defray half of the expenses of the treaty although unwilling for participation in the negotiations to be considered as an acknowledgment that

10. *Ibid.*, 589.
11. Of the three Georgia commissioners James Jackson was the only one of prominence and with whom Hawkins had future relations. He had been a Revolutionary officer, had recently resigned from the United States Senate to aid in rescinding the Yazoo act, and was soon to become Governor of the state. As governor he had much correspondence with Hawkins which, on the whole, was cordial and indicates that in spite of decided differences of opinion each developed respect for the other.

treaties between Georgia and the Creeks had been super-
seded at New York.

From the day of their arrival the Georgians were disin-
clined to be conciliatory toward the United States commission. The militiamen who accompanied them were presumably for the purpose of safeguarding supplies furnished
by the state; but Hawkins, Pickens, and Clymer feared that
their presence would convince the Indians that Georgia intended armed coercion.

The invitation of the United States commissioners to the
Georgians to share their tents and accommodations was declined and an official coolness was evident. Violent exception
was taken to the regulations Hawkins and Clymer had posted
on the garrison gates. Though Hendricks soon became reconciled and was willing to cooperate, his colleagues outvoted
him, continued in opposition, and protested the actions of
the Federal commission almost daily. Questions of jurisdiction constantly arose and were the subject of frequent correspondence.[12] Hawkins, as chairman of the United States
commission, had the responsibility of answering the complaints of the irate Georgians who claimed their state had
been insulted. He retained his composure and dignity despite condemnation and in a series of able answers insisted
upon carrying out his instructions to the letter. One of the
points made by the Georgia commissioners was that, since
Coleraine was within the boundaries of the state, regulations
of the United States commissioners were in violation of its
sovereignty.

The attitude of Hawkins demonstrated a high degree of
moral courage. From the beginning of his public career there
is nothing to indicate that he ever condoned mistreatment
of the Indians or fraud against them. As a matter of wise
national policy, and worthy national morality, he had ever
urged fair dealing and attempts toward conciliation. Under
the Confederation and the Constitution, he steadfastly held,

12. *American State Papers, Indian Affairs,* I, 590-593.

Indian relations were the prerogative of Congress. Congressional committees and Federal commissions had given him so much experience that he had become well acquainted with Southern Indians, better acquainted probably than any American citizen who had not actually lived among them. In 1796, however, he had not developed enough personal affection for these people to justify the charge of prejudice in their behalf against his fellow citizens. He had no unfriendliness toward Georgia or any member of that state's commission. His actions at Coleraine were unquestionably based on honest convictions and a desire to fulfill his official engagements with integrity and efficiency. Nevertheless, the rapidly developing controversy between Federal and state commissions did not necessarily have the complete and unquestioned totality of virtue on either side. The Federal commission maintained a calmness and dignity often absent within the Georgia commission, but the latter had on its side some reasonable argument.

Obviously the Creeks were a source of apprehension and even great terror to Georgia. Protected states, with their boundaries well defined and free from troublesome Indians, could not realize the anxiety of Georgians who felt that representatives of the protected states in Congress were incompetent to decide an issue so vital to Georgia's interests. Regardless of whether or not Congress had the sole right to deal with Indian tribes, it had been customary to recognize agreements between Indians and individual states when such agreements were mutually respected, and, at times, Federal agents had attempted to persuade the Creeks to abide by agreements with Georgia. Also, Georgia felt thoroughly justified in protecting herself, especially since Congress had done little for her protection.

Prior to 1790 no treaty between the Creeks and Congress had been negotiated. A series of treaties between Georgia and these people, begun as early as 1733, had occasioned no general opposition until the Treaty of Augusta in 1783, but this treaty and those signed at Galphinton in 1785 and at

Shoulderbone in 1786 had been rejected by McGillivray on the ground of inadequate Indian representation and were repudiated at New York in 1790. Demanding acceptance of their validity, Georgia held that the Tallassee country was already cleared of the Indian title and was not subject to further negotiation. In 1789, General Benjamin Lincoln, Colonel David Humphreys, and Cyrus Griffin had come to Georgia under authorization of Congress to sign a treaty. They failed, but reported that after careful investigation the above-mentioned Georgia treaties ". . . were all of them conducted with as full and authorized representation, with as much substantial form, and apparent good faith and understanding of the business, as Indian treaties have usually been conducted."[13] Such were the major differences at Coleraine.

Frequent resort to long written communications failed to clear up differences between the two commissions. Colonel Hendricks was reconciled by the arguments of the Federal commissioners to the point of accepting their invitation to camp with them and eat at their table. Jackson and Simms, however, elected to remain on board the schooner *Fair Play*, which had brought the Georgia supplies and was moored in the river.[14]

Disorder developed upon the arrival of the Indians. On June 10, Chief Big Warrior demanded redress for the death of his brother at the hands of whites three years before. The Federal commissioners returned a conciliatory answer and a minor crisis was averted. In spite of the regulations of Hawkins and Clymer, and Colonel Gaither's promise to carry them out to the letter, white men and half-breeds were getting into the Indian camp, and the Indians were doing some drinking. About twenty of them returned to their camp drunk one night from a visit to the garrison where they had been supplied with whiskey by the soldiers.[15] The Indians on the whole, however, were friendly to the United States

13. *Ibid.*, 616.
14. *Ibid.*, 594.
15. *Ibid.*, 596. Commissioners to Seagrove, June 14.

commissioners and their fears of the Georgians, had been somewhat allayed by the posted regulations.

On June 16 the conference formally opened when four hundred Indians marched under the flag of the United States, danced the eagle tail dance and saluted the Federal representatives by having four dancing warriors wave eagle tails six times above their heads. The six principal kings and headmen shook hands with the commissioners and handed them pipes of peace. Hawkins addressed the Indians with words of friendship and presented the Georgia commissioners to them. Peace pipes were smoked again, the Indians were given a salute of sixteen guns, and warmed with free liquors. At length they retired to their camp to meet on the morrow. The chiefs dined with the commissioners and after more "wine and spirits" and pipes they assured the government officials that their representation was full and qualified to speak for the nation.

Timothy Barnard, Alexander Cornells, James Burges, and Langley Bryant were selected by the Federal commissioners as interpreters. Philip Scott was added to this group at the request of the Georgians. Fusatchee Mico (White-bird King) was the Indian spokesman.[16]

The Georgia commissioners presented Hawkins a copy of the talk they wished to make. Though certain parts were objectionable to the representatives of the United States, they approved it with slight change. On June 18, Hawkins introduced the Georgians to the Indians in the conference square as "The three beloved men of Georgia," and asked for them a courteous hearing. James Jackson delivered the talk, dwelling on violations of the treaties with Georgia and asking for the restoration of property stolen by Indians from Georgia citizens to the amount of one hundred ten thousand dollars. During Hawkins's talk the Indians applauded his every word, though many of them understood little he said, but they heard General Jackson in silence, except to ask

------

16. *Ibid.*, 579.

who signed the Treaty of Galphinton, and to laugh when he requested damage for hogs lost by the Georgians.[17]

A copy of Jackson's talk was given to the Creeks and for three days they remained in their camp to consider it. On June 21, they returned to the square. White-bird King, speaking at length, said the Indians had come at the invitation of President Washington to meet the Federal commissioners; had only Georgians been present they would not have come as the Treaty of New York was the Indians' agreement with President Washington.[18]

The Creeks were unwilling to listen to suggestions that lands be sold to Georgia, and for several days even protested that they had never relinquished as much land as was given Georgia in the Treaty of New York because McGillivray had misinformed them as to the boundary line. Hawkins, however, insisted that the line, as yet not run, should conform to the treaty, to which they at length reluctantly agreed.

Negotiations between Georgia and the Indians had definitely failed, but the conference continued until June 29, 1796, when the Treaty of Coleraine was signed. Composed of ten articles, it confirmed the Treaty of New York; called for the running of the line agreeable to that treaty; gave the United States a tract of land five miles square on the south side of the Altamaha River for a military post, and similar grants on the Oconee for trading or military purposes; and provided that the Creeks furnish two chiefs and twenty warriors as hunters and guides for the commissioners of the United States and Spain who should be appointed to run the line between the United States and Spanish Florida. The Creeks agreed to respect the treaties of Hopewell and Holston between the United States and the Cherokees, Chickasaws, and Choctaws. All property or persons seized since the Treaty of New York were to be returned to Georgia, and the governor was empowered to send three agents to claim and receive such property and persons. The Indians would be

---

17. *Ibid.*, 598.
18. *Ibid.*, 599.

supplied six thousand dollars and two blacksmiths with the necessary tools of their trade.[19]

The wishes of Georgia were by no means met. On July 1, the Federal commissioners wrote an explanation to Governor Jared Irwin informing him of the pacific disposition of the Creeks, but also that "The expectations formed by your State, relative to the purchase of certain lands guaranteed to the Indians are frustrated. The representation of the Creek nation came instructed by the whole nation not to part with the lands."[20] The commissioners, however, were of the opinion no improper persuasion had caused the Indians to take such a position.

> From the long, repeated, and friendly conversation we have had with the chiefs, we have been able to draw from them some information, which we owe to our situation to give freely to you. It is, that it will require some time, and a considerable degree of prudence, to impress on the Indians, a confidence in the uprightness of the views of your Government, and in the friendly and peaceable intentions of its citizens, who inhabit the frontiers. And until such confidence is established, we are of opinion that all attempts to acquire land from them, by fair and open purchase, will be ineffectual.[21]

On July 3, presents were distributed to the Indians and they prepared to return to their homes. While looking over some of the surrounding country in the Indian lands, Hawkins found a cache of a thousand pounds of dried beef which the Indians had prepared from supplies they had secured early in the negotiations. This was an emergency ration in case of attack, further evidence of their distrust of the Georgians.

On July 6, after giving instructions for disposal of surplus supplies, the United States Commissioners bade adieu to Coleraine and departed for St. Marys by row boat.[22] The

---

19. *Ibid.*, 586-587, 609-610.
20. *Ibid.*, 611.
21. *Ibid.*
22. *Ibid.*, 612.

negotiations were over but repercussions continued and Georgians were greatly agitated over the results. The day before the signing of the treaty seven protests were presented to Hawkins by the Georgia commissioners. They objected to: the regulations of the United States commission as an infringement of Georgia's rights and as prejudicial to the state's interests at the conference; the removal of deliberations from the bower erected for that purpose in the square to Seagrove's home; the exclusion of the Georgia commissioners; and the authorship of the Indians' answer to Georgia. They also complained of Seagrove's failure to deny rumors of Georgia's unfriendly purposes, the place and time of holding the treaty conference, and the cession of lands claimed by Georgia to the United States. Finally since Georgia obtained no benefits, they protested the unfairness of the assessment against the state of half the expense of the negotiations.[23]

In their letter of July 1 to Governor Irwin the Federal commissioners answered and contradicted each of the protests and closed with these words:

> We deem it unnecessary to say more on this subject, but, to conclude, that it is remarkable, throughout the protest, that every sentence is at war with some other, and that the conclusions drawn, always destroy the premises.[24]

The argument continued. Private citizens took it up. A newspaper campaign of vilification of the United States commission was carried on by the Georgia commissioners and other citizens of the state. Judges charged juries, grand juries made presentments, the General Assembly adopted resolutions, governors issued proclamations, all bearing on the negotiations, and the Treaty of Coleraine was debated on the floors of Congress.

On July 29, an executive order from the state house at Louisville provided for publication in the *State Gazette* the protests of the Georgia commissioners, the Treaty of Gal-

---

23. *Ibid.*, 613.
24. *Columbian Museum & Advertiser*, August 5, 1796.

phinton, an extract from the Treaty of Shoulderbone, and an extract from the report of United States commissioners Lincoln, Humphreys, and Griffin, in 1789. As each of these documents had been used in the arguments of Jackson, Simms, and Hendricks, the whole controversy was well aired from the Georgia viewpoint.

In the October term of the Superior Court of Chatham County, Georgia, the grand jury utilized a portion of its presentment to comment upon the treaty and to charge the Federal commissioners with speculation. The jurymen accepted Jackson's version without question.

> We present the usurpation of powers, by the Commissioners of the United States, to make rules and regulations for the citizens of this state, during the late treaty at Coleraine: Regulations without exception of persons, which equally effected the Commissioners of this state, within her own limits, and the lowest citizen, which must have tended to lessen the state in the eyes of the Indians, and to prevent the state's succeeding in her object of obtaining the Oconee lands, and which regulations, superceded the laws of the land and civil jurisdiction. It appearing that citizens were arrested by military process, instead of constituted authority, which if admitted to be proper at Coleraine, may as a precedent, be also practiced on future occasion, in the city of Savannah, or any other part of the state.
>
> We are also of opinion, that the mysterious conduct of the late commissioners of the Union, and the superintendent of Indian affairs, covered some individual speculating designs against the interests of this state.[25]

On August 25, a resident of Coleraine addressed a long letter to James McNeil of Augusta, in which he condemned the Federal commissioners for their part in the treaty. This letter was published unsigned in the *Augusta Chronicle* and copied by other papers in the state. The writer, claiming

---

25. *Augusta Chronicle*, October 29, 1796. Among others accused of complicity in land fraud was Justice James Wilson of the Supreme Court of the United States.

personal observation, accused Hawkins, Clymer, and Seagrove with having prevented the Georgia commissioners
from achieving their objectives because the Federal officials
were "under the influence of Yazoo." He praised the actions
of Jackson and Simms. Hendricks, he reported, was at first
influenced by "much flattery and deception," but eventually,
"as an honest man well attached to the interests and constitutional rights of this state, did join his colleagues, and enter
a protest on the part of the state against the delusive and
unconstitutional proceedings of the Federal Commissioners. . . ." The letter ended with the charge that "those
who are concerned in the pretended purchase of Yazoo
lands, have been deeply concerned in this shameful business. . . ."[26]

The United States commissioners had defenders, however. In answer to this letter, a citizen, calling himself "Tombigbee," wrote:

> As to the fact, whether "Jackson and Simms," or "Hawkins,
> Clymer and Seagrove" injured the state at the late intended
> treaty: I am certain no man who has been much in public
> life as yourself, would resort to such documents to prove
> the one or the other position:- for, what do they contain,
> in the order they appear, but opinions, abuse and prophecy?
> - Yet, if you chose to expose yourself, let it not be done at
> the expense of truth and other people's reputation. It is a well
> known fact that an appropriation of shares was made to Mr.
> Seagrove, by the Georgia Mississippi Company, and that he
> positively refused to accept them - nor had he, or any one
> for him, any advantages resulting from such or any other
> appropriation: as to the idea of Mr. Hawkins or Mr. Clymer
> being concerned in the late sales of Western territory, it is too
> preposterous for reasoning upon, and could only originate
> from the virulent spirit of that party who cannot rest content
> with their fulminating repeal and their Gothic destruction
> of public records, but must have recourse to the most disin-
> genuous misrepresentations and chicane, to continue that
> furor which their influence and assiduity disseminated, and
> which to their great mortification is rapidly subsiding.[27]

26. *Augusta Chronicle*, September 24, 1796.
27. *Ibid.*, October 1, 1796.

Another unidentified resident of Coleraine had prophesied even before the treaty was signed that Jackson would be unsuccessful in securing lands for Georgia.

It is my opinion that Jackson and Simms have damned the treaty- it seems to me the former is deranged, his arrogance overleaps anything I have ever seen. From his want of temper he disgusted the Indians as well as the Federal Commissioners. Declamatory invective made up all his oratory, and per-vaded his whole deportment upon this important mission. Colonel Hendricks' conduct is much approved; and had his measures been pursued the lands might have been obtained. He associated with all the gentlemen engaged in negociation, and gained their esteem. I think he ought to protest against the proceedings of his colleagues, but I am afraid he will not. Jackson's mean endeavors to shift the blame off his own shoulders will, I fear be too successful with the misguided people; but, be assured that the Federal Commissioners and Mr. Seagrove continued to do every thing in their power, as long as Jackson kept within tolerable bounds. You may rely on this account of affairs, although I cannot at present descend to particulars. *Some little matters have turned up here which* may probably flop his career in a short time.[28]

Judge Benjamin Taliaferro, charging the grand jury of Hancock County, Georgia, at the September term of the Superior Court, made certain observations upon the treaty. He pointed out that whether or not the interests of Georgia had been violated was a matter to be decided by the General Assembly. Citizens should attempt to prevent strife with the Indians, and those who would take the law into their own hands to stir up horrible and bloody strife should be condemned. No individual was competent to determine whether war with the Creeks was preferable to peace as this was a power lodged with the general government. When the government decided upon war, he said, it was prepared, but when war was brought on by the act of private citizens the government was perplexed and unprepared. "Let us en-deavour then to preserve peace with those people so long as

28.. *Ibid.*, September 24, 1796.

we are under treaty with them, or if we are forced into hostilities, let it be fairly in our power to evince to mankind that we are not the aggressors; then may we with propriety expect the aid and the cooperation of the nation to afford us the necessary protection."[29]

Benjamin Hawkins, leaving this stormy debate behind him, journeyed north to report his actions to the President of the United States. Washington, with a confidence in his appointee engendered by long acquaintance and some degree of intimacy, accepted readily Hawkins's version of the proceedings and was well pleased with the conduct of the commissioners. He reported to Congress on December 7, that though Georgia's desires had not been accomplished, the treaty was a success and by means of it "the general peace may be more effectually preserved."[30]

Georgia remained unreconciled and attracted some support in Congress. Because of the opposition of the state's Senators, the treaty was ratified with the proviso that no violation of the rights of Georgia was contemplated. President Washington retired to private life on March 4, 1797, but his successor, John Adams, proclaimed the treaty and emphasized the proviso:

> That nothing in the third or fourth articles of the said treaty shall be construed to effect any claim of the state of Georgia, to the right of pre-emption in the land therein set apart for military or trading posts, or to give to the United States, without the consent of the said state, any right to soil or the exclusive legislation over the same, or any other right than that of establishing, maintaining and exclusively governing military and trading posts within the Indian territory mentioned in the said articles, as long as the frontier of Georgia may require these establishments.[31]

Georgia continued to object, however, and as late as May, 1797, a committee of the House of Representatives, appointed

29. *Ibid.*, October 1, 1796.
30. *American State Papers, Foreign Relations*, I, 30.
30. *American State Papers, Foreign Relations*, I, 30.
31. *Augusta Chronicle*, April 22, 1797.

to discuss the official protests of the state, reported the following resolutions:

> That the United States will make compensation to the State of Georgia, for the loss and damage sustained by that State, in consequence of the cession of the County of Talassee, made to the Creek nations, by the treaty of New York, unless it shall be deemed expedient to extinguish the Indian title to the land.[32]

Georgia was not compensated but was promised repeatedly that Indian titles should be extinguished as soon as practicable. To Georgians, irked by Federal delay, "as soon as practicable" appeared to mean "never." The resultant feeling of bitterness was not conducive to a cordial reception of the chairman of the United States commission when it fell his lot to return to the state as agent of the Creeks.

32. *Ibid.*, June 9, 1798.

CHAPTER VI

A Journey Through the Creek Country

O NE of Washington's early presidential interests was the attainment and preservation of friendship with the Indian tribes. In 1792, in an address to Congress he voiced the opinion that " . . . the employment of qualified and trusty persons to reside among them as agents, would also contribute to the preservation of peace and good neighborhood."[1]

By an act of the Congress of the Confederation in 1786 two superintendents of Indians affairs had been provided for. With the admission of Tennessee as a state in 1796 the position of superintendent in the Southern District lapsed. Hawkins was appointed by Washington "Principal Temporary Agent for Indian Affairs South of the Ohio River," and so signed himself throughout the administration of President John Adams. He never bore the title "superintendent" which has so often been attributed to him.[2]

An account of Hawkins's appointment written in 1812 with clarity and apparent intimate knowledge by an ardent, but anonymous, defender of the agent explained:

> After Col. Hawkins returned to the seat of government from the treaty of Colerain with the Creek Indians; he represented to President Washington that he thought that tribe of Indians might be kept at peace, under proper management, by an Agent of Indian affairs; but that a great sacrifice must be made by a man of talents, who ought to fill the office and reside constantly among the Indians. General Washington

---

1. *American State Papers, Foreign Relations*, I, 19.
2. R. S. Cotterill, "Federal Indian Management in the South, 1789-1825," *Mississippi Valley Historical Review*, XX, 335.

replied, "You have on no occasion heretofore refused your
services when necessarily called for by the general government, I wish you to sacrifice a few years of your life in making the experiment which you have suggested, and try the
effects of civilization among them." This proposition left
Col. Hawkins no room for retreat. He accepted the appointment . . . .[3]

James Seagrove had been agent of the Creeks since 1792.
There is no record of friction between him and Hawkins
at Coleraine. That Seagrove had been criticised at times by
both Georgians and Creeks is not sufficient evidence to im-
peach him for lack of ability. The nature of Hawkins's report
to the President can only be surmised. At any rate, less than
five months after the Treaty of Coleraine Hawkins had super-
seded Seagrove and was back in the Indian country with his
authority expanded to take in all the Southern Indians.

On January 6, 1797, Seagrove wrote to Richard Thomas,
clerk in the Indian Department, and mentioned having written to Creek chiefs explaining why he was no longer agent.
" . . . it is with the Nation, if they wish my services, to call
a meeting of the principal chiefs and draw up a clear and
spirited remonstrance to the President which will have the
desired effect." He suggested that Thomas dress these sentiments in proper style. " . . . let it be full and expressive of
my services to them & my own country." He concluded by
hinting at "base and foul play."[4]

Hawkins informed the Secretary of War that this letter
was false and absurd. His opinion was that Seagrove either
could not or would not serve upon terms the government
required. He further criticised his predecessor for having
lived at St. Marys and Coleraine and suggested that anyone
thinking the former a suitable place for the Agency " . . . might
be suspected of selfishness and being capable of sacrificing the
public good to their own ease and emolument . . . . There

3. *Republican & Savannah Evening Ledger*, Sept. 15, 1812.
4. *Letters of Benjamin Hawkins 1796-1806*, (Savannah: Georgia Historical Society *Publications*, IX, 1916), 251.

is unquestionably some difference between a seaside residence, with a handsome sallary [sic] & a large contingent fund, surrounded with one's friends, and a residence among the Indians."[5]

Other complaints Hawkins made against Seagrove were that he kept the Indians quiet by constantly giving them public goods, thus encouraging mendicancy, and that his accounts were in such bad shape his deputies sometimes went several months without pay.

After his dismissal, Seagrove set up a store at Coleraine and attempted to lure the Creeks away from both Panton, Leslie & Company and the United States factory.[6] He evidently held some resentment toward Hawkins but in 1799, in a letter to Methology, a Creek chief, he advised cooperation with the United States:

> As to your complaints against colonel Hawkins, the superintendent, and his deputies, it is a matter on which I can give no opinion, it being my sole object to endeavour to preserve peace between our countries and to avoid anything personal.[7]

Unquestionably, during the early years of Hawkins's Agency there was some sentiment favoring Seagrove. Governor Sargent of Mississippi, who was ever jealous of Hawkins and carried on an extensive correspondence campaign against him, wrote to Secretary Pickering in September, 1798, that he had learned through Andrew Ellicott, who had his information from Gayoso, Spanish Governor of Florida, that "It would seem . . . the Creeks though Disgusted with Colonel Hawkins, have a patiality [sic] to Mr. Seagrove."[8]

In November, 1796, Hawkins arrived at Hopewell, the scene of his first treaty negotiations, and the home of his

---

5. *Ibid.*, 262.
6. Hawkins, *Letters*, 309-310. See Chap. XI for discussion of Factory System and Panton, Leslie & Company.
7. *Augusta Chronicle*, July 6, 1799.
8. Dunbar Rowland, editor, *The Mississippi Territorial Archives, 1798-1803, Executive Journals of Governor Winthrop Sargent and Governor William Charles Cole Claiborne*, I, 46.

good friend and recent colleague, General Andrew Pickens. Illness and the cordial reception he received at the hands of General and Mrs. Pickens made him loath to leave. Among the first specific duties assigned to him were to run the Cherokee line agreeable to the Treaty of Holston and the Creek line in conformity to the Treaty of Coleraine. The date fixed for the Cherokee line was March 10, 1797. He determined, therefore, to utilize the intervening time in seeing the country, acquainting himself with his wards, and in spreading information among the Creeks and Cherokees as to the policy of the government and plans of the President for their future welfare.[9]

Accordingly, he set out from Hopewell on November 24, travelling on horseback with pack animals carrying supplies and equipment. Though a stranger to the country, he was acquainted with Indian treachery and knew of their dislike for whites. Nevertheless, even while he travelled through a wild and sometimes dangerous region there is nothing to indicate that he carried arms of any kind.

From Hopewell he travelled south and west through Cherokee lands, stopping frequently to meet and converse with those he met, half-breed traders and Cherokees alike. He was dependent upon them for shelter and refreshment, for information and guidance. His journal, replete with minute detail, is a valuable storehouse of information about the country and the people with whom he came in contact.[10] On the second day of his journey he crossed the Chattooga River, from South Carolina into Georgia. His ultimate destination was the Creek country along the Chattahoochee, but he did not neglect the Cherokees and journeyed at length in their territory.

On November 26, passing ten horses laden with deer skins, he remarked that this made "thirty-one wagon loads" [sic]

9. Hawkins, Letters, 13.
10. Fortunately nine manuscript volumes of this journal have been preserved in the library of the Georgia Historical Society and have been published by that organization under the title The Letters of Benjamin Hawkins.

brought out of that section of Cherokee Georgia that season.[11] On this day he crossed the scenic Tallulah River and turned toward the headwaters of the Chattahoochee.

Hawkins's purposes were to introduce his new wards to the benefits of civilization and to influence them to produce agricultural commodities. Two days after his passage of the Tallulah, an Indian hunter conducted him to the hut of a half-breed woman.

> She treated me hospitably. She was poor, she said from trouble and difficulty not from want of industry. She had been greatly incommoded by the misunderstanding between the Red and White people. She knew not where to fix down, and this uncertainty continued until it was too late to make corn, she planted some, but too late. She showed me a wound in one of her arms which she got on a visit to some of her friends who lived in the neighborhood when the town was attacked by some white people from Tugalo. I mentioned the plan contemplated by the government for bettering the condition of the Red people, she replied she had once made as much cotton as produced a petticoat, that she would gladly make more and learn to spin it, if she had the opportunity.[12]

In this same locality Hawkins found that the Indians bartered two chickens which they had raised for two and a half yards of cotton binding worth two cents, and sometimes traded a bushel of corn for a pint of salt. He was told that an Indian woman had just returned from a journey of seventeen days to the white settlements, where she traded a bushel and a half of chestnuts for a petticoat.[13]

As Hawkins traversed the Cherokee portion of Georgia he saw constant evidence that white encroachments were driving the Indians to new hunting grounds. His journal frequently mentions deserted villages, in many of which cotton and corn stalks were still standing and the ubiquitous peach trees were growing.

---

11. Hawkins, *Letters*, 16.
12. *Ibid.*, 18.
13. *Ibid.*

On November 29, he encountered Christian Russell, a Silesian trader among the Cherokees who was preparing to set up a tanyard at the Cherokee town of Etowah. Hawkins informed him of the law regarding licenses for traders and warned him to apply for one.[14]

The next day Hawkins had the interesting experience of finding himself in a village temporarily inhabited only by women. He was told by a Negress, who acted as interpreter, that the men were all in the woods hunting. He explained to the women the President's policy and his object in sending him into their country. They knew how to grow cotton, they said, and would grow more and follow Hawkins's instructions and the President's plan. "They exhibited to me a sample of their ingenuity in the manufacture of baskets and sifters, out of cane, the dies of the splits were good and the workmanship not surpassed in the United States by white people. I recommended to them to be attentive to Mr. Dinsmoor."[15]

Most of the Cherokees to whom Hawkins talked seemed anxious to follow his advice to plant the soil. They expressed the desire to remain permanently and peacefully in their villages and, "they were willing to labour if they could be directed how to profit by it." The women did most of the manual labor, and in one village Hawkins found them planting corn, sweet potatoes, pumpkins, beans, peas, cymblins, gourds, watermelons, muskmelons, collards, and onions. Salt was to them a great necessity and was held very dear, as they raised hogs, cattle, and poultry, which they could not preserve without it. They also made a little sugar and cotton, and manufactured baskets, sifters, pots and "earthen pans." The men supplemented the products of the women's labors with

---

14. There is no evidence that the tanyard was established. It was not many weeks before Russell was asking Hawkins for a license for trade among the Creeks.
15. Hawkins, *Letters*, 20. Silas Dinsmoor was Temporary Agent to the Cherokees.

deer skins and venison. Even so, the old men, women, and children were poorly clothed.[16]

> They in the morning told me that many men had been sent into their nation to their chiefs but I was the first who thought it worth while to examine into the situation of the women. I had addressed myself to them, and talked freely and fondly to them, and they were sure I meant to better their condition. They would follow my advice. They told me they were healthy, and lived to old age, some few had the ague and fever, but that generally they were never too unwell to labour, even when they bore children they were their own midwives and would most of them turn out the next day after delivering themselves and pursue their ordinary occupations.[17]

One constant complaint of the Indians was that the coming of the whites destroyed their game and lessened their opportunities of a livelihood. Deserted villages gave evidence of the disappearance of game, although Hawkins glimpsed deer and saw many signs of turkeys. While it is unquestionably true that the advance of civilization did drive out wild-life, the Indians themselves were not strict conservationists. Probably the practice that played most havoc with the Indian game was the sale of deerskins to traders. In the summer of 1796, Hawkins was told some Cherokees had mixed three bushels of buckeye root with two bushels of clay, pounded the mixture up, and placed it in Limestone Creek in northwest Georgia. Fish were poisoned for eight miles downstream and from sixty to eighty Indians gathered as many dead fish as they could carry away.[18]

Hawkins had no complaint with the meals he had among the Cherokees. One breakfast menu he mentioned was good bread, pork, potatoes, peas, and dried peaches.[19]

The adults, as soon as they learned his identity, received the agent of the United States cordially and with manifest

16. *Ibid*, 21-22.
17. *Ibid.*, 22.
18. *Ibid.*, 23.
19. *Ibid.*

pleasure, but children were terrified at the sight of a strange white man. They had heard the old people tell of raids by the whites and had thus grown up in great fear of pale faces.

On December 5, Hawkins reached the Tallapoosa River, called Aquonausete by the Cherokees, and was in the country of the Upper Creeks. That evening he met the first Creek and was cordially received, his fame having preceded him. He also had his first visual evidence of the hardiness of the red man. In a mountainous region of what is today east Alabama, with a December rain falling, one of the guides took off his shirt, spread it on the wet ground, pulled a small, badly-worn blanket over himself and slept soundly through the night. Hawkins slept none too comfortably under a shelter and covered with a blanket, bearskins, and an oilcloth coat. The Cherokees while travelling ate little and used no salt. Wissoetaw, or parched corn meal pounded fine, was their sole ration. A handful mixed in a pint of water made a meal. Hawkins professed a fondness for wissoetaw with a little sugar added.[20]

The agent spoke little of the Creek tongue and had no interpreter, though one of the Cherokee guides could converse slightly in the Creek language. The first house he visited belonged to a chief who had been at Coleraine accompanied by his twelve-year-old daughter. The chief was hunting, but recognition of Hawkins by the daughter assured him of a welcome and he was given a clean hut and provisions. Among the supplies was some sofkey, or saufkee, the Indian name for lye hominy, a staple product among the Creeks. Despite this cordial and generous treatment, Hawkins's first impression was that the Creeks were much poorer than the Cherokees.

The next day he arrived at the village of New York, or New Yaucau, named after the treaty of 1790. Here he found the home of James Sullivan, a trader, and was received courteously by David Hay, the assistant, in Sullivan's absence. Hawkins conversed unsatisfactorily with the Indians

20. *Ibid*, 26.

in the village, using as his interpreter a Negro woman who was not very intelligent. This was the second time in a little over a week that he had been compelled to use a Negro woman as an interpreter, evidence that some slaves had either been stolen from the whites, or had run away into Indian country. Across the river from New York lived Tuskena Patki, the White Lieutenant, one of the principal Upper Creek chiefs. Though the chief was on the hunt, Hawkins visited his family and found it poorly supplied with food, again in contrast to the well stocked Cherokees.[21]

On reaching the town of the Hillabees, Hawkins found a Scotch trader, Robert Grierson, who had long been in the country and was well established with large holdings of lands, forty slaves, three hundred cattle, and thirty horses. Like most of the traders Grierson had an Indian family. The agent was received hospitably by the old Scot who was superintending the picking and ginning of his cotton for which he anticipated thirty-four cents a pound in the Tennessee market. Influenced by Grierson's example the Hillabee Indians were farming and raising stock, one half-breed owning one hundred and thirty head of cattle and ten horses. There were four villages connected with the Hillabees, and one hundred and seventy warriors belonged to the town.[22]

Grierson's agreement to accompany Hawkins to the important council town of Tookaubatchee was the occasion of Hawkins's issuing his first order. The departure was delayed when two of Grierson's horses were stolen in the night. Stephen Hawkins, another trader, volunteered to seek the thieves and was given authority:

> . . . to take with him such aid as he may deem necessary, and to pursue and apprehend the said offenders, wherever to be found within the agency South of the Ohio. And I do hereby require of the agent of the Cherokees, his assistants and all others in authority to be aiding and assisting in the premises.[23]

21. *Ibid.*, 29.
22. *Ibid.*, 29-30. Near this town Hawkins observed Indian women picking up red oak acorns for making oil which they used as food.
23. *Ibid.*, 32.

On December 13, Hawkins and Grierson passed through Tookaubatchee and arrived at the home of Alexander Cornells, half-breed assistant agent and interpreter, who resided four miles down the river. This was the district of the Abbecoos of the Upper Creeks, and the towns numbered twenty, most of them on, or near, either the Coosa or the Tallapoosa rivers. Nearly all had traders and Hawkins found among them Americans, English, Scotch, Irish, French, one Dutchman, one Jew, and a Spaniard, besides half-breeds and one native Indian trader. Since these men were influential in the success or failure of any Indian policy, Hawkins made a careful study of them. In his journal he listed forty-six traders by name and classified them as to honesty, sobriety, and whether they owned property or were in debt to Panton, Leslie & Company. About a fourth of them were addicted to drunkenness and a similar proportion in debt to Panton, Leslie & Company, and dishonest in their relations with the Indians.[24]

As the purpose of Hawkins's journey into the Upper Creek country was to acquaint himself first-hand with his new wards in their natural surroundings, he used the opportunity while in Alexander Cornells' home to converse at length with Grierson and his half-breed assistant, both men of intelligence. They were naturally biased in favor of the Creeks, and it may be that Hawkins, who had always demanded fair treatment of the Indians, needed no extra encouragement for his efforts in their behalf. Certainly he was cordially received and possibly flattered by frequent references to his fairness at Coleraine and Hopewell. Later he was often to be criticised by his fellow countrymen for exaggerated efforts in the interest of his charges and overindulgence of them, but he was sincere and could never have acknowledged, or even recognized, any basis for such criticism. It is possible, however, that his first impressions, fixed in his mind and

24. *Ibid.*, 168. Panton, Leslie & Company was an English trading firm operating in Florida and on the Gulf Coast under Spanish authority. See Chap. XI.

encouraged by Cornells and Grierson, may have given his critics some justification for their complaints.

Hawkins reported: "I have had much conversation with him [Cornells] and Mr. Grierson on the subject of my mission, as they possessed and could give the best information now to be had in the nation." He was informed that the Indians had improved a great deal in twenty years, were less cruel, milder in manners, and more inclined to be friendly with their neighbors. They had also advanced in industry and showed increased interest in husbandry. The Creeks had particularly exhibited a desire for peace since the Treaty of Coleraine and referred appreciatively to the conduct of the United States commissioners at the conference.[25]

Intrusion on hunting grounds and horse stealing were the two practices most conducive to unfriendly relations between the races. Cornells and Grierson complained that the stealing of Indian livestock by depraved whites had become a well-organized system, and heroic measures would be necessary to put a stop to it. Another evil deplored was the neglect and desertion of Indian wives and children by white men who had married in the nation.[26]

Within two and a half miles of Tookaubatchee there were four islands in the Tallapoosa River which had been cultivated. In the shoals around them moss covered the rocks and the shallow waters were frequented in summer by horses, cattle, and deer, grazing together. In the winter large flocks of swans, geese, and ducks gathered there. Hawkins told of sturgeon, trout, perch, rock fish, and red horse running together in one creek which emptied into the river.[27] The hunting grounds of the Upper Creeks seemed better stocked than those of either the Cherokees or the Lower Creeks. Since these people preferred the hunt to any other form of labor, it is no wonder they were jealous of white intrusions on such well-stocked grounds.

25. *Ibid.*, 35.
26. *Ibid.*, 35-36.
27. *Ibid.*, 37-38.

As he penetrated farther into the country of the Upper Creeks Hawkins noticed decided improvement. More land was cultivated, stock was better and more numerous, houses cleaner and more comfortable, and the Indians seemed willing, even anxious, to cooperate with the government in a program of farming and handicrafts. The presence of many half-breeds, some of whom held high tribal positions, and white men with Indian families had some influence on this change of tribal customs.

On December 18, Hawkins and Alexander Cornells visited Richard Bailey, a white man living five miles down the river. Bailey had an Indian family and was a man of much influence in the nation. On his excellent farm he gathered honey from twenty beehives and planted cotton which his wife and daughters spun and made into clothes. He possessed seven Negroes, two hundred cattle, one hundred fifty hogs, and one hundred twenty horses. An Englishman, he had formerly worked in Savannah, but had spent forty years pleasantly and profitably among the Creeks.[28]

The next day on the way to the house of Charles Weatherford, half-breed brother-in-law of McGillivray, Hawkins passed a Uchee village and a half mile farther a Shawnee town. These Indians were living peacefully with the Creeks, though the Shawnees retained the language and customs of their tribesmen of the Northwest.

A day later Hawkins was at Weatherford's residence on a high bluff on the left bank of the Alabama River below the confluence of the Coosa and Tallapoosa. Weatherford, one of the principal chiefs of the Upper Creeks, was a man of some wealth with a particular interest in breeding fine horses. He maintained a race track near his home.[29] Hawkins thought him a most undesirable character and doubted his legal ownership of some of the horses he raced.

Near Weatherford lived Mrs. Durant, the oldest sister of Alexander McGillivray, whose husband was a dull man

---

28. *Ibid.*, 39-41.
29. *Ibid.*, 42.

with some Negro blood. With their eight children they were housed in dirty and uncomfortable quarters. They possessed eighty slaves but the Negroes were burdensome because of poor management. Panton, Leslie & Company had refused to supply Mrs. Durant further with goods and this emphasized her poverty.

Hawkins next visited Hickory Ground, the former residence of General McGillivray. He spent a night in the neighborhood with Nicholas White, a trader.

> . . . agreeably, except the conduct of my deputy Alex Cornell, who forgetting himself, got drunk, and was a little disorderly. This morning I began to correct the abuse in my own family. I told my deputy that he was a chief of the land and in the service of the United States, he knew well how to conduct himself, and I was surprised at the impropriety of his conduct, he must reform, and not give me the pain of seeing him again playing the part of the drunken Indian.[30]

Christmas day found Hawkins again at the Bailey home. The clean, kind, and jocose Mrs. Bailey served excellent food, plus an occasional drink of Bailey's "good rum," and the day passed pleasantly. Hawkins, though not averse to an occasional glass of grog, was a temperate man and commented favorably upon Bailey's sobriety and his ability to handle the neighboring Indians even when they were drinking.[31]

While dining on pork, chicken, duck, rice, and potatoes, Hawkins was reminded that eleven years before he had eaten Christmas dinner among the Indians at Hopewell, and, " . . . that the table was covered with a great variety of wild meat and fowls, the company large, that all of them are still living, and that the conversation then was the means of establishing a peace with these Indians, and of bettering their condition. I remember well that the sentiments I then enter-

---

30. *Ibid.*, 45.
31. *Ibid.*, 47.

tained were the same I still possess, and am labouring to carry into effect."[32]

The spirit of Christmas had entered the Indian country. It was customary for all the neighboring slaves to gather at the home of Mrs. Durant or Mrs. Weatherford on Christmas day. This year the gathering was at the Durants'. "And there they had a proper frolic of rum drinking and dancing . . . . the white people and the Indians met generally at the same place with them and had the same amusement."[33]

It was the opinion of Hawkins that Negroes among the Indians, with few exceptions, were an expense and burden to their owners. "They do nothing the whole winter but get a little wood, and in the summer they cultivate a scanty crop of corn barely sufficient for bread."[34]

One of the principal objects of Hawkins's journey was to ascertain the Indian attitude toward the government's plan to help them learn and adopt the white man's culture. He received conflicting, and therefore not altogether satisfactory accounts. Mrs. Bailey doubted the practicability of carrying the benevolent views of the government into effect. Her daughter had learned to spin among the white people, but many of the Indian women, while industrious, were neither clean, provident, nor careful.

> This I [Hawkins] replied might be owing to want of information and means of helping themselves. She said she did not know whether it was so or not, but of one thing she was certain, they all had water enough, and yet they never kept their husbands clean, even the white men, and this was really a source of vexation to her, and put her under the necessity of scolding the men whenever she saw them, for not making their wives wash their linen; and the women for their want of cleanliness.[35]

32. *Ibid.*, 48.
33. *Ibid.*, 48-49.
34. *Ibid.*, 49.
35. *Ibid.*, 48.

The intimation that the white man's civilization might not prove acceptable and beneficial to the Indian was unpleasant to the new agent. He was committed to a policy of social and economic betterment for his wards. No consideration, other than an earnest desire to help the Indian, would have caused him to bury himself in the wilderness in the face of family opposition.

A few days after his talk with Mrs. Bailey he received a more encouraging report. Emautle Hutke, White Chief, spent a night with him.

> This old man told me he had a great regard for the white people, that ... the Indian had, notwithstanding his obstinacy received much useful instruction. That now they had more comforts, to which they were strangers to, cloathing, [sic] comfortable houses, and plenty of bread.
>
> He remembered when the part of the nation where he lived had not a blanket or a hoe, and his father remembered the introduction of the knife and the hatchet. He remembered when there was not a horse in the nation and rum used to be packed by the traders and sent down with the skins, he remembers the first horse and mare that was brought in the nation by a trader and that the Indians were afraid of them.
>
> And now he said they had hoes, axes, knives, guns and other necessaries, and he was glad I intended to increase the number, and trade them other useful things.[36]

On the last day of the year 1796, Hawkins completed his tour of the Upper Creek towns, reached the Chattahoochee River and entered the Lower Creek country. On January 5, he visited the council square at Cusseta, attended by James Darouzeaux as interpreter, was cordially received by the Micos and chiefs, and partook of the ceremony of the Black Drink, a concoction of herbs offered as a token of friendship. Hawkins told the Indians of the government's plan to introduce among them the white man's customs and to better their condition. They were also informed of the transfer of Colonel Gaither and his garrison from Coleraine

36. *Ibid.*, 49-50.

to the Oconee River and of plans for strengthening the garrisons on the frontier as a protection to them and a guarantee of the observance of treaty agreements. The Creeks were assured that the Cherokees had agreed to accept plans for their betterment.

> They all heard me with attentive silence, untill I mentioned the raising and spinning of cotton. One of them laughed at the idea, but the Fusatchee assent [sic] to all and said it must be done.
> The objection made to it by the men, is, that if the women can cloathe [sic] themselves, they will be proud and not obedient to their husbands.[37]

Hawkins remained on the Chattahoochee, generally at Coweta, until February 2. For a month he spent his time in talking with the Indians, visiting the surrounding towns, and in writing his journal. He met and became friendly with most of the important kings and chiefs of the lower Chattahoochee towns. His careful observations of the people and the country were recorded meticulously. His journal abounds with interesting accounts of topography, Indian agriculture, abundant wild life, and Indian customs.

On January 23, while visiting the town of Coweta Tallahassee, he

> . . . was shown in an old field some stakes to which the Cherokees had been tied in the last war they had with the Creeks about 40 years past when taken prisoners. Three of the stakes remain. Here the captives were tied and here they received their doom, which with the exception of young lads and a few women was the tortue [sic] till death.[38]

The next day Hawkins witnessed a sample of Creek thievery and realized in an emphatic way that even the property of the agent was not safe when one of his horses was stolen. Though the young men of the town claimed to know

---

37. *Ibid.*, 56.
38. *Ibid.*, 63.

the identity of the culprit, many days passed before the horse was returned.

Finding at Coweta an intelligent Creek woman who spoke English, he decided to use her as an example to the other women and through her to get his plan of aiding the Indians started.

> I have promised her to cloathe [*sic*] her and her two children at the expense of the United States, annually and to furnish her with the means of living comfortably, on condition that she will have her daughter taught to spin, and assist herself, to interpret to the women, and whatever may be devised for their benefit. She readily assented and has promised to be governed in all things by those who have the direction of Indian affairs.[39]

The experiment failed. More than eight years later Hawkins noted under the above entry in his journal that she did not carry out her promise "nor could she be prevailed on to use any other means than lying whenever she saw a white man."[40]

Before leaving the Chattahoochee town on February 4, 1797, and journeying east toward the Flint River, Hawkins heard that Edward Price had arrived at his Coleraine post with goods for the Indian Department "much damaged by bad weather on the passage." The agent's badly-needed baggage was in this damaged consignment.[41]

Price complained that he had been greatly embarrassed by Creeks who came begging for supplies. Some of these Indians had refused to go to Coleraine when invited the year before; but, since they had been accustomed to go to James Seagrove and receive public supplies, they had come demanding similar handouts from Price. Hawkins supported the factor and informed his charges that such mendicancy must cease, that while he was in charge of Indian affairs they should expect to receive only their annuities promised by the treaty.

---

39. *Ibid.*, 65.
40. *Ibid.*, 65 note.
41. *Ibid.*, 66.

From the 9th to the 21st of February, Hawkins visited Timothy Barnard, one of his assistants, at his home on the lower Flint. He then journeyed east and reached Fort Fidius, newly-built garrison on the Oconee commanded by Colonel Gaither where he remained for about two weeks writing reports and catching up on his correspondence.

Hawkins had been in the Indian country slightly over three months. His time had been spent largely in travel and in the endeavor to become acquainted with his charges and to acquaint them with his plans. He had meant his journey to be one of observation, and not the routine of his work. Nevertheless, a study of his report of March 1 to the Secretary of War shows that he attended to the following numerous details: correspondence with the Society of Quakers in regard to the training of Indian boys; correspondence with the United States factor about his long delayed and damaged baggage; holding up of the Creek annuity until plans for a meeting of chiefs could be arranged; communication with the War Department concerning intrigue among the Indians; arrangements for the return of, and actual receipt and delivery of stolen horses; consideration of the complaints of the Indians regarding white trespasses; report of the execution of murderers among the Creeks at his instigation; the determination, on his own initiative, to run the Cherokee line before running that conforming to treaties with the Creeks; denial of licenses to resident traders who had not conformed to the laws; advice to the Secretary of War as to the best method of licensing traders; granting passes to white men to traverse Indian country; encouraging the Indians to neutrality in the war between Spain and England; and, finally, completing arrangements for running the Cherokee line. The life of an Indian agent Hawkins soon found was not easy, and, if his duties were well performed, it was a full-time job with long hours and few holidays. He was firm in his resolution to help the Indians, and the magnitude of the task challenged his enthusiasm.

When the day of his departure for Tellico Blockhouse to run the Cherokee line arrived, Hawkins's tour of the Creek country came to an end. He was no longer a stranger to the Creeks, nor they to him. He must now spend some weeks among the Cherokees, but the Creeks anticipated his return.

Chapter VII

Tracing Boundary Lines

THE Cherokee "experiment line," temporarily located in 1792 by a commission appointed by William Blount who had negotiated the Treaty of Holston some months before, was never satisfactory to the Indians, who claimed that it did not conform to the terms of the treaty. Therefore, though no attempt had been made to survey the Creek line agreeable to the terms of the recent Treaty of Coleraine, Hawkins selected the Cherokee survey as the most pressing and March, 1797, as the month to begin arrangements. Generals Andrew Pickens and James Winchester had been named as his colleagues on the Cherokee commission. On March 7 he requested Lieutenant Colonel Gaither, commandant at Fort Fidius, to furnish a mounted escort of dragoons to accompany him to Tellico Blockhouse on the Tennessee River.[1] On the same day Pickens and Winchester were informed of his plans, and Silas Dinsmoor, Cherokee agent, was instructed to be ready to accompany the commission with an interpreter.[2]

Hawkins realized that his duties with the line commission would continue for some months. He therefore gave his assistants, Timothy Barnard and Alexander Cornells, and Edward Price, the factor, careful and detailed instructions as to the conduct of affairs at the Agency while he was away.[3]

He reached Hopewell, the home of General Pickens, on March 16 but, finding the General unprepared for an immediate departure, he spent a pleasant week in the home of his old friend before setting out across the mountains for

---

1. Hawkins, *Letters*, 93-94.
2. *Ibid.*, 94-95.
3. *Ibid.*, 96-99, 101-102.

Tennessee. Hawkins kept a journal and described in minute detail the journey through Cherokee lands to Tellico, which was reached on March 31.

General Winchester had been informed of the plan to meet at Tellico but, professing unfamiliarity with the country, he misinterpreted his instructions and failed to meet Hawkins and Pickens there.

> It is my intention not to be present [he wrote Dinsmoor] especially as I have no acquaintance with the Creek nation, nor no geographical knowledge of that country, but shall hold myself in readiness to attend the runing [sic] and establishing of the Cherokee and Chickasaw lines.[4]

Hawkins considered Winchester's ideas as "pretty extraordinary." He could not conceive of a man, sufficiently prominent to be assigned to such a position, not knowing where Tellico Blockhouse was, or one who could fail to realize " . . . that we could never be so absurd as to come from the Creek line, two hundred and fifty miles, here, for the purpose merely of meeting him to accompany us back again."[5] On April 5 Hawkins wrote in the "Journal of the Proceedings of the Commissioners Appointed to Ascertain and Mark the Boundary Lines Agreeable to the Treaties Between the Indian Nations and the United States":

> We received information of a confidential nature as to the informants that General Winchester would not be here; that a postponement of the runing [sic] of the line by some means or other was in contemplation by some persons interested in intrusions on Indian rights.[6]

Hawkins and Pickens informed James McHenry, Secretary of War, on April 11, that if there was any expectation of delaying the line under the idea that the presence of all three was necessary in order " . . . to give time to the intruders to plant

---

4. Ibid., 146.
5. Ibid., 147.
6. Ibid., 146.

crops, we will frustrate it."[7] On April 24 they intimated to McHenry that General Winchester's absence was deliberate and requested permission to proceed without him.[8]

Inevitably, the determination of Hawkins to perform his duties with complete adherence to his instructions caused him to run counter to the interests of certain white men. He was unwilling to compromise and insisted upon literal conformity to agreements with the Indians. He was supported without reservation by Pickens. During the five years since the treaty of Holston many white men had encroached upon Cherokee lands. Some of them had consciously and purposely done so; others were there either through misinformation, or because of an honest uncertainty as to where the line was.

Every possible obstruction was placed in the way of the commissioners. On April 16, it was recorded:

> The Commissioners received, for several days past, information of an intention to prevent them from executing the trust reposed in them, either by the non-attendance of General Winchester, or by attacking the Indians, to bring on a war.[9]

Eight days later, Hawkins and Pickens made positive charges against Winchester:

> We are well aware of the speculative pursuits of the General, and if we were not, he seems determined to betray himself; he knows we are at Tellico, where the military force is now stationed, or in the neighbourhood of it, and he affects ignorance of everything, offers his services to get an additional escort, surveyors, assistants, &c., to go to Duck River to save time. There are no troops in his neighbourhood, and he knows we are not going to Duck River.[10]

Obstacles were also placed before the commissioners by John Sevier, Governor of Tennessee, and by Captain Richard

---

7. *Ibid.*, 120.
8. *Ibid.*, 130-131.
9. *Ibid.*, 155.
10. *Ibid.*, 159.

Sparks, 3rd Regiment, United States Army, who was in command of the troops in Tennessee. Full cooperation was received only from Colonel David Henley, agent for the War Department, stationed at Knoxville.

Governor Sevier informed Hawkins and Pickens on April 13 that the citizens of Tennessee were alarmed over the rumors of large bodies of Indians assembling on the frontier. Sevier stated that he had taken great pains to keep peace with the Indians, and threatened, unless immediately informed why so many were assembling, to order out the Tennessee militia to protect the citizens of the state. He complained:

> It is reported that you are appointed Commissioners to ascertain and mark the boundary line between the United States and the Indians, and altho' the State of Tennessee is so materially and essentially interested in the event, no official information thereof has been communicated to its executives, neither by the Executive of the United States or the Commissioners, *if they be such*.[11]

The commissioners replied to Governor Sevier on April 16:

> We think, Sir, that . . . a knowledge that the agents in the Indian department were here, ought to have been sufficient to remove all cause of alarm from the citizens of this state . . . . We are appointed . . . 'Commissioners to ascertain and mark the boundary lines agreeable to treaties between the Indian nations and the United States,' and we are now here on that business . . . . We shall take care that in the execution of this trust our fidelity shall correspond with the confidence reposed in us by the appointment.[12]

Following this exchange of communications there seems to have been no further outward conflict between the commissioners of the United States and the Governor of Tennessee. Sevier, nevertheless, was resentful and did nothing to further the negotiations or make the running of the line less difficult. Hawkins was informed that the Governor's letter

11. *Ibid.*, 156-157. Italics mine.
12. *Ibid.*, 157-158.

had been copied and circulated widely before it had reached the commissioners. It had aroused some citizens and had encouraged those with grievances against the United States to embarrass the commissioners and to obstruct the running of the line.

The attitude of Captain Sparks caused more difficulty. He was not only non-cooperative, but ordered George Strother, Ensign Commandant at Tellico, not to obey the orders of the commissioners.[13] The conduct and communications of Sparks were such as to cause Hawkins to write him briefly and succinctly: "Sir: I have just received your letter of the 10th. It requires no comment from me, as I submit the propriety of your conduct to your reflections."[14] This was followed by a letter to Colonel David Henley:

> . . . I am of Opinion that Captain Sparks has behaved himself as is unbecoming an officer and a gentleman; as he has remained in Knoxville you have probably learned more than I have; you will be able to judge whether you think the executive can safely trust the important command of this frontier to such a character. I have been informed that in your presence he said he did not care a dam for his commission.[15]

The commissioners had been authorized to issue instructions to Captain Sparks, and on the day the above letter was written he was ordered to furnish an escort of thirty privates, two commissioned and four non-commissioned officers, with mounts and equipment. Sparks yielded to the firmness of Hawkins and Pickens, and eight days later they wrote to the Secretary of War that the escort had been furnished and that Sparks had visited them with an explanation of his past conduct and the promise of future cooperation.[16]

On April 3 David Campbell, one of the Tennessee commissioners who had run the "experiment" line in 1792, called

---

13. *Ibid.*, 122.
14. *Ibid.*, 152.
15. *Ibid.*, 125.
16. *Ibid.*, 130-131.

on Hawkins and Pickens and offered to accompany them and point out the line to them. Twelve days later a deputation of Tennessee citizens, knowing the inaccuracy of this boundary and fearing that the real line would force them from their farms, visited the commissioners. They admitted that formerly the lines had not been run for accuracy but to protect the citizens who had settled in the Indian country. In fact, the line run by Campbell had been "run to see how the citizens could be covered, as they were then settled on the frontier." The citizens agreed that the time had come when the law must be obeyed, but they suggested that the enforcement be applied to the future and not to the past. Finding the commissioners determined to run the line accurately, they requested that they at least be permitted to harvest their crops already planted.[17] Hawkins reported the answer of the commissioners as follows:

> . . . that as to the small grain, we would see that they saved that and their fruit, but for anything else, it did not depend on us; in case of doubtful settlement for want of the line, it would be reasonable to expect our indulgence, but where the intrusions were manifest violations of the Treaty of Holston, no indulgence ought to be expected . . . .[18]

This reply is typical of Hawkins's insistence upon absolute conformity to instructions. He, however, assured the settlers that since the line could not be completed before June, they would have adequate opportunity to make their crops. This assurance was accepted by the settlers, and they agreed not to make trouble for the party.

Silas Dinsmoor had been sent to Knoxville to superintend the construction of an instrument for taking latitude which a "mathematical instrument maker" was constructing. When he returned on April 18, the first official act of the survey party was the taking of the latitude of Tellico Blockhouse with the new "semicircle."[19]

17. *Ibid.*, 153.
18. *Ibid.*, 153-154.
19. *Ibid.*, 158.

The principal chiefs of the Cherokees had been invited to meet the commissioners and to accompany them as they ran the line. The Indians, professing a fear for their safety, were slow to assemble, but began straggling in on April 19. Gaining confidence, they came in increasing numbers until, when the conference began on April 25, one hundred and forty-seven chiefs and warriors were present.

It has been charged by his critics that Hawkins was over-indulgent to the Indians. His actions during this conference do not sustain such charges. Silas Dinsmoor was given the responsibility of furnishing with supplies and presents those Indians invited to attend the conference. He was instructed that those who had come without invitation should be sent home or made to support themselves during their stay. When Hawkins was asked to furnish the chiefs with whiskey he answered:

> . . . no, not one drop till the business they convened on was completely adjusted. They replyed this was not usual, they hitherto were indulged and expected a continuance. He rejoined he saw but little good in their past transactions, that he did not come to continue abuses, but to remedy the past, and he should, for himself, make a point of doing what he judged proper regardless of the past. After some hesitation, the chiefs agreed the decision was just and they expected some good from it, as heretofore much injury had been done them when in a state of drunkenness.[20]

After a four-day conference the Indians agreed to aid in running the line according to the treaty and appointed commissioners from the nation to accompany the United States Commission. On April 29, 1797, the party left Tellico. Hawkins remained with it until September. Though the line was not then completed he returned to Georgia and reached Fort Wilkinson on the Oconee River on September 12. The citizens of Tennessee were dissatisfied with Hawkins's work. In November James Byers, United States factor at Tellico, wrote to Edward Price, who held the same position at Cole-

20. *Ibid.*, 159.

raine, that two Indians had recently been killed by some whites who had been removed from Cherokee lands. He added:

> . . . to manifest their disapprobation of the justice of government in forcing them from their plundered possessions- The immaculate government of Tennessee, dissatisfied with the line established by the late commissioners have had it run again by a holy pack of insurgents - who report the line imperfect - and Colo. Hawkins a liar - a set of brutes as they are to endeavour to smurge [sic] the reputation of a man, who has more sense, honor and honesty, than the whole state of Tennessee put together.[21]

Some months later Hawkins wrote to a friend of his experiences on the Cherokee line:

> I cannot express to you the difficulty and fatigue I underwent in ascertaining and marking the line, and the anxiety I had at seeing a number of my fellow citizens certain victims of their own folly by intruding on the rights of the Indians . . . . A something crept into the State of Tennessee, which leaped over the bounds of decency and law, and determined to put the government to defiance; it had already taken such a growth when I arrived there as to be alarming in a high degree, and nothing but the prudent precaution of the President in sending Colonel Butler there with a respectable force checked it.[22]

For the duration of Hawkins's stay among the Cherokees there were outbreaks of violence, some of which, no doubt, were due to Georgia's sale of Yazoo lands and in particular to the machinations of Zachariah Cox, who was speculating in western lands. The Indians often complained of this speculator and addressed a memorial to President Adams on the subject. The Chickasaws and Choctaws were particularly apprehensive. On April 25, Hawkins wrote from Tellico.

> . . . I am taking necessary measures to quiet the minds of the Indians on this head, but the impression is made that our

---

21. Indian Office files, National Archives.
22. Hawkins, *Letters*, 254. Hawkins to Mrs. Eliza Trist.

fellow citizens are eagerly grasping after their lands, and mean if they can, at some short period, to possess them.[23]

He also expressed fear that such speculative activities might cause the Indians, if they should be encouraged by a foreign power, to engage in a general war. Hawkins opposed the settlements established by Cox and refused him a license to trade. He was not sure the latter course was wise, however, and asked James McHenry to advise him on this score, saying ". . . there cannot much, if any, injury arise to the government in permiting [sic] Mr. Cox to trade."[24]

Later, when Cox presented to Hawkins a plan for the use of armed force to seize the lands of the Tennessee Company, Hawkins replied:

> . . . I think it unequivocally my duty to assure you that I deem the plan, as exhibited to me, to be unfriendly to the Indians and destructive of that confidence which I know they have in the justice of the government, and delusive to such of my fellow citizens as would be weak enough to embark in the execution of it under the expectation of obtaining land for their service.[25]

The agent's impatience with Cox continued and he often expressed in his correspondence a desire for his arrest. He wrote General Pickens on November 19: "I expect Cox is arrested before this; his plan is evidence of his guilt, and it is high time he and his accomplices had met the punishment due to their crime."[26]

The expulsion of William Blount from the United States Senate took place while Hawkins was in Tennessee. This affair was a distinct shock to Hawkins because of his relationship to it and his long acquaintance with Blount. Just what the nature of the contemplated plot was has not been divulged. The principal evidence against Blount was a letter

---

23. *Ibid.*, 132; see also 163-164.
24. *Ibid.*, 135.
25. *Ibid.*, 189-190.
26. *Ibid.*, 243.

written by him to James Carey on April 21, 1797. Carey, an interpreter among the Cherokees, was at the time with Hawkins on the boundary survey. Hawkins was referred to in the letter and thus was unwillingly involved.

Blount was en route to Philadelphia to take his seat in the Senate when he wrote the letter. Referring to some matters that Captain John Chisholm had taken up with the British Minister, Blount said he expected to be at the head of the "business" if the plan matured. "You must take care . . . not to let the plan be discovered by Hawkins, Dinsmoor, Byers, or any other person in the interest of the United States or Spain." Carey was urged to do all in his power to strengthen Blount with the Indians, but ". . . by no means [to] say anything in favor of Hawkins." He was asked to use every endeavor to injure the agent and his assistants, and to blame the "experiment" line of 1792, not on Blount, but ". . . upon the late president, and as he is now out of office it will be of no consequence how much the Indians blame him." Rogers, a ferryman on the Clinch River, was to use his influence ". . . to get the Creeks to desire the president to take Hawkins out of the nation, for if he stays . . . and gets the goodwill of the nation, he can and will do great injury to our plans."[27]

On July 6, 1797, a special committee of the Senate recommended unanimously the expulsion of Blount from that body. The next day the House of Representatives impeached him of high crimes and misdemeanors, and on July 8 he was expelled from the Senate by a vote of twenty-four to one. The vote against expulsion was cast, not in the belief of the innocence of Blount, but because it was felt that such procedure would stop the impeachment trial.[28]

Hawkins, though he was brought into the affair through no fault of his own, and in a way that might have done in-

27. *American State Papers, Foreign Relations*, II, 76-77. James Byers was United States factor at Tellico.
28. *Annals of Congress*, I, 38-46, 447-466; *Augusta Chronicle*, July 29, 1797.

jury to his reputation, seemed reluctant to discuss his former friend's expulsion. When he mentioned the affair he usually did not refer to Blount by name. In some of his correspondence, however, he comments hesitantly on the incident.

He wrote to a friend in North Carolina: "I have since I left you . . . witnessed the downfall of a character I highly valued. . . ."[29] And to another he said:

> . . . the man, my old friend, formerly very much in my estimation, and until the last year or two of my being a member of the Senate, deemed to be of the purest integrity; he is before the tribunal which has and will do him justice, and there I leave him.[30]

His former friendship and his desire not to take part in the controversy did not prevent Hawkins, however, from expressing officially his contempt "of those dirty intriguers and their villainous attempts to involve the government in difficulties and distress."[31]

Hawkins was slow in passing judgment and did so only after he was convinced by the evidence in his hands. There were some changes in the Indian department as a result of the revelations in the Carey letter, but the agent acted with calmness and only after mature deliberation. He was instructed by the Secretary of War to examine into Carey's complicity and to report his findings to the War Office. Secretary McHenry was informed that upon receipt of instructions he had left the line survey and returned to Tellico to examine Carey. The report of the examination was transmitted but was not recorded in Hawkins's journal.[32] Its contents can be surmised from the fact that Samuel Richy was appointed by Hawkins to serve as official interpreter of the Cherokee language.[33] It is worth noting that the examination of Carey took place before the results of the Senate investi-

29. Hawkins, *Letters*, 252.
30. *Ibid.*, 254.
31. *Ibid.*, 182.
32. *Ibid.*, 181.
33. *Ibid.*, 194.

gation were known but too late to have had any effects on that investigation.

During the course of the conference with the Cherokees in April the chiefs had made a special point of the Indian claim to the ferry over the Clinch River, and had requested that John Rogers be retained as ferryman.[34] Since Rogers was mentioned in the Blount letter, Hawkins wrote to him on July 16:

> As you are a man with a large family of Indian children, and I wish much they may do well, and by your coming to Clinch you can do well for them, I am desirous of your saving yourself if you can. You must upon receipt of this, send me an exact statement of every thing, and if your statement should be true, I will retain you in the post assigned you, and contribute to make you and your family easy in your circumstances. You will see it depends on yourself. We have some other letters, and Carey and others have been examined. I promised Carey you should have an opportunity to acquit yourself, and by this letter I fulfill my promise.[35]

Rogers, however, as had Carey, failed to extricate himself from the implications of Blount's letter and was replaced as ferryman on the Clinch by James Richardson.[36]

In the 1790's and the early 1800's there were many routine administrative jobs associated with the direction of Indian affairs, and Indian agents were not provided with the luxury of permanent offices and amanuenses. The wide-flung regions over which Hawkins presided and the resultant necessity of his being often on the trail made his official duties of a formal nature particularly arduous. In addition to the journals, he laboriously copied in letter books his official, semi-official, and private correspondence. The abundance of this correspondence is amazing, since much of it was written while Hawkins was in the forest. He must have spent many hours with quill in hand, seated on a log, dependent for light upon

34. *Ibid.*, 161.
35. *Ibid.*, 188-189.
36. *Ibid.*, 193.

a camp fire or a tallow candle. Almost daily he wrote reports and answered letters, and made copies of them for his letter books.

During the months spent on the Cherokee line Hawkins was never allowed to forget that the survey was incidental to his many other duties. Cherokees were constantly involved with Tennesseeans and Creeks with Georgians, horses were being stolen, slaves ran away to Indian country, speculators stirred up all of the tribes, murders were committed, and the Creeks and Chickasaws were almost on the verge of a conflict. All of these affairs were brought to the agent's notice and the Indians, at least, expected him to solve all of the problems involved. He conferred with Indians and with whites, handled Indian annuities, kept an eye on the business transactions of traders and factors, and directed his assistants among the four nations.

Conditions among the Creeks seemed to indicate an urgency for his return to the Creek country. Accordingly, he left Tennessee early in September for Fort Wilkinson on the Oconee River in Georgia. The next few months were spent with the Creeks. January 1, 1789, was set as the date for the assembling of the commissioners for running the Creek line in conformity to the treaties at New York and Coleraine.

Hawkins had some difficulty in persuading the Creeks to agree to the running of the line, as many of the younger warriors were opposed. Eventually, however, his influence and the aid of some of the older chiefs led to the appointment by the nation of six commissioners whom Hawkins immediately confirmed.[37] General Pickens, the other United States commissioner, did not attend. James Jackson, who as one of the Georgia commissioners at Coleraine had engaged in bitter controversy with Hawkins, was governor of the state. At Hawkins's suggestion, he sent Colonel Andrew Burns and Colonel J. Clements to attend the line survey on the part

---

37. *Ibid.*, 236, 243.

of Georgia.[38] On February 16 Hawkins reported to Secretary McHenry that the line had been run from the Tugalo River over Currahee Mountain to the main south branch of the Oconee River. Though about sixteen families of Georgians were found on the Creek lands and forced to move out, McHenry was told ". . .I am happy in being able to assure you that there was no diversity of opinion among us, and that the line was closed in perfect harmony."[39]

Hawkins next served as a member of the commission to survey the boundary between the United States and Spanish Florida, under the treaty agreement of 1795. Andrew Ellicott had been commissioned as the surveyor on the part of the United States and descended the Ohio and Mississippi rivers to New Orleans in 1796. He encountered opposition from Spanish officials, but eventually ran the line as far as Pensacola, where he requested Hawkins to meet him in April, 1799.[40]

Ellicott and his party reached Pensacola on June 20 and five days later were joined by Hawkins. The morning after Hawkins's arrival they held an audience with Governor Folch, the Spanish Governor of East Florida. The audience was cut short when Folch dismissed the Americans in order to see two self-styled Seminole Indians who had come to oppose the running of the line.[41]

The Indians, both Creeks and Seminoles, under the influence of the Spaniards, had for some time shown a disposition to oppose the marking of the boundary. In fact, President Adams in a message to Congress in December, 1798, had called attention to this hostility and had suggested the possibility of recalling Ellicott.[42] Hawkins, in the meantime, had entered into an agreement with Governor Folch for the protection of the surveyors.

38. *Ibid.*, 242, 286.
39. *Ibid.*, 287.
40. Andrew Ellicott, *The Journal of Andrew Ellicott*, 199. Hereafter to be cited as *Ellicott's Journal*.
41. *Ibid.*, 202.
42. *American State Papers, Foreign Relations*, I, 48.

The agent was of the opinion that the so-called Seminoles who had waited on the governor were from the Creek nation. This opinion was confirmed shortly by friendly Creeks who informed him that the visitors had come from Tallassee among the Upper Creeks and had been sent to Pensacola by their chief Tame King. They left Pensacola after talks with the governor which were unfriendly to the United States.[43]

Before beginning any boundary survey it was customary, and almost necessary, to hold conferences with the Indians through whose hunting grounds it was proposed to run the line. The Spanish officials suggested that such conferences be held in Pensacola, but Ellicott, on the advice of Hawkins, insisted on the Conecuh River at the point where the boundary would cross it. His reasons for such insistence were that Pensacola ". . . would have given them [the Spanish] considerable advantages over us in point of intrigue, at which they were habitually dexterous; and what was equally to be dreaded, the delay that might reasonably be expected from intoxication, in which the Indians always indulge themselves at treaties where liquor is to be had. . . ."[44]

Hawkins and Ellicott, therefore, left the Florida town and sailed to the head of Pensacola Bay. There they met Chief Mad Dog of the Creeks and made arrangements with him for the conference. Governor Folch was, of course, expected to attend the conference but Mad Dog insisted that he would not because ". . . he knows what I shall say to him about his crooked talks. His tongue is forked, and as you are here, he will be ashamed to show it. If he stands to what he had told us, you will be offended, and if he tells us that the line ought to be marked, he will contradict himself; but he will do neither, he will not come."[45]

True to Mad Dog's prophecy, Governor Folch had an attack of "diplomatic gout" en route and returned to Pensa-

43. *Ellicott's Journal*, 203-204.
44. *Ibid.*, 203.
45. *Ibid.*, 204.

cola. Mad Dog's philosophical comment was that "a man with two tongues can only speak to one at a time."[46]

Other Spanish officials did arrive, however. Among them were Colonel Maxant, personal representative of Governor Folch, and Captain Minor, the Spanish line commissioner. On May 5, Ellicott and Hawkins held a conference with the Spaniards. Hawkins informed them ". . . that many crooked talks had some time since been sent out among the Indians, that they had been taught to believe that his Catholic Majesty had no desire to have the line determined or marked." Whether these talks had been sanctioned by Spanish officials, Hawkins did not know. He was of the opinion, however, that only the Spanish officers could dispel this belief of the Indians.[47]

The following day, Mad Dog, as speaker of the Creeks, called the chiefs together and, in the presence of the Americans the Indians were informed by Captain Minor that Spain wished to have the boundary run. Neither Hawkins nor Ellicott found any fault in this declaration, and the next day Mad Dog assured the line commissioners that the Indians were satisfied and would supply an escort as provided by the Treaty of Coleraine.[48]

A camp for the surveying party was established on the Conecuh River. It was not until May 22 that the guide line to the Chattahoochee was begun, and the following day Hawkins and Ellicott set out for Pensacola in a canoe, arriving three days later. The reason for the return was distrust of Governor Folch and the desire to be near whatever intrigue might be hatching. Their suspicions were well founded. Within a few days a report reached Hawkins that a large body of Creeks were on the way to see Governor Folch. The Governor, embarrassed by the presence of the Americans, could not say to the Indians what he had intended. He told them that, since they were from the north of the boundary line,

46. *Ibid.*, 205.
47. *Ibid.*
48. *Ibid.*, 206.

they should seek presents from Hawkins and Ellicott. Hawkins informed the Creeks that he had not invited them to Pensacola and they were therefore not entitled to any presents or supplies. They were, however, given a few and ordered to return to their town immediately.[49]

Nearly a month had been spent in Pensacola by Hawkins before the Indians were finally dismissed. During this period he wrote a number of letters to Folch and handled the situation in such a way as to elicit from Ellicott praise for "that firmness, caution, and candour, for which he has been so justly esteemed."[50]

By the middle of June Hawkins felt it was safe for him to leave and he returned to Coweta. He sent Burgess, one of the assistants, to join the surveying party and to keep the Creeks quiet on the lower Chattahoochee, but the Indians collected around the camps, stole horses, and in various ways obstructed the running of the line. No serious incident occurred, however, but Burgess informed Ellicott that he had news that the Creeks would attack the party when it left for the St. Marys River. Worried by this rumor and still suspicious of the Spaniards, Ellicott sent urgent messages for Hawkins to join the party.[51]

Early in September, Captain Minor dismissed his military escort and most of his Spanish laborers and insisted upon an immediate departure for the St. Marys. The party was then at the mouth of the Flint River. Ellicott refused to move further until Hawkins arrived.

On September 14 Hawkins reached camp and preparations were made for the start for the St. Marys on September 20. On the seventeenth notice was received from Indian Willy, a friendly Creek who lived a few miles up the Chattahoochee, that a party of twenty Creeks was at his place. They claimed to be Choctaws. That afternoon the Indians crossed the river above the camp. The surveying party was quickly armed

49. *Ibid.*, 207-209.
50. *Ibid.*, 209.
51. *Ibid.*, 217.

and under Hawkins's direction was drawn up for battle. Big Lieutenant, the Creek chief in command of the Indian escort, tried in vain to persuade the hostile Indians to disperse. As they approached nearer the camp, Hawkins informed them that any act of thievery or hostility would mean the immediate death of the culprits. The Indians did not attack, but during the night they drove off horses and cattle and pillaged a small schooner which Ellicott had anchored in the river. The next morning the surveying party retreated. Ellicott and his party went down the river in the schooner; Captain Minor and the Spaniards went overland to Pensacola, and only Hawkins remained to quiet the Creeks.[52]

The line was never run. Ellicott sailed around Florida to St. Marys and from there located and built a mound at what he considered the headwaters of the St. Marys River. He laid the whole blame for the failure of the survey to the treachery of the Spanish officials. The perpetrators of the attacks on the commission were Upper Creeks from Tallassee under the command of Tame King and were the same Indians who had been in Pensacola on Folch's invitation.[53]

Hawkins, on the other hand, while knowing of the Spanish deceit, placed part of the blame on Ellicott himself. While he was still on the Flint at the scene of the recent disorder, he wrote one of his assistants:

It is not yet explained to me why the commissioners made a halt of three months on the Chattahoochee. You know how seriously I pressed them not to remain more than two, and that in that case they might proceed in perfect safety, as they would be moving in the season of the Boos-ke-tah, when all the discontented would be attending the ceremonies of the annual festival, which always occurs in the month of August. The baggage I saw at Ko-ne-cuh was great, and I was surprised to see Americans, who have been accustomed to travel through the woods, encumber themselves with such unnecessary and useless baggage. One fact I will relate.

52. *Ibid.*, 217-223.
53. *Ibid.*, 224-226.

The flat irons, alone, for the commissioners weigh 150 pounds and it takes four horses to move Mr. Ellicott's washerwoman.[54]

Though the Indian disorder was encouraged by the Spaniards and probably abetted by the culpable delay of the commissioners themselves, Hawkins, as agent, was responsible for the punishment of the perpetrators. He consistently took the view that most of the Indians would abide by their obligations and that all should not be condemned for the crimes of the few. As soon as possible the chiefs were informed of the crime and satisfaction was demanded of them. In November Tustunnugee Haujo reported to Hawkins the results of his demands:

I am ordered . . . to bring you this stick, It is the only way of the red people when they punish any people to do it with sticks; and then to send them to those interested in the punishment and throughout the land to proclaim the deed done.[55]

Upon receipt of Hawkins's demand a council had been called at Tookaubatchee and it was there agreed that all who had taken part in the molestation of the survey party should be punished. The house of one of the leaders was surrounded:

We pulled down and set fire to his house, we beat him with sticks until he was on the ground as a dead man, we cut off one of his ears with a part of his cheek and put a sharp stick up his fundament.[56]

Thus was atonement done. Justice was executed in the Indian manner and Benjamin Hawkins applauded the cruel execution, and insisted that others be punished likewise. When asked by the Indians if they as individuals could be held responsible for such deaths under tribal laws, he answered:

If the sticks are used by the Law of the whole nation and a man dies, it is the Law that killed him, it is the nation who

54. Caroline Mays Brevard, *A History of Florida from the Treaty of 1763 to Our Own Times*, (Deland, 1924), I, 14. The location of this letter is not given, neither is the date, nor the person to whom it was written.
55. Hawkins Papers, Georgia Department Archives and History.
56. *Ibid.*, Tustunnugee Haujo to Hawkins, Nov. 4, 1799.

killed him. If anyone complains and asks for satisfaction, this is your answer, Your relation was a rogue and a mischief maker, the law says such people must have the sticks, and that is their pay . . . It is the pay of the nation.[57]

Hawkins was not a cruel man; neither was he crude. No doubt his sensibilities were deeply offended. The circumstances back of the attack on the survey party inclined him perhaps to sympathize with the Indians. Nevertheless, he was responsible to his government for order and law enforcement in a wild domain. Where the justice of the white man did not prevail, and would not have been understood, he could subscribe to the Indian manner of punishment if it were effective. Where civilization has come in contact with primitive peoples, those nations have been most successful in managing their aboriginal wards which did not attempt too quickly to divorce the native from his tribal customs. Hawkins was unquestionably a successful agent. No doubt his success was in large measure due to his willingness to compromise with the Indians where there were incompatible differences between their customs and those of the white men.

---

57. Hawkins to Creeks at Coweta, November 4, 1799. Hawkins Papers.

CHAPTER VIII

Life on the Agency

HAWKINS had been in the Indian country as Principal Temporary Agent only a few months when President Washington retired from office. President Adams as Vice President and presiding officer of the Senate had known and served with Hawkins in that body. He was therefore acquainted with his qualifications for the position he now held and continued him in office as a matter of course. There is nothing to indicate that his removal was ever contemplated by Washington's successor.

For some years Hawkins did not establish a permanent residence but spent his time among the Indians in their villages and at army posts in the Indian country. During this peripatetic period of his agency he was often at Cusseta, Coweta, Tookaubatchee; but he preferred Fort Wilkinson on the Oconee and spent much of his time there.

Though Hawkins had served with Thomas Jefferson in Congress and had corresponded with him at intervals for more than fifteen years, he had no assurance, other than his belief that Jefferson was sympathetic with what he was trying to do, that he would be continued in his position after March, 1801. There are two slightly contradictory explanations by prominent Southern historians of why he was reappointed.

Professor H. M. Wagstaff, a North Carolina historian, explained the reappointment as follows:

Nathaniel Macon, probably the staunchest Republican in Congress . . . became Jefferson's dispenser of federal patronage in 1801. Macon at first wanted to make the test of Republicanism the standard by which officers were chosen but was soon led by the astute Jefferson not to enter upon a proscriptive policy toward the better known and most influential Federalists. With this plan matured, and an understanding between Macon and Jefferson, William R. Davie and Benjamin Hawkins were approached in June 1801, and offered a commission to negotiate with the Southwestern Indian tribes. Hawkins at once accepted and was thereafter lost to the Federalist party.[1]

The second explanation is that of William E. Dodd:

> . . . Jefferson wrote Benjamin Hawkins, an ardent Federalist who had lost caste in North Carolina in 1796, asking him to recommend fit persons for appointment to vacancies in North Carolina . . . . This of course was an attempt to conciliate another powerful opposing influence in the South. Hawkins was won and he was continued many years in the lucrative office of Indian Commissioner to the Creek Nation.[2]

These explanations have one thing in common; namely, they are predicated on the assumption that Hawkins was a Federalist and that Jefferson considered him so. It is true that he was appointed a treaty commissioner with William R. Davie in June, 1801. So was General Andrew Pickens. Hawkins and Pickens had served on various commissions together since 1785, and there seems little basis for placing any political significance upon this appointment. It was natural and logical. Of more importance is the fact that Hawkins at the time was already serving as Principal Agent and with Jefferson's approval. He may have "lost caste in North Carolina in 1796." He certainly had been absent from North Carolina since that date and was consequently an illogical choice to recommend "fit persons for vacancies" in the state. Five years among the Indians had hardly left time for participation in partisan politics. Hawkins's original appointment may have been due to his Federalist affiliations, but his continuation in office was more likely the result of demonstrated ability.

1. Wagstaff, *Federalism in North Carolina*, 40.
2. Dodd, *Nathaniel Macon*, 171.

When his commission from President Jefferson was delivered Hawkins had a new title. He was no longer Principal Temporary Agent but Principal Agent on a permanent basis. A new period of his administration of Indian affairs began. He felt then that he could establish a permanent location for his Agency and build a home. One of the stipulations of the Treaty of Coleraine was that the Federal government might set up reservations five miles square on the rivers in the Creek country for trading purposes or military posts. Hawkins selected such a site on the Flint River for his home. The Agency reservation was marked out on both sides of the river in what are now Crawford and Taylor counties in Georgia. Hawkins's home was on the east bank, and on the opposite bank was located Fort Lawrence.[3]

There on the banks of the Flint the duties of his office were administered by Colonel Hawkins. There he lived among the Indians as neighbor, as friend, as benefactor, and as representative of the United States. He was often spoken of as the father of the Creeks, and he sometimes fell in with this idea and referred to them as his sons and daughters.[4] Hawkins was a born dirt farmer and cultivated a large plantation on the Agency reservation. It was well stocked with horses and cattle and worked with Negro slaves some of whom he brought with him from North Carolina. The Agency was manorial in extent, and the agent was a benevolent lord.[5]

The Flint was an excellent choice of location for the permanent Agency. It was in the midst of the country of the Lower Creeks yet accessible to the white settlements in Georgia. Fort Hawkins on the Ocmulgee, built in 1806 as a factory and military post and named for the agent, was only a day's journey to the east. To the west a slightly longer journey would carry one into the center of the towns on

---

3. Ruby Felder Ray Thomas, *Historic Spots and Places of Interest in Georgia*, 44-45.
4. Hawkins, *Letters*, 232.
5. See further Merritt B. Pound, "Benjamin Hawkins, Indian Agent," in *Georgia Historical Quarterly*, XIII, 392-409.

the Chattahoochee, and across the Chattahoochee lived the
Upper Creeks. Better still, it was possible to visit many of
the Lower Creeks by water, and Hawkins often used this
mode of travel. It was not unusual to see Indian canoes or
dugouts pulled up on the banks of the Agency; and Hawkins
spent many hours and days in company with Indian com-
panions, paddling along the placid waters of the Flint, or up
the broader Chattahoochee.

The agent loved the wild beauty of his adopted country.
His letters and journals are filled with descriptions of the
land. Not often do these accounts indicate his true enthusiasm for the forests as Hawkins was generally matter-of-fact
in his writing. Seldom did he become rhetorical; and yet,
when writing of the country, there is evident an underlying
satisfaction and serenity. He often was discouraged with
men and because of his ill health frequently contemplated
resignation from office, but he never indicated a desire to leave
the land. The Indians were his first thought; agriculture, his
recreation and hobby as well as his part-time vocation. Thoroughly convinced that the future of the Indians lay in
cultivation of the soil rather than in hunting, he was especially interested in showing them what their lands would produce under proper tillage.

Political and administrative aptitudes had been acquired
by Benjamin Hawkins. Agricultural interests were natural
with him, and his early life was spent on the farm among
successful farmers. In much of his correspondence with
Washington, Jefferson, and Madison about political affairs
he also discussed crops, weather conditions, and insect pests.
He was interested in anything that grew. To Jefferson he
wrote on March 8, 1787: ". . . I expect I shall be able to
send you a few plants of the Dionaea Muscipula sometimes
this spring. . . ."[6]

6. McPherson, "Unpublished Letters of North Carolinians to Jefferson," *North Carolina Historical Review*, XII, 254; see also Hawkins to Madison, July 3, 1789, Madison Papers, XI, 75, in Library of
Congress.

On June 10, 1790, Hawkins, in a letter of congratulations to Daniel Smith upon his recent appointment as secretary of the Southwestern Territory, expressed his interest in the West, and offered Smith the following advice:

> Let me advise you to impress as early as possible on your Citizens the necessity of attending to home manufactures, [sic] Your relative situation with the commercial part of the United States is such that this is indispensable to your prosperity. You can raise fruit trees of all sorts, grapes of all sorts for wines . . . clothing of cotton flax wool and silk. - You never can have much money but you have facility in acquiring the necessaries and comforts of life from the richness of your soil and mildness of your climate unknown to any other country in my recollection. Recommend therefore by your own example the raising nurseries of fruit trees and having them planted throughout your whole country. - I have often lamented the unaccountable inattention of our people to the raising of the comforts of life, [sic]   One hour devoted only weekly to the planting vines, trees and garden stuff is quite sufficient to start any plantation with an abundance of these things.[7]

It was easy, and perfectly natural, for the composer of this letter to take an interest and pleasure in introducing the Indians to agriculture and industry.

Hawkins was particularly successful in the culture of grapes and strawberries. In 1793, while in Warrenton during a recess of the Senate, he wrote Jefferson that he was sending him thirteen varieties of grapevines, mostly European. Each vine was labeled with complete instructions for planting and care. He also mentioned sowing wheat, clover, and timothy; planting apple and peach trees, and "preparing a large nursery to stock my plantation with all the varieties within my reach."[8]

7. Carter, *Territorial Papers*, IV, 26-27.
8. McPherson, "Unpublished Letters of North Carolinians to Jefferson," *North Carolina Historical Review*, XII, 266-268.

In May, 1795, he wrote President Washington from Warrenton:

> The season here promises to be favorable for croping [sic]
> and our agricultural prospect considerable. We have been a
> little retarded in the Tobacco crop, by the fly injuring our
> plants, yet I believe there will be enough in pretty good
> time. The frost . . . has destroyed the most valuable of our
> fruit, peaches, apples, cherries and quince. But did not injure
> the grapes, gooseberries, currants, raspberries, strawberries,
> plums, whortleberries and blackberries.[9]

From his arrival in the Indian country, Hawkins constantly
encouraged his charges to substitute the plow and the hoe
for the weapons of the trail and the chase. The year 1797
gave him little opportunity to practice agriculture for himself. In the spring of 1798, however, while temporarily
domiciled at Coweta Tallahassee, he began farming operations.
In March of that year he wrote Alexander Cornells and advised him to plant his corn "the next full moon; it will be a
good time, and I find the Indians all plant too late; we are
beginning to plant some now; I have planted peas, cymblins,
cucumbers and garden stuff."[10]

On May 5, he recorded in his journal: "Planted cabbages,
the season remarkably dry; I watered them and covered them.
Planted corn in new ground, coultered both ways & checked
Planted potatoes. Our little crop late from necessity."[11]

President Jefferson in his message to Congress of December, 1801, reported that Hawkins had introduced sheep
among the Creeks and that these Indians were also raising
horses, cattle, and goats. Among the improvements credited
to Hawkins were the settlement of the Indians in villages
in new ground, the fencing of fields, and the use of fifty
plows. Hawkins had introduced the plow and had instructed
the Indians in its use in 1797. A nursery of peach trees among
the Lower Creeks had produced 5,000 trees and another had

---

9. *Ibid.*, 166-167.
10. Hawkins, *Letters*, 299.
11. *Ibid.*, 309.

recently been established among the Upper Creeks. Prior to the establishment of these nurseries, Hawkins had raised peach trees and distributed them at his own expense. Short staple cotton was being grown in small quantities and some had been marketed in Tennessee. Experiments in the growing of sea island cotton were being carried on under Hawkins's supervision. Flax, rice, wheat, barley, rye, and oats had been introduced. "Apple trees, grape vines, raspberries, and the roots, herbs, and vegetables, usually cultivated in good gardens, have lately been introduced, and they all thrive well."[12] He also had a personal patch of tobacco.

Hawkins recorded in his journal in December, 1796, an interesting description of cotton culture among the Creeks. He had been in Georgia only a short time and there is no evidence that he had any experience in growing this staple elsewhere, but he showed no hesitancy in advising the proper methods of cultivation. One can well wonder from whence came the knowledge which allowed him to speak with such authority and assurance.

> I took a view of Mr. Grierson's farm, he had planted the last season two acres of cotton in drills, 4 feet asunder; the land apparently not very good, high dry and gravelly, the cotton grew well, many of the stalks 8 feet high. I saw he had not thined [sic] it sufficiently, not toped [sic] any part and that it was mixed with the Nankin. I viewed his cotton house, the staple of the cotton good, tho' not so much so as it would have been, had it been thined and toped. The bowls or pads would then have been larger. I advised him in the next season to pursue the proper course and to separate the seed, and as from his information the black seed cotton will not do here, to plant only the green seed . . . . He has a treadle gin, well made, sent him from Providence. I saw some defect in the puting [sic] it up, which I directed him how to remedy. He informs me he finds no difficulty in hiring the Indian women to pick out the cotton . . . .[13]

---

12. *American State Papers, Indian Affairs*, I, 647.
13. Hawkins, *Letters*, 30.

In April, 1809, Hawkins wrote to Governor Irwin of Georgia that much of his fruit had been destroyed by severe cold, the thermometer reaching twenty-six on March 28. "We have had no rain since the 12 March and as you are a farmer you know our situation. The agency is crowded with applicants for implements of husbandry and domestic manufactures and with Indians learning to weave."[14]

During his stay in Georgia, Hawkins became especially proficient in the culture of the strawberry. Dr. William Baldwin, resident of Milledgeville, visited the Agency in 1812. He was so amazed at what he saw in Hawkins's strawberry patch that he published his account in the local newspaper and, lest he be classed as a second Baron Munchausen, he named two "gentlemen of high respectability" as witnesses. He reported that on April 27 three hundred berries could be counted on a single root and on that day one hundred were gathered "perfectly ripe." This was the native fruit, *Fragaria Virginica*. In another patch Hawkins was growing a foreign species which was producing very large berries. Baldwin figured that on the basis of production on the two plots, an acre would produce "the enormous quantity of 80 bushels, which would serve a large village with this delicious fruit for at least two months."[15]

In the same issue of the paper in which this account was published two columns were devoted to letters concerning the culture of this fruit at the Agency and to a description by Hawkins of his methods of cultivation. With the utilization of barnyard manure and intensive spading, he had increased the yield of the native plants from ten small berries to the root to three hundred much larger ones. His fame as a horticulturist spread. Dr. Baldwin wrote: ". . . I have no doubt [it] would contribute to the health of our fellow citizens in general, and particularly those of the Southern States,

---

14. Hawkins Papers.
15. *Georgia Journal*, August 26, 1812.

were the cultivation of them upon your simple plan adopted. . . ."[16]

Hawkins was also proud, and justly so, of his vineyards. As a mark of particular favor and respect he often sent his Georgia friends cuttings from his grape vines.

Frequent public references were made to the advance of the Indians during Hawkins's incumbency, not only in agriculture but in industry as well. Several of Jefferson's messages to Congress commented upon this advance. In December, 1805, he reported:

> Our Indian neighbors are advancing, many of them with spirit, and others beginning to engage, in the pursuits of agriculture and house hold manufacture. They are becoming sensible that the earth yields subsistence with less labor and more certainty than the forest, and find it their interest from time to time to dispose of parts of their surplus and waste lands for the means of improving those they occupy, and of subsisting their families while they are preparing their farms.[17]

Again, in October, 1807, Jefferson wrote: " The great tribes in our Southwestern quarter, much advanced beyond the others in agriculture and household arts, appear tranquil, and identifying their views with our, in proportion to their advancement."[18]

Madison, also, as President, made similar references in some of his messages to Congress. His message of November, 1809, commented: "With our Indian neighbors, the just and benevolent system contained towards them, has also preserved peace, and is more and more advancing habits favorable to their civilization and happiness."[19]

Favorable editorial comment in the Georgia papers was

16. *Ibid.*
17. *American State Papers, Foreign Relations,* I, 67.
18. *Ibid.,* I, 70.
19. *Ibid.,* 76. Though few such presidential messages mention Hawkins personally, the frequency of the comments seems to argue the efficiency of the administration of the man who was in charge of such an important part of the Indian population.

not lacking. On January 24, 1806, the *Georgia Republican*, Savannah, reported:

> Our readers are no strangers to the enlightened and inde-fatigable exertions of Colonel Hawkins to ameliorate the conditions of the aborigines of the Country, by introduc-ing among them the blessings of the civilization. - The suc-cess with which these efforts have been attended in the short period of ten years is without parallel in the history of savage nations.

In this same paper there is related a conversation between Hawkins and Istehoce, a Creek chief, which may be indica-tive of one of Hawkins's weaknesses in his dealings with the Indians. Istehoce is quizzing Hawkins as to his acceptance of the Biblical story of Eden. Istehoce does not believe the story and so does not have the white man's hatred of snakes. He agrees to accept the white man's plan for the Indians, however, as being to their advantage, but warns Hawkins that some of his tribesmen are playing the snake and "unless you take and mash their heads . . . you will not succeed in your plans."

In the summer of 1808 the report spread that Hawkins had been driven from the Agency by Indians.[20] Hawkins learned of this report and as evidence that he was at home and that the Indians were still practicing the arts of civilization under his tutelage he wrote on August 5:

> The plan of civilization is progressive. We are clothing and feeding ourselves. The tin ware we use; and hats; shoes and boots, and the saddle I ride on, are made in the Agency; and all the leather we use or want is tanned at the Agency. My family of eighty persons are all clothed in homespun.[21]

In May, 1808, Henry Dearborn, Secretary of War, paid trib-ute to the work Hawkins was doing:

> I have received the blanket manufactured by Upaulike and family of the Creek Nation. It is an honorable & pleasing

20. *Republican & Savannah Evening Ledger*, August 27, 1808.
21. *Ibid.*, August 27, 1808.

specimen of the progress of civilization among those Nations who have been fortunate enough to be within your Agency. A few years more of persevering attention will no doubt demonstrate the error of those opinions which have so generally prevailed in our Country, on the subject of the civilization of the aborigines - Generations yet unborn will have abundant reason for blessing the memory of your character for having contributed so essentially to the melioration of their condition.[22]

A medal was sent to Upaulike as evidence of his proficiency in the arts of civilization, and Hawkins was instructed to present the family with two blankets from the public stores for one sent to the President.

Colonel Hawkins was unmarried when he took up his abode with the Indians and though it was customary for white men living there to take Indian women as wives or mistresses, there is no evidence that he ever did so. He was critical of of such arrangements only when the white men mistreated their wives or deserted their Indian children, but he felt that for the United States agent to take an Indian wife would lessen his influence among these people.

Within a few months after Hawkins's arrival the mother-in-law of his assistant, Timothy Barnard, came to him and offered him one of her daughters, a young widow, for as long as Hawkins wished her. His reply was:

> You have offered me your daughter. I take it kind of you.
> Your daughter looks well, is of good family . . . . You know
> I am principal Agent of the four Nations. I do not yet know
> whether I shall take one of my red women for a bed-
> fellow or not, but if I do, if it is for a single night, and she
> has a child, I shall expect it will be mine . . . .[23]

Hawkins, by his own admission, was willing to consider taking the young widow; but the old mother would not agree that

22. Indian Office, Secretary of War Letter Book B, 377-378, National Archives.
23. Hawkins, *Letters*, 83.

the wife and "children should be under the direction of the father, and the negotiation ended there."[24]

This incident took place in February, 1797. In November of the same year while Hawkins was at Cusseta and confined to his bed "with the gout or rheumatism," the Queen of Tookaubatchee came to his bedside and offered herself to him. "I shall be proud of you if you will take me. If you take a young girl into the house I shall not like it, but I wont say one word; maybe I can't love her, but I wont use her ill." Though the young queen was only twenty-three, plump, full-breasted and neat in appearance, he refused her proposal.[25]

Most of the white men among the Indians had no association with the women except those they lived with, but Hawkins visited with them, treated them kindly, and occasionally invited them to dine at his home. He had no high opinion of them, nevertheless.

> They have a great propensity to the obscene in conversation, and they call everything by its name, and if the concurrent testimony of the white husbands can be relied on, the women have much of the temper of the mule, except when amorous, an [d] then they exhibit all the amiable and gentle qualities of the cat.[26]

Though Hawkins could, and did, perform the marriage ceremony for others on occasion, there was no one in the Agency to perform a similar service for him. Conditions in the trans-Ocmulgee region were not unlike those of the seventeenth century Virginia frontier when the circuit-riding parson preached the first wife's funeral, married the second wife, and christened the baby on the same day. Hawkins took for his common-law wife a woman named Lavinia Downs. Just who she was, where she came from, and when she began to live with him is unknown, though when she was

24. *Ibid.*, 85.
25. *Ibid.*, 255.
26. *Ibid.*, 256.

married to Hawkins on January 9, 1812, she was the mother of six of his children.[27]

Lavinia was a friend of Edward Price's family, and it is likely that Hawkins met her either at Coleraine or at Fort Wilkinson. A letter from Price to Hawkins, written probably in December, 1798, seems to indicate that she had lived with Hawkins before that time. "Lavinia is with us, sleeps alone and says she cant help feeling her solitary situation these cold nights."[28]

In 1812, Hawkins's chronic ill-health led him to fear that he would not long survive. Accordingly he was married, and his will distributing his estate among six children, a wife, and a nephew was drawn up on the same day.[29] Though the marriage ceremony was long past due, there is every evidence that he was a kind, faithful husband and an affectionate father. The absence of a publicly-spoken and legally-recorded vow did not lessen his feeling of obligation and responsibility toward his wife and children.

Hawkins spent much of his time in removing from Indian lands white men who had come there without proper authority to take advantage of the Indians. His hospitality, however, was well known, and the legitimate traveller was accorded a cordial welcome. Visitors were frequently entertained and transients of any race were assured a cordial reception and excellent fare in abundance. Traders, Indian department officials, and army officers were so frequently

---

27. Lewis Lawshe & Others *vs.* Francis Bacon & Wife. Suit in the Crawford County Superior court 1834. Papers in Georgia Department Archives and History.

28. Indian Office, Letter Book Fort Coleraine and Fort Hawkins, 1795-1812, 176, in National Archives. Letter not dated but the one following it in the Letter Book is dated December 14, 1798. Hawkins had written Price on October 23, 1797, asking that Price send him some woman to superintend his household as "a long continuance of the fatigue I daily experience would be more than I can bare [*sic*]." The letter was delivered by a man named Downs who was temporarily in the employ of Hawkins. It is possible that Price carried out the Agent's request by sending him a kinswoman of his messenger. Ms. letter, Indian Office files, National Archives.

29. Hawkins's will filed for probate in the Jones County courthouse. A copy in the Georgia Department of Archives and History.

at the Agency as to cause little comment. The French General Moreau spent some time there in the spring of 1808, and when he left was escorted through the nation toward Charleston by the agent himself.[30]

On October 16, 1810, Ichabod E. Fisk, A. M., native Vermonter, for some years the rector of St. Marys Academy, died in Hawkins's house and was buried on the Agency. Afflicted with an "inflammation of the lungs or stomach," he had arrived in July en route to Mississippi. Hawkins, with his usual hospitality, gave asylum to this kindly, cultured, and ill gentleman and cared for him until his death.[31]

Dr. William Baldwin, prominent citizen of Milledgeville, was thanked by Hawkins in May, 1812, for "having done me the favor to make [himself] one of my family during the spring."[32] Henry Ker wrote that "At night (Feb. 14, 1815) I put up at Colonel Hawkins's where I was well received. This gentleman had a fine plantation . . . . " Ker also referred to his host as "the gentleman who so kindly entertained me the preceding night."[33]

William Hawkins, the agent's nephew, lived with him, was accepted as one of the family, was given a child's share of the estate and made joint executor with Lavinia, Benjamin's wife.[34]

There is little in Hawkins's correspondence to indicate his religious philosophy. He certainly did not think of himself as a missionary to the Indians. He often cooperated with certain Quaker societies[35] which were interested in Indian education; but, whatever his religious views, he did not attempt to force them upon the Creeks. He was to them teacher,

---

30. *Republican & Savannah Evening Ledger*, April 26, 1808.
31. *Georgia Journal*, October 3, 1810.
32. *Ibid.*, August 26, 1812.
33. Henry Ker, *Travels Through the Western Interior of The United States*, 341.
34. Copy of the will of Benjamin Hawkins, Georgia Department of Archives and History. Wheeler records that another nephew, Philemon Hawkins, III, resigned as captain of artillery and came to live on the Agency in 1815. In poor health, he died shortly after his uncle. *Sketches*, 429.
35. Hawkins, *Letters*, 126, 127.

friend, lawgiver, even judge—but never priest. The nearest approach to an acknowledgment of a religious creed that his correspondence reveals is contained in a letter to James Madison in 1803. It reads as follows:

> Tell Mrs. Madison we are all Quakers in the Indian Agency and there is little or no difference now between our annual meetings and the annual meetings of our white brethren, we are full as silent, as grave, and circumspect here as in Philadelphia. We are under the guidance of reason, and they under the light of the gospel, in pursuit of the same object . . . . If our doctrine of hereafter is uninformed in the opinion of our white friends, we will exchange our *guide* for their *light* and subscribe to whatever they recommend provided they will assist us here, to preserve the birthright portion of the planet we inhabit. To this end the little that we require is, that the followers of the meek and humble Jesus will believe we are their neighbours, and treat us accordingly.[36]

In spite of the fact that much of the life of Hawkins was spent out of doors, on the farm and on the trail, he was never in robust health. He wrote Madison in September, 1784, from Sweet Springs in Botetourt County, Virginia, lamenting his indisposition throughout the summer. The cause of his poor health was unknown to him. He had been at Sweet Springs since July on account of his health and was contemplating going to Georgia in the hope that the climate would benefit him.[37] Jefferson was informed in October, 1793, that he had been ill with a fever.[38] In November of 1797, Hawkins wrote: ". . . I had one visitor sorely afflicted, a severe attack in my left leg and foot of the gout or rheumatism for 6 or 10 nights; sometimes not able to turn in my blankets. . . ."[39] In February, 1798, he was still sick.[40] On April 16: "I am unwell; I can ride, but make an

36. Madison Papers, XXV, 93, in Library of Congress.
37. *Ibid.*, V, 22.
38. McPherson, "Unpublished Letters of North Carolinians to Jefferson," *North Carolina Historical Review*, XII, 266.
39. Hawkins, *Letters*, 252.
40. *Ibid.*, 290.

awkward foot at walking, my left leg and foot being swelled and painful."[41] A week later he felt his "health was declining,"[42] and evidently it was, for he was never entirely rid of his aches and pains from that time on.

Agriculture, rheumatism, and the formal routine of Indian administration left little leisure at Hawkins's disposal. He spent many hours, nevertheless, studying the Indian language and customs, and was the author of *A Sketch of the Creek Country 1798-1799*, a work of no little importance. Hawkins was serious minded from his youth. Life among the Indians was a serious affair; and, in order to retain the respect of these people, he was ever on his dignity with them. Other than agriculture, reading and study, and the improvement of his plantation, the pleasures of Hawkins are not recorded. Living in a sportsman's paradise, there is nothing to indicate that he ever fired a gun or baited a hook. It may be that Hawkins got his pleasures from the contemplation of nature and the realization of a life of service to his fellow man. Most of his extant letters are official or semi-official, and they are uniformly serious and dignified in tone. The little of his personal correspondence that has been preserved reveals a sense of humor and a warm personality. Occasionally these personal communications were both garrulous and facetious, especially when written to old friends back in North Carolina. In November, 1797, he wrote such a letter to his friend William Faulkener.

> Will you assure Mrs. F. that I often wish her health and happiness; that if she is fond of grandure and will send her son to me, I will give him a queen, or if he, by her permission, prefers the custom of the Oriental country, I will give him half a dozen, with fortunes suitable to their rank, each a pestle and mortar, a sifter and fanner, an earth pot, pan and large wooden spoon, with one hoonau (half petticoat), as low as the knee, and iocoofxuttau (Short shift), not so low as the tie of the hoonau; earrings surrounding each

41. *Ibid.*, 302.
42. *Ibid.*, 306.

of the rims of the ears, a necklace, a string of broaches before, with one hatchetau (or blanket) and as much tuefull-wau (binding) as will club the hair; they will each have a full portion of the temper of the mule, except when they are amorous, and then they will exhibit all the lovely and amiable qualities of the cat.[43]

Mrs. Eliza Trist was evidently one of his favorite correspondents. On the same day that Hawkins wrote to Faulkener he wrote her a long letter, apparently in answer to an equally garrulous one he had received. It was friendly and chatty. Interesting customs of the Indians were explained, and much space was taken up with remarks about mutual friends of whom Mrs. Trist had written Hawkins:

> . . . Do not forget, I pray you, that I am to be your gardener and Walker the shepherd. Mrs. Easton, she is a deserter; however, as she has set up the manufactory of babes, we must forgive her; she will succeed; they will all imbibe the good qualities of the mamma, and make others happy by it.
>
> And Mr. Matlock, success to his establishment; pray, bespeak the birth [berth?] of godfather for me, and if I cannot attend, I hereby vest you with the authority to appoint a proxy for me, who, in my name, shall have full power to renounce the devil, and all his works, and the vain pomp and glory of this wicked world &c., &c.
>
> Pray authorize your son or Mr. Venable to give one kiss to the amiable daughters where you are in remembrance of me, and accept one yourself from Mr. V. as the perpetual pledge of the sincere affection of your friend & obedient servant.[44]

Friendly, neighborly letters these were. Benjamin Hawkins was no recluse. He loved people and greatly enjoyed the companionship of his social and intellectual equals. He must have often suffered severe attacks of nostalgia, and it is difficult to explain his resignation to a life among half-civilized Indians and half-breeds except on the basis of his realization of the worthwhileness of his life work. Though there is little evidence that he was ever conscious of any self-sacrifice, he might aptly be described as a missionary of civilization.

43. *Ibid.*, 252-253.
44. *Ibid.*, 256-257.

CHAPTER IX

Control of the Indians

I N addition to his direction of agents among the Cherokees, Choctaws, and Chickasaws, and his assistants among
the Creeks, Colonel Hawkins was charged with the responsibility for the general conduct of the "Four Nations"
and the supervision of the United States factories and factors. His duties were many and varied.

The laws of Georgia did not extend into the Creek country, and, except for Hawkins and his assistants, the only representatives of the United States in this region were a few
small military garrisons. Hawkins at times exercised legislative, executive, and judicial functions over both Indians
and white inhabitants. He also served as diplomatic agent
for the United States and his copper-colored wards. As routine duties he issued passes to travellers and licenses to traders;
distributed goods and annuities to the Indians; apprehended
and returned runaway and stolen slaves; returned stolen
cattle, horses, and even dogs; adjudicated disputes of ownership between Indians, Indians and whites, and between whites
living in Indian country; demanded, and secured, punishment for criminal offences; directed posses and military expeditions; officiated at conferences; settled disputes between
the Indians and the states; and, in his capacity as a Federal
officer, performed the marriage ceremony.

It is needless to say that all duties were not executed with
uniform perfection or with satisfaction to all concerned. His
territorial jurisdiction extended over a vast area; his assistance was inadequate, and his charges varied from the simple
and primitive to the extremely vicious and incorrigible.
Hawkins stood in the way of individuals who, actuated by

cupidity and the desire of personal aggrandizement, wished to take advantage of the Indians, and of the states which wished to extend their boundaries and territorial jurisdiction in ways he considered unauthorized. On the other hand, he insisted upon the Indians' living up to regulations, and with impartiality he demanded that wrongs committed should be atoned for. Naturally he made enemies. Under such circumstances it is doubtful if anyone could have avoided doing so. Hawkins realized his limitations. In 1799 he wrote to Governor Jackson of Georgia: "I find it an arduous undertaking with a few assistants to make the impressions I wish on the minds of my red charges who are scattered over a wild country of at least 300 miles square."[1]

It is difficult to escape the conclusion that but for his sincerity and honesty Hawkins could not have retained the affection of the great majority of the Indians and the respect of the whites who knew him for his long tenure of office.

Life among the Indians was not without dangers. There were frequent rumors that Hawkins had been driven out of the Indian country, but there is no evidence that he was ever actually attacked.[2] In May of 1798, while at Coweta Tallahassee, he was informed that a large body of malcontents were on the way with hostile intent. He was advised to flee but he retired to his tent. During the night he was guarded by the principal chiefs of the nation, and even the women declared their determination to take up arms in his behalf. The rumored attack did not materialize and from that time on the agent was sometimes threatened but never actually subjected to physical violence. The respect the Indians had for an official of the government, combined with their affection for the man himself, kept him safe even in periods of extreme unrest.[3]

Prior to the administration of President Jefferson, Haw-

---

1. *Columbian Museum & Savannah Advertiser*, Feb. 4, 1800.
2. Dunbar Rowland, editor, *The Mississippi Territorial Archives, 1798-1803*, I, 107-108.
3. Hawkins, *Letters*, 310-312.

kins had jurisdiction over and responsibility for, all of the Indians south of the Ohio River. His charges included the Cherokees, Chickasaws, and Choctaws, as well as the Creeks, and he was called *Iste-chate-lige-osetate-chemis-te-chaugo* (The Beloved Man of the Four Nations). In 1798 the Mississippi Territory was created and Winthrop Sargent was appointed governor. This appointment was a continuous source of embarrassment to Hawkins. Samuel Mitchell, agent to the Choctaws, was particularly displeasing to Sargent, who referred to Mitchell as "a knave and a fool" and secured his dismissal in 1799. John McKee, who had served as Cherokee agent from 1794 to 1796, was appointed by Hawkins to Mitchell's place and Mitchell was transferred to the Chickasaws.[4] Governor Sargent, nevertheless, was still dissatisfied and continually complained to the State and War Departments.

The first official notice of a conflict of jurisdiction came in May, 1798, when Timothy Pickering, Secretary of State, wrote Sargent calling his attention to the act of Congress which made the Governor of Mississippi superintendent of Indian affairs in the Southern District. Pickering felt that Congress had overlooked the fact that Hawkins had been given this position. He therefore suggested to Sargent that ". . . it will be expedient to leave the general superintendency of the Southern Indian to Colo. Hawkins, who is a respectable and amiable man and much beloved by the Indians . . . I have noticed the matter only by apprising you of it, to prevent any injurious clashing of powers."[5]

Prior to the receipt of this letter, Sargent had requested a ruling on his jurisdiction over the Indians,[6] and, immediately after receiving Pickering's suggestions, wrote in reply that he still feared a clash of powers and asked for more detailed instructions.[7] In still another letter he complained: "The In-

---

4. Cotterill, *Federal Indian Management*, 335-336.
5. Carter, *Territorial Papers*, V, 35-36.
6. Rowland, *Mississippi Territorial Archives*, I, 20.
7. *Ibid.*, 20-21.

dian Business as it at present stands, embarrassed between Colo. Hawkins and myself, I beg leave to recommend it to your serious consideration. . . ."[8]

The question of jurisdiction was further complicated by the fact that Sargent was under the Secretary of State while Hawkins was responsible to the Secretary of War. This caused Sargent to take the position that though in the Northwest Territory the governor in his Indian relations had "been a mere cypher," he did not intend to submit to Indian control by subalterns in Mississippi.[9]

Pickering suggested that Sargent work out the question of authority through correspondence with Hawkins. "I am persuaded that between you and Colo. Hawkins no difficulties will arise. . . ."[10]

Sargent ordered Mitchell to correspond directly with Hawkins, who had appointed him, but to send him a duplicate of all communications.[11] The subsequent dislike of Sargent for Mitchell and the fact that Pickering later suggested to the War Department that in the future Hawkins and his deputies be instructed to communicate with Sargent when they were in Mississippi seem to indicate that the orders were not carried out.[12]

In December, 1798, Sargent requested of Pickering permission to discharge Mitchell,[13] and in February, 1799, he informed Hawkins that Mitchell was spreading rumors that the agent had been driven from the Creeks.[14]

For awhile Sargent's bombardment of the State Office with complaints slowed down, but in October, 1800, he again complained to the Secretary of War of a conflict of jurisdiction and said that he could get no reports from Hawkins or from the agents among the Choctaws.[15]

---

8. *Ibid.*, 22.
9. *Ibid.*, 30-33.
10. Carter, *Territorial Papers*, V, 45-46.
11. Rowland, *Mississippi Territorial Archives*, I, 35.
12. Carter, *Territorial Papers*, V, 51-52.
13. Rowland, *Mississippi Territorial Archives*, I, 93-95.
14. *Ibid.*, 107-108.
15. *Ibid.*, 288-290.

Not only was Sargent perturbed over conditions but even Henry Dearborn, President Jefferson's Secretary of War, was ignorant as to the exact status of Hawkins. A letter addressed to the agent from the War Office in March, 1801, stated:

> The general superintendence of Indian affairs in the South, being confided in you, and the records and papers of the War Office having been destroyed by fire, I wish you to furnish me with a Copy of the Instructions under which you have hitherto acted, and with a detailed report of the state of the objects under your charge.[16]

Sargent was succeeded by W. C. C. Claiborne as Governor of Mississippi in 1801, but the conflict of the powers continued. In February, 1802, Secretary Dearborn informed Claiborne that under the presidential regulations governors of the territories were Indian agents, and all sub-agents should correspond with them. He added, however: "Colo. Hawkins and the Agents of the Factories at Tillico [sic] in Tennessee and in Georgia will communicate with the Secretary of War as usual."[17]

In answer to this letter Governor Claiborne expressed the opinion that some of the Creeks should be under his jurisdiction, but, since it was evident that the President intended for Hawkins to handle both Lower and Upper Creeks, he would confine his attention to the Choctaws.[18]

When Silas Dinsmoor, Cherokee agent, was succeeded by Return J. Meigs in 1802, he took the place of John McKee as Choctaw agent. To complicate matters still further he was instructed by Dearborn to correspond directly with Colonel Hawkins as he had previously done.[19]

In January, 1803, William Hill, an assistant agent for the Creeks, left Fort Wilkinson for Washington with a letter

---

16. Indian Office, Out Letter Book A of Secretary of War, 37-39.
17. Rowland, *Mississippi Territorial Archives*, I, 416-418.
18. Dunbar Rowland, editor, *Official Letter Books of W. C. C. Claiborne, 1801-1816*, I, 87.
19. Carter, *Territorial Papers*, V, 146-150.

of introduction from Hawkins to James Madison and instructions to explain to him conditions in the Indian country.[20] Hill, probably unwittingly, was the direct cause of the reduction of the territorial jurisdiction of Hawkins. In February Dearborn wrote Hawkins:

> The papers of this office having been destroyed by fire, I had not the means of knowing the particulars of your instructions as Agent &c until the arrival of Mr. Hill at this place. It appears that when you received your appointment, it was contemplated that your agency should extend to all the Indian nations within the United States, east of the Mississippi, but by the establishment of a territorial Government in the Natchez country and other changes in the circumstances of the adjacent country, it has become expedient that a different arrangement should take place respecting the Indian Agencies, and in order that there should be no interfering authorities with the several agencies it is thought advisable to consider Msrs Dinsmoor and Mitchel's Agencies as attached to Governor Claiborne's direction - that Colonel Meigs correspond immediately with this Department, and that your Agency in future be confined to the Creeks and Seminoles within the boundaries of the United States.[21]

From the date of the receipt of the above letter Hawkins's title was simply Agent to the Creeks. In January, 1806, however, he was instructed to consider the Cherokee country lying between the Creek line and the Apalachee River as attached to his Agency.[22]

The policy of the United States toward the Indians within its borders was expressed by President Washington in his message to the Second Congress in October 1791:

> It is sincerely to be desired that . . . an intimate intercourse may succeed calculated to advance the happiness of the Indians, and to attach them firmly to the United States.

---

20. Madison Papers, XXV, 26.
21. Indian Office, Secretary of War Letter Book A, 331; Carter, *Territorial Papers*, V, 190. Hill later became deranged and was placed in confinement at Fort Wilkinson. He committed suicide by tying rawhide around his neck, attaching it to a rafter, and jumping from a keg of nails. *Georgian Republican*, March 18, 1806.
22. Indian Office, Secretary of War Letter Book B, 150.

In order to do this, it seems necessary - That they should experience the benefits of an impartial dispensation of justice; That the mode of alienating their lands . . . should be defined and regulated to obviate imposition. . . .

A system corresponding with the mild principles of religion and philanthropy, towards an unenlightened race of men, whose happiness materially depends on the conduct of the United States, would be as honorable to the National character as conformable to the dictates of sound policy.[23]

In thorough accord with this policy, Hawkins attempted at all times to carry it out. As a first step in its accomplishment he felt it necessary to gain the confidence of the Indians. His fair-minded service on treaty and line commissions led them to accept him as their friend. He devoted his energies to retaining their confidence and good will.

Among the Southern Indians the Creeks were the strongest, the most warlike, and most often and most seriously embroiled in difficulties with the white men. In their relations with Georgia and the United States they had been led by more astute and capable leaders than had the other tribes. There can be no doubt that Hawkins for these reasons considered the Creeks his most important charge. Even when charged with the supervision of all the Southern tribes he made the Creek country his headquarters and set up his residence there.

Upon his arrival in Georgia Hawkins found two major divisions among the Creeks and a further decentralization of control because of the comparative independence of each town of the nation. Under such conditions it was well nigh impossible to locate responsibility for crimes and depredations. One of the great sources of conflict between Georgia and the Creeks had been the failure of some chiefs and certain towns to recognize agreements entered into by other chiefs. In 1799 Hawkins wrote:

The Creeks never had, till this year, a national Government and law. Everything of a general tendency, was left to

23. *American State Papers, Foreign Relations*, I, 16.

the care and management of the public agents, who heretofore used temporary expedients only; and amongst the
most powerful and persuasive, was the pressure of fear from
without, and presents.[24]

During 1798 Hawkins had tried diligently to remedy this
condition. Following the excitement caused by the punishment of the banditti who had assaulted the line commissioners
of the United States and Spain in September, 1799, Hawkins
convened the national council and reported to the assembled
chiefs "his opinion of the plan indispensably necessary, to
carry the laws of the nation into effect."[25]

The plan was accepted. The Creeks agreed to classify
the towns and to appoint a warrior over each class to see to
the execution of the law, to absolve from blame any and all
persons causing death to a criminal being punished under
the law, and to place all white mischief makers of any nation-
ality under the agent. They agreed further that the agent
might use the troops of the United States or call upon whatever number of Indians he might think proper to enforce
the law.[26]

The new scheme of government was so successfully inaugurated that Hawkins's report with his description of its
actual operation was made a part of the message of President Jefferson to Congress in December, 1801. As described
in this message, the national council met once a year, generally in May, at the call and upon the date set by Hawkins.
Each town was asked to send deputies and generally sent
five or six. The first order of business was a report on the
state of the nation by the agent. Next the agent advised
the council as to what action it needed to take and demanded
the punishment for crime committed and compensation for
treaty violations. In many respects the relationship of Hawkins to the council was similar to that of the President to
Congress.

---

24. Benjamin Hawkins, *A Sketch of the Creek Country 1798-1799*, p. 67.
25. *Ibid.*, 67.
26. *Ibid.*, 68.

The council selected a speaker for an indefinite term. Sessions were continuous throughout the day and night until the council adjourned. The council hall was living quarters as well as legislative chamber. When an Indian became sleepy he rolled up in his blanket and slept; when he was hungry he ate; but he did not leave the chamber until the meeting was over. Debate continued until action was agreed to or definitely postponed. When an agreement was reached it became the "will of the nation" and was proclaimed by the speaker to the agent and all the chiefs. If the will of the nation had any bearing upon inter-racial or inter-tribal relations, Hawkins recorded it and made it known. Food was furnished by the agent from the public stores and either he or one of his assistants was always present while the council was in session.[27]

Such an arrangement made the agent tremendously effective in the internal affairs of the Creeks and gave him a power over them that had not been approximated since the death of McGillivray in 1793. He became, in effect, the first chief of the nation and his influence was paramount over the native chiefs.

The towns still retained a good deal of autonomy. Each had its own government, its own presiding chief, called Micco or King, and except when the national council was in session it acted independently.[28] This town independence was frequently a source of trouble to the agent and increased the burden of maintaining complete peace and enforcing the law uniformly. Attached to some of the towns there might be several villages under the same Micco. There were twelve towns among the Lower Creeks, twenty-five among the Upper Creeks, and seven Seminole towns in 1799.[29]

The national council of the Creeks met at Tookaubatchee on the Tallapoosa River. Here Hawkins met with the chiefs

27. *American State Papers, Indian Affairs*, I, 647.
28. Hawkins, *A Sketch of the Creek Country*, 68.
29. *Ibid.*, 24-25.

annually except in periods of disorder when it was some-
times necessary to call extraordinary sessions. Among the
Southern tribes, at least, this relationship of the United
States agent to the Indians was unique.

Individual Georgians and officials of the state at times
applauded the work of Hawkins when it seemed to them
his efforts were conducive to peace and order on the frontier. Many, however, were skeptical of introducing agriculture and industry among the tribes if those pursuits of civilization implied the promise of permanent occupation of the
lands the Indians held. The drive to the west, the urge for
expansion, was ever present among Georgians. Like most
Americans since the settlements at Jamestown and Plymouth
they felt that the savage—something less than human—must
be removed from the path of civilization and must not be
allowed to thwart the development of the white race. The
Indian was not utilizing the land to its capacity; he could
live anywhere; he was obstructing progress, and he must
make way! Some few Georgians, on the other hand, held
to the idea that if the Indians were induced to give up hunting for agriculture they might be willing to cede surplus
lands. James Jackson, as commissioner of the state at Coleraine, had violently opposed the promise of permanency
of occupation; but, as governor of Georgia, he wrote to
Hawkins in April, 1800:

> The object you have in view may if accomplished operate
> beneficially both for the United States and for themselves, by
> changing the habit of hunting to cultivation and manufac-
> turing, reducing the necessity they now feel for large tracts
> of uncultivated lands, and thereby inducing a relinquish-
> ment of most of them which ultimately must increase the
> population and consequent wealth and strength of the
> Union.[30]

As was so often the case where the Indian stood in the
way of the white man's desire for new lands, Jackson's inter-

30. Governor's Letter Book, March 28-June 28, in Georgia Department
Archives and History.

est in the benefits to the Indians was incidental to his major interest of reducing Georgia lands held by the Creeks. Occasionally, however, a public character in American history actually thought in terms of the Indians, their interests, and their equity in the land where they were born. Benjamin Hawkins was such a character. In February, 1792, as a member of the United States Senate, he expressed a critical attitude toward the policy of the United States:

> During the war we acknowledged the Indians as brothers, told them of our difficulties, and embarrassments arising from our contest with Great Britain, assured them of our disposition, tho' unable, to furnish them such comforts as they had been accustomed to receive, urged them to be patient, and declared that when success crowned our efforts, they should be partakers of our good fortune; They were then acknowledged to be the possessors of the soil on which they lived.
>   At the close of the war . . . we seem to have forgotten altogether the rights of the Indians. They were treated as tenants at will, we seized on their lands . . . and did not even think of offering them compensation for any claims. . . .[31]

Thomas Jefferson had written Hawkins from Paris in August, 1786, and suggested the difficulties presented by the official attitude toward these people.

> The attention which you pay to their rights also does you great honor, as the want of that is a principal source of dishonor to the American character. The two principles on which our conduct towards the Indians should be founded, are justice and fear. After the injuries we have done them, they cannot love us, which leaves us no alternative but that of fear to keep them from attacking us, but justice is what we should never lose sight of & in time we may recover their esteem.[32]

As agent, Hawkins was sometimes forced to use threats of coercion to induce respect for law, but his major interest

---

31. McPherson, "Unpublished letters of North Carolinians to Washington," *North Carolina Historical Review*, XII, 162-165.
32. Jefferson Papers, XXIII, 3995, Library of Congress.

was in recovering the esteem of the Indians for the government. Jefferson, as President, once even expressed the fear that Hawkins, overlooking his obligations to his country, might be pursuing the interests of the Indians to an extreme.[33]

Instruction of the Indians in the arts of civilization was a pleasure to Colonel Hawkins. Other duties, probably more immediately necessary, but much less pleasant, were keeping order, executing the law, and settling disputes between the Indians and the Georgians. In February, 1798, Mrs. Elizabeth Hilton of Jackson County, Georgia, befriended two Indians. One of them criminally attacked her. When the matter was reported to Hawkins, he had the guilty Indian arrested and placed in the jail in Oglethorpe County where he was apprehended "to be dealt with as the law directs."[34] The prisoner, Tuskegee Tustunnugee, was at the time representing the Creeks as a commissioner seeking the murderer of a white man and was a chief in the nation. A week later another of the Creek commissioners, Emautlau Haujo, one of the leading chiefs of the nation, addressed a letter to the Georgia authorities in his colleague's behalf. He asked that in the interest of peace the Indian be befriended.

> Colo. Hawkins our great beloved man, he will tell you, that our unfortunate Chief Tuskegee Tustunnegau [sic], was the friend of the white people. . . . He has one enemy and one only, rum, he will get drunk, and then he is ungovernable, yet even when drunk he has obeyed the voice of our beloved man, who, as the representative of our father the President when he was called on to submit to the laws he obeyed . . . yet the man was a principal chief of our land greatly beloved, and a public Commissioner and one of that Commission which had been lately fired on, one killed and two others wounded by white men, and we had not received satisfaction.[35]

33. Andrew A. Lipscomb, editor, *The Writings of Thomas Jefferson*, X, 357-358. Jefferson to Andrew Jackson, Feb. 16, 1803.
34. Hawkins Papers.
35. *Ibid.*

Hawkins was willing to let the law take its course. Tustunnugee himself offered no resistance to his arrest, saying, "I will submit. I am a man. If I get a rope it is my fate."[36] Hawkins supplied an interpreter for his defense and there let the matter rest, but in March he reported that the chief had been restored to his nation "by the kind interposition of the frontier people."[37]

Upon his release Tustunnugee made the following talk:

I forfeited my life and the people restored it to me; I was ashamed that I, who had delighted in doing good acts to the white people, should violate their laws. I suffered much, not from fear of death, because I am above fear, but because I had done an injury to white people in company with our great beloved man and the beloved man of Georgia, which put me to shame. If our beloved man had not taken my knife, raisor and moccasin all from me, I should have put myself to death. I now rejoice that I am alive to tell how I have been treated, that the great body of the people of Georgia are friendly to the Indians; that the Governor of Georgia sent a guard to take care of me; that this guard, tho' but few in number faithfully obeyed their orders, and when his jail was attacked by a number of bad men, the Governor's guard saved my life; they fired on their own people and wounded two, one of them badly. My people have lost four of their beloved chiefs by white men and never retaliated; I expected I was the fifth, but I am saved, and I hope for the good of the white people; I will now die sooner than cease to be friendly to them.[38]

There is no evidence that Tustunnugee ever again failed in his friendliness to the white people. He remained a staunch supporter of Hawkins and the Georgians throughout his life. Governor Jackson, however, felt that justice had miscarried and demanded his rearrest. To this demand Hawkins replied:

I can never doubt the purity of your intentions in making that demand which you conceive founded in justice. But

---

36. Hawkins, *Letters*, 292.
37. *Ibid.*, 298.
38. *Ibid.*, 301.

the magistrate having liberated that chief and restored him
to his country and friends, I doubt the propriety of my
acting on the presumption of this procedure being extra
judicial. It is a new case and important in its consequences
altho' I could have satisfied the nation and his friends of
the justice of the decision in the case even of his execution
in the first instance. Yet being liberated and restored by the
magistrates it would be difficult if not impractical to explain
satisfactorily to them this second operation.[39]

This letter indicates Hawkins's attitude toward justice in
the Indian country. He was always anxious for the demands
of the law to be executed, but the execution had to be regular
and by methods that the Indian could understand. "I am
determined never to forgive any man, red or white, who
sheds innocent blood, and I expect to see the day when all
who shed innocent blood shall be put to death, and that an
honest man may go where he pleases and be not afraid."[40]

Frontier life is inevitably disorderly. A conflict of cul-
tures naturally develops. Civilized people in contact with
nature in the raw often temporarily forget the conventions
of civilized society and become semi-barbaric in their relations with primitive races. Where the original inhabitants
are unwilling to give ground the disorder is aggravated. On
the Creek-Georgia frontier a conflict of jurisdiction added
to the lawlessness. A large part of the correspondence of
Hawkins is taken up with demands of Georgia for the punishment of Indians, and the even more frequent demands of
the Creek chiefs for redress of grievances against the Georgians. Where the Indians were the culprits and the guilty
could be determined they were often apprehended and punished by their own people by a primitive code closely related
to the old Mosaic law. White lawbreakers presented greater
difficulty. It was harder to determine guilt and the Georgia
authorities seemed oftentimes reluctant to exact the severe
penalties of the law against white men as long as Indian depredations continued. The Indians, on the other hand, often

39. Hawkins Papers.
40. Hawkins, *Letters*, 298.

acquiesced in the agent's demands for the punishment of their own criminals; but when a white culprit went unpunished for long they could not be restrained from taking the law in their own hands.

The Indians were notoriously fickle in carrying out their obligations in spite of lip service to law observance. Always among them were young warriors, individualists, who could not, or would not, see that their chiefs in council could bind them to any agreement to which they had not personally subscribed. It was natural that a lawless element of white people should gather on the frontier. It was thus impossible for Hawkins, with three or four assistants and widely scattered Federal garrisons, to keep order. He was often criticised. To one such critic he replied:

> If you in the course of your researches have found out the secret of making Indians fulfill their public engagements where there is no law, and it belongs to individuals to take personal satisfaction, and to the family of the individual to avenge the rong [sic] and you will communicate that secret to me, I hereby bind myself and my successors in office to send you six princesses in full dress.[41]

Among the more common crimes committed in the Indian country were murder and the stealing of Negroes, cattle, and horses. Neither whites nor Indians had a monopoly on any of these crimes. In January, 1803, Hawkins wrote to Governor John Milledge of Georgia that he had learned of the killing by whites of an Indian accused of horse-stealing: "The apprehending and punishing an Indian according to law is a thing not to be complained of by the Chiefs of the Creek Agency, and is easily explained to them, but the case reported is not free from suspicion of unfairness at least, however I shall forbear saying anything at present on it as it is in the Province of the law to give it a name."[42]

---

41. *Ibid.*, 59-60. Hawkins to Major Freeman, January 8, 1797.
42. Hawkins Papers.

In September he wrote again:

> We have now a regular tribunal of justice established in the
> agency to which the Indians and white people are in the
> habit of resorting for the settlement of their claims. This
> court meets annually in May and sits as long as there is any
> business before them. Honest claimants have now no excuse
> for having recourse to reprisal, to obtain their due. The
> chief [sic] of this agency have manifested in several in-
> stances lately as great a desire to do justice to the white
> people as to obtain it from them. I wish all complaints
> against the Indians could get into some regular channel of
> the agency. . . .[43]

Violence between the races continued throughout the administration of Hawkins, and until the Indians were finally
removed. Neither perfect order nor perfect understanding
was ever attained. An Indian murderer unapprehended and
unpunished would cause criticism of Hawkins and likely lead
to reprisals by the whites. Similarly, the murder of an Indian
by whites would cause the Indians to retaliate. Nevertheless
the entire period from Hawkins's appointment until the War
of 1812 was one of comparative peace. White men, on peaceful pursuits, came and went through Indian country with
relatively little anxiety and Indians were often within the
territorial jurisdiction of Georgia. Absolute elimination of
violence was too much to expect. Hawkins, himself, was
often discouraged because of conditions, but his vigilance
spared many lives of both races.

Next to murder, the most serious source of disorder was
horse stealing. The average Indian could not resist the desire to ride off on a fine horse that came into the field of
his operations, and the Indian horses wandering close to the
borders proved too great a temptation for some whites to
resist. There were white men always ready to buy stolen
horses from the Indians if the price was sufficiently low. In
March, 1797, Governor Jackson wrote Hawkins that he had
paid the unreasonable price of two hundred dollars to Chee-

---

43. *Ibid.*

haw King for a horse stolen by Georgians "rather than run the risque of retaliation."[44]

Hawkins, realizing the dangers resulting from this practice, established strict regulations regarding it. No Indian was allowed to buy or sell horses or cattle except the titles be examined and the sale approved, but on several occasions he complained to the Governor of Georgia that as long as white men on the frontier continued to buy horses from the Indians they would continue to steal and sell them.[45]

In February, 1802, he worked out an elaborate plan of branding "to serve as a guide to the agents as well as the honest dealers in horses and cattle." Horses were to be branded on the right side of the neck in inch-and-a-half letters, and cattle on the right hind quarters in two-and-a-half inch letters. In Tennessee, on the west side of the Cumberland mountains, stock was to be branded A; other Tennessee stock to be marked B; North Carolina owners were to use the letter C; South Carolina, D; Georgia was divided into three sections using the letters E, F, G, respectively. For the settlements on the Tombigbee River the mark was to be I, and for stock on the Mississippi the letter K.[46] Governor Tatnall wrote Hawkins in March, 1802, praising this plan and announced that he would publish it and instruct all stock owners in Georgia to follow directions.[47] There is no evidence that this plan was adhered to, and stock continued to be stolen.

These regulations were for the purpose of keeping track of stock that had strayed or been stolen, but one of the most constantly perplexing problems to confront the agent resulted from citizens of Georgia purposely putting their cattle across into Indian country for grazing, in violation of treaty

44. Governor's Letter Book, Feb.-May, 1797, Georgia Department Archives and History.
45. Hawkins Papers, Hawkins to Gov. Milledge, Jan. 3, 1803; also, Hawkins to Gov. Jackson, Aug. 2, 1798.
46. Ibid. Hawkins to Gov. Josiah Tattnall, Feb. 13, 1802.
47. Governor's Letter Book A, Georgia Department Archives and History.

agreements. In August, 1805, Hawkins transmitted to Governor Milledge an Indian complaint that white men were stealing cattle between the Ocmulgee and the Oconee.[48] In December, 1808, Tuskeegee Tustunnugee warned Hawkins that unless the white people refrained from putting their cattle across the Ocmulgee River the young men of the nation could not be restrained and it would be impossible to guard the safety of travellers through the Creek country.[49]

Tustunnugee Hopoie and Tuskeegee Tustunnugee, speakers of the Lower Creeks, wrote Hawkins jointly in March, 1809:

> When we are disturbed about our affairs it gives us some consolation to see and converse freely with you. We have unceasingly exerted ourselves to get our affairs right by keeping our young men within the bounds of good neighborhood; and let us do what we can . . . with regret we state to you that much of our embarrassment arises from the improper conduct of our white neighbors who have placed their stock over to range on our lands contrary to the assurances of their government.[50]

Hawkins reported this complaint to Governor Jared Irwin, and he, by proclamation, ordered all white trespassers out of Indian country, but trespassing continued.[51]

Another frequent source of discord between the races was the violation of fishing rights by Georgians. They not only fished in Indian waters themselves, but even refused to allow the Creeks to approach their own streams for the purpose of taking fish.[52] Hawkins, in these cases, threatened to turn the violaters over to the district court of the United States. Governor Irwin again cooperated and ordered the state courts to prosecute "all such persons as are guilty not only of fishing in the River with Traps against the consent of the Indians and also against the positive provisions of the

---

48. Hawkins Papers.
49. *Ibid.*
50. *Ibid.*
51. *Ibid.*, October 15, 1809.
52. *Ibid.*, Zachariah Booth to Hawkins, "Ocmulgee high fauls Jones County," March 24, 1812.

Treaty between the United States and them, but of whipping and abusing them in the most vindictive manner."[53]

Governor Irwin had confidence in Hawkins's desire "to do ample justice to the citizens on all occasions."[54] He supported the agent's efforts to keep peace and order on the frontier and yet conditions were often such that Chief Tuskeegee Tustunnugee could truthfully remark: "Your situation for a while was of that sort, which got you blaim [sic] from both sides. . . ."[55]

Neither praise nor blame could deter the agent from attempting to carry out his avowed purpose of doing "ample justice." He strove earnestly to bring about peace and friendship between the two races in the interests of both, and he tried to solve each conflict justly without regard to the color of the skin of the parties to it.

53. Executive Order to Justice of Inferior Court, Randolph County, April 7, 1812, Georgia Department Archives and History.
54. *Columbian Museum & Savannah Advertiser*, Nov. 17, 1807.
55. Hawkins Papers, Tustunnugee to Hawkins, Dec. 21, 1808.

CHAPTER X

Treaties:
Negotiations and Enforcement

DESPITE Georgia's resentment of the terms of the Treaty of Coleraine, the Creek line in conformity to it was drawn early in 1798. James Jackson, who had served as a Georgia commissioner at the treaty conference and was the most severe critic of the United States commissioners present, was shortly afterward elected governor of the state. To him the boundary line commission reported on February 22, 1798, that the line had been drawn and "the Continental [*sic*] Commissioner Coll. Hawkins and the Indians showed every Disposition to run the line agreeable to existing Treaties."[1]

Article seven of the Treaty of Coleraine required that all prisoners and property taken by the Indians should be surrendered and that Georgia might appoint commissioners to secure the return of such property and prisoners. In February, 1798, Hawkins wrote Jackson recommending the appointment of such commissioners, and in July he again wrote the governor promising these commissioners his complete support,[2] but no action was taken on these recommendations.

The terms of the treaty did not make clear whether Georgia Negroes who had fled to the Indians of their own free will came under the meaning of this article. Hawkins, in order to circumvent discord which might arise over the interpretation of article seven, took a step highly advantageous to Georgia. He insisted that the chiefs agree to re-

---

1. Report of the Line Commissioners to Governor James Jackson. MS. in Telamon Cuyler Collection, University of Georgia Library.
2. Hawkins papers.

turn all runaway Negroes upon payment by the owner of twelve dollars and a half for each slave.[3] Though this fee for Negroes sometimes changed, because of the difficulties in capturing runaways, Hawkins's agreement with the Creeks was accepted by Georgians, and his correspondence often reported Negroes delivered to him by the Indians to be restored to their owners upon the payment of the necessary fee for capture and food.

When Negroes were delivered at the Agency, Hawkins would inform the Governor of Georgia, who, in turn, would often cause the letter to be published in the papers of the state.[4] On one occasion Hawkins reported that it had been necessary to capture a fugitive named Moses twice, and therefore his master must pay double expenses.[5]

At another time a Negro woman was pregnant when she was brought to Hawkins's house. Subsequently she and four others were returned. "Mary has been a long while with me and attended the while she had a child, and I have furnished them some clothing, but I deem their labour while here a compensation for what [I] have done for them and for their clothing."[6]

In 1805, Phill, one of the Hawkins Negroes, reversed the usual procedure and ran away to the east into Georgia. Halstead, the factor at Fort Wilkinson, announced his capture and he was returned to the Agency.[7]

Georgia never relaxed the pressure it put upon the Creeks to secure more of their lands, and in the fall of 1800 another conference to clear the Ocmulgee River fork and the Tallassee country was contemplated. Hawkins was instructed to cooperate with commissioners whom Georgia might appoint. James Jackson again refused to make appointments and ex-

3. *Ibid.*, Hawkins to Jackson, August 2, 1798.
4. *Georgia Republican*, August 19, 1806.
5. Hawkins to Gov. Mitchell, November 16, 1812. Cuyler Collection, University of Georgia.
6. Hawkins Papers, Hawkins to _____ (no address), February 9, 1807.
7. Indian Office, Factory Letter Book, Halstead to Hawkins, National Archives.

plained in a message to the General Assembly that such an appointment would be an acknowledgement of the relinquishment of the claims the state had insisted upon since the Treaty of Galphinton.[8] In December the Secretary of War instructed Hawkins that, if the latter felt the cession advisable, he should prepare the Indians for it, otherwise negotiations were to be postponed.[9] Georgia's attitude had already killed the possibility of success and so the conference was not held.

It was Jefferson's expressed policy to keep Hawkins as one of the commissioners at every treaty conference with the Southern tribes. He, accordingly, was present and, together with James Wilkinson and his old friend Andrew Pickens, signed a treaty with the Chickasaws on October 24, 1801, re-defining the lands of the tribe. On December 7 the same commissioners negotiated and signed a similar treaty with the Choctaws at Fort Adams. The report of the commissioners on the latter treaty was lost in the Duck River in Tennessee when the post rider from Natchez was drowned there. In February, 1802, the Secretary of War wrote Hawkins for another report.[10]

In March, 1797, a special committee in the Senate of the United States had reported that Georgia had no valid claim to its western lands. This report was based on the act of Parliament of October 7, 1763, which gave to the colony the lands south of the Altamaha River but also provided that "All lands and territories lying to the westward of the sources of the rivers . . . are reserved under the sovereignty . . . of the King." Georgia, it was further stated in the report, never claimed western jurisdiction until after the Revolution. It was recommended, however, that since a conflict had arisen between Georgia and the United States it be settled amicably by commissions appointed by the President and the Governor of Georgia.[11]

---

8. *Augusta Chronicle*, November 22, 1800.
9. Indian Office, Secretary of War Letter Book A, 5, National Archives.
10. *Ibid.*, 163.
11. *Augusta Chronicle*, March 25, 1797.

In October of 1797 the Georgia legislature defeated a bill to cede to the United States all lands west of a line drawn due north from a point on the thirty-first parallel twenty-five miles west of the Chattahoochee.[12]

In 1802, Georgia finally appointed commissioners, one of whom was ex-Governor James Jackson, and the state sold its western land claims to the United States with the understanding that the Indian lands within the state would be cleared at the expense of the United States as soon as this could be done peaceably. The promise of the United States to extinguish Indian land titles was a repudiation of the policy implied in the Treaty of New York, and was the principal reason Georgia was willing to sell.

The treaty of Fort Wilkinson was the first step in carrying out this pledge of the United States. At the time, "Some of the Western Creeks were disposed to make trouble over the encroachment upon the lands of their nation, but the very efficient Indian Agent, Col. Benjamin Hawkins, proved equal to the occasion and pacified the malcontents."[13]

To negotiate with the Creeks, President Jefferson had appointed General James Wilkinson, General Andrew Pickens, and Colonel Hawkins. They assembled at the designated place on the Oconee River on May 8, 1802.

Two days later Governor Tatnall of Georgia was informed that in response to his request the treaty negotiations would be delayed until the legislature could be convened. While Hawkins and Pickens remained with the Indians, who had begun to arrive, General Wilkinson journeyed to Louisville for an interview. On May 21, Governor Tattnall wrote appreciatively of this interview and expressed his gratitude at the evident desire of the commissioners to promote the interests of his people.[14]

When the commissioners learned that the special session

---

12. *Ibid.*, October 14, 1797. The legislative journals of Georgia for 1797 were not published.
13. Ulrich B. Phillips, *Georgia and States Rights*, 49.
14. *American State Papers, Indian Affairs*, I, 671.

of the Georgia General Assembly was not to convene until June 10, they considered it necessary to begin the conference without Georgia's being officially represented. Accordingly, the negotiations began on May 24. After many delays the Treaty of Fort Wilkinson was signed on June 16, 1802.[15]

Not all lands desired by Georgians were secured. The payment of $25,000 in merchandise and in debts assumed, plus an annuity of $3,000 and an additional $1,000 to the chiefs for ten years, also seemed too great. Nevertheless, it was the best that could have been done under the circumstances. The commissioners explained the situation to Secretary Dearborn:

> Having employed with zeal, but without effect, every fair means in our power to accomplish the specific objects of our instructions, we turned our attention from these objects, to one of more importance, in point of intrinsic value, viz: The extinction of the Indian claims within the Oakmulgee fork, from the Rock Landing, up to the High Shoals of the Apalachy river. . . . The great difficulty to be surmounted was, the passage of the Oconee; and the extension of our front, in contact with the unextinguishable claims of the Indians, above the confluence of the Oconee and Oakmulgee, appeared to be the next most desirable object. In prosecuting these views, we had to combat, not only the jealousies, distrusts and fears, natural to the Indians, but also, an apprehension, serious and alarming to the old chiefs, that, if they ceded any part of their country, their young warriors might resist it, and joining the partizans of Bowles, divide the nation, wrest the government from those who at present administer it, and, by some hasty and imprudent act, involve the country in ruin.[16]

Hawkins and Wilkinson remained at Fort Wilkinson for another month engaged in the difficult task of distributing the goods among the various towns.

In January, 1703, the Senate unanimously ratified the Treaty of Fort Wilkinson. On that day the Georgia Senators wrote to the Governor: "This unanimity, we flatter our-

---

15. *Ibid.*, 669.
16. *Ibid.*, I, 680. William Augustus Bowles. For discussion see Chapter XI.

selves will induce the General Government, to a further interposition in our favor, to obtain the remainder of the lands contained in the fork of the Oakmulgee and Oconee."[17]

In April Governor John Milledge commented upon this treaty in a message to the General Assembly.

> The state has, for the first time under its national government, acquired an accession of jurisdictional territory, the treaty of Fort Wilkinson, concluded the 16th June, 1802, having been unanimously ratified by the Senate of the United States, and accepted, ratified and confirmed by the President, under the seal of the general government, on the 11th of January last. . . . The first treaty held under the general government with the Creek Indians, was that of New York, where the treaty making power adopted the precedent respecting the ratification of Indian treaties. That treaty is well known to us all - it dismembered the state of that part of her dominion called Tallassee County, and not until the Treaty of Fort Wilkinson, under a change of national administration, did we get restored to us a small portion of that County of which we have been deprived. But we need not doubt that there exists a disposition on the part of the general government to heal, by every means in its power, the wound made on the jurisdiction of state right.[18]

Certain Georgians were naturally disappointed that the Indians had not been persuaded to make the Ocmulgee River the boundary line, and criticism of the commissioners resulted. It was rumored that General Wilkinson had charged that had it not been for Hawkins and Pickens the Indians would have accepted the Ocmulgee line. Concerning the rumor, General David Anderson wrote in defense of Hawkins "from a love of justice and without any other motive."

> Eulogism is no part of my aim. I would only wish that the citizens of Georgia, who have imbibed these mistaken prejudices, would stop, inform themselves of the truth: that they may be grateful to the man who advocates their rights, and not withhold the tribute of justice from an Agent, who

17. *Columbian Museum & Savannah Advertiser*, Feb. 4, 1803.
18. *Augusta Chronicle*, May 7, 1803.

is not only disposed to serve them, but who is eminently qualified for that purpose in a way so desirable, both on the part of Georgia, and the United States. . . .[19]

Hawkins, himself, addressed a letter to Governor John Milledge in October in which he defended his friend Andrew Pickens against similar charges.[20]

Georgia's impatience to expand westward would have resulted in dissatisfaction with any treaty which did less than clear completely the Creeks from the boundaries of the state.

General Wilkinson was instructed to run the boundary lines with the Choctaws at his discretion and "with such aid as you may obtain from Colonel Hawkins."[21] In April, 1803, he was ordered upon completion of the Choctaw line to report to the Creek nation "where in concert with Col. Hawkins" he was to make another attempt to induce the Creeks to an extension of their cessions to the Ocmulgee boundary at least.[22]

In August Wilkinson wrote to Dearborn:

I have not heard from Col. Hawkins . . . but reports in this quarter are unfavourable to the pending negotiation with the Creeks (whether founded on Facts or prejudice, which rages here against the Col: is doubtful) I shall therefore quicken my pace. . . .[23]

This proposed treaty was not negotiated. Hawkins's next assignment was for running the line in conformity to the treaty of 1802. In October he was instructed to make necessary arrangements, to notify the Creek chiefs and Governor Milledge, and to try to satisfy both Georgia and the Creeks.[24]

Hawkins, William Freeman, surveyor, General John Clark, Major David Adams, and Major Jesse McCall, Georgia

---

19. *Ibid.*, Sept. 24, 1803.
20. Hawkins Papers
21. Carter, *Territorial Papers*, V, 175. Dearborn to Wilkinson, September 17, 1802.
22. *Ibid.*, 214.
23. *Ibid.*, 236-237.
24. Indian Office, Secretary of War Letter Book A, 381-382.

commissioners, with William Robertson, secretary, and three Creek chiefs, assembled at High Shoals on the Apalachee River on January 20, 1804. After a difference of opinion between Hawkins and two of the Georgia commissioners as to where the line should begin, Hawkins's interpretation prevailed and the line was commenced. With only part of the line run by February 3, Hawkins informed the Georgia commissioners that on account of the disposition of the Indians it would be unsafe to run the southern portion of the line,[25] and the survey stopped.

Again the agent was criticised by Georgians but the three Georgia commissioners published a letter in his defense in which they said: " . . . the calumny which has been levelled, by a number of the citizens of Georgia, against Col. Hawkins . . . is undeserved . . . ."[26]

After the survey had been stopped and the Georgia commissioners had returned home, Hawkins continued for two months among the Creeks seeking their cooperation in the completion of the line. Three meetings were held with the chiefs before he could report that the Indians had agreed to send four persons to aid in recommencing the survey in April.[27]

In the meantime the insistence of Georgia for more lands resulted in the Secretary of War informing Hawkins that $12,000 had been deposited to his credit in the Bank of Savannah for the purpose of negotiating with the Creeks. He, in company with General David Meriwether, was instructed to secure additional lands from the council at Tookaubatchee when it assembled in May. He was also authorized to draw on Halstead, the factor at Fort Wilkinson, for goods to the amount of $2,000.[28]

25. Cuyler Collection, University of Georgia, MS. Journal of the Line Commissioners.
26. *Augusta Chronicle*, Feb. 18, 1804.
27. Cuyler Collection, University of Georgia, Hawkins to Governor Milledge.
28. Indian Office, Secretary of War Letter Book A, 458m; Also *American State Papers, Indian Affairs*, I, 693.

After many years of neglect, Georgia had finally applied to the President for authorization to appoint agents to claim property of citizens of the state held by the Indians.[29] These agents had first been provided for in the Treaty of New York, and again at Coleraine. Hawkins was asked to give them every aid in his power.[30] Since early after his arrival in 1796 Hawkins had suggested to governors of Georgia at various times that they appoint such agents and had offered his cooperation in effecting their purposes but to no avail. In June, 1804, John Clark, Jesse McCall, and David Adams were appointed and ordered to report at Tookaubatchee on June 20 at the council meeting that had been set for that day instead of in May as was usual. They were also to consult with the agent immediately. They were informed that if, in the opinion of Hawkins, the presentation of their claims would prejudice the chances of securing more lands, the claims were not to be pressed.[31]

Clark, McCall, and Adams arrived at the designated time and presented their credentials to Hawkins, solicited his aid, and asked that he present their demands at the proper time. Hawkins expressed a desire to do all he could but was fearful that Georgia's claims had been too long delayed.[32] He was of the opinion, however, that they should be presented to the council and this matter was considered there at the same time as the overtures of Hawkins and Meriwether for more lands.

On July 2, Major Adams, speaking for Georgia, presented claims under every treaty to which either the state or the United States had been a party since that at Augusta in 1783.[33] Hopoie Micco, the speaker, returned an evasive answer the next day and put off the final decision until another meeting

---

29. Indian Office, Secretary of War Letter Book A, 384-385.
30. *Ibid.*, Letter Book B, 5.
31. Executive Order, Gov. Milledge, Louisville, June 7, 1804. Georgia Department Archives and History.
32. Hawkins Papers, Georgia Commissioners to Milledge, June 23, 1804.
33. *Ibid.* Georgia Commissioners' Demands, July 2, 1804.

of the Indians at Coweta which was scheduled for July.[34] The following day, after having breakfast as the guests of Colonel Hawkins, the Georgia commissioners departed for home.

Before Major Adams returned for the answer to Georgia's demands, Hopoie Micco was taken ill. The Indians again put off a definite answer on the grounds of the speaker's absence. Hawkins, however, demanded the immediate return of six Negroes known to be among the Creeks. He promised the usual reward of $12.50 for each but insisted that if the Indian warriors did not bring them in he would take them with white soldiers. Adams agreed to be satisfied with the return of these slaves. At any rate, he realized the futility of further demands and departed with expressions of solicitude for the recovery of the speaker and of expectancy that all property would be returned in due time.[35]

In August Hawkins reported to Governor Milledge that he had been two months among the Indians, during which time he had held three separate conferences. He felt the result, "considering the great diversity of opinion among the Indians, has been as favourable as I had a right to expect, and we have shaped a course which in the end, will enable the government to obtain from them all that could be reasonably expected at this time. I believe Ocmulgee will be your boundary, before the termination of the year, as high up as the three forks at least and probably to its source."[36]

He stated also that the upper towns had expressed unanimous willingness to make a cession of the Ocmulgee lands, and that the opposition had dwindled. He requested Milledge in the interim to use his influence to keep down frontier disturbances, and especially to stop the market for stolen horses as being contributory to ill feeling.[37]

As a result of the divergence of opinion among the Creeks, Hawkins suggested to the Secretary of War that aid, or en-

---

34. *Ibid.*, Hopoie Micco to Georgia Commissioners, July 3, 1803.
35. *Ibid.*, Proceedings of the Conference at Tookaubatchee, August 8, 1804.
36. *Ibid.*, Hawkins to Milledge, August 15, 1804.
37. *Ibid.*

couragement, at least, be given to those Indians who were willing to make concessions to the wishes of the Georgians. After consultation with the President, the Secretary replied:

> It should be understood that we act between the Indians only as friends & mediators, but not as parties in their disputes with each other - the Government ought not to be pledged to enter into a war in favor of or against any party in their more national disputes - The Creek nation being a collection of the remnants of several tribes, their local disputes may originate in the difference of descent, of manners or language and if they choose to divide into two or more tribes, we can have no particular interest in opposing them or in intermeddling with their interior Government any further than by friendly advice.[38]

Not until September 28 did the Georgia commissioners report to the Governor. At that time they acknowledged failure in their endeavors. "It is obvious," they said, "that the Indians are procrastinating the business, and that they never intend to return the property." They suggested that the only possibility for Georgia to receive remuneration for stolen goods was to get a land cession in settlement; otherwise, "it must be by compulsory measures."[39]

The Creeks had promised Hawkins and Meriwether that they would send a deputation to Washington in the fall and there make an agreement for the land cession west of the Oconee River. Because of the illness of Hopoie Micco, the speaker, this journey was put off for another year. Meanwhile, Hawkins, acting under his commission of April, 1804, negotiated alone and signed a treaty at the Agency on November 3, 1804. By the terms of this treaty the land in the forks of the Oconee and Ocmulgee rivers, as high up as the High Shoals of the Apalachee River, was to be ceded to the United States. The Indians were to receive $200,000 in stock paying six per cent per annum, the principal to be held in trust by the Secretary of War and the interest to be

38. Indian Office, Secretary of War Letter Book B, Nov. 10, 1804, 26-28.
39. Hawkins Papers, Clark to Milledge, Sept. 28, 1804.

paid semi-annually.[40] A tract of land on the east side of the
Ocmulgee four miles long and two miles wide was reserved
by the Creeks, and Hopoie Micco insisted that the following
be written into the treaty:

> You are the agent for the President: you have been long in
> our land doing good for us; you are an old chief among us;
> we appoint you our agent, to see justice done us in our af-
> fairs, as well as the white people. The tract of land at the
> Oakmulgee old field is ours; we have reserved it for a
> place to meet and trade with our white friends; and we
> want you to see justice done to our merchants and traders,
> and ourselves, as well at that place, as in the nation, and
> to take the direction of every thing then, for the benefit
> of both parties, in such a way as you may think best, and
> I wish to put this into the treaty this day concluded, that
> the President may see it.[41]

Hawkins wrote Governor Milledge that he had been desirous of getting more lands, so much in fact, "That Georgia
might be satisfied for ten years at least and my department
freed from the irritation arising from the continued pressure
for land." He, however, was fortunate to get as much as
he did because of Indian ill will produced by outrages on the
frontier. He had made another demand for the return of all
Georgia property but had been requested not to press the
matter until the treaty had been signed and ratified, after
which the chiefs promised to restore all stolen goods.[42]

Georgia was, of course, still not completely satisfied with
what Hawkins had accomplished. Nevertheless, it was the
culmination of nearly three years of negotiations. A letter
from a Georgia congressman to a friend in Augusta in December probably expressed the attitude of most Georgians.
He said the price agreed to was too high, dissatisfaction was
great, and ratification was doubtful. "We will however hope

---

40. *American State Papers, Indian Affairs*, I, 691.
41. *Ibid.*
42. Hawkins Papers.

for the best, and nothing on our part shall be omitted to restore ratification."[43]

In presenting this treaty to the Senate, President Jefferson called attention to the fact that Hawkins had exceeded the payment authorized in his instructions.

> The commissioner has been induced to go beyond this limit, probably by the just attention due to the strong interest which the State of Georgia feels in making this particular acquisition, and by a despair of procuring it on more reasonable terms, from a tribe which is one of the most fixed in the policy of holding their lands.[44]

The treaty was rejected in the Senate because both the amount to be paid the Creeks and the manner of payment were objected to. When Hawkins was informed of these facts he was instructed by Dearborn to persuade the chiefs to accompany him to Washington in the summer, if possible, and to arrive not later than October 10, 1805, at all events.[45] In June the agent was ordered to drive intruders from Creek lands by military force, if necessary, until after the treaty in the fall. In this letter the Secretary of War expressed his hopes for the conference. "If the Oakmulgee, can once be established as the Boundary, I trust, I shall not live long enough, to hear any contention for any other boundary line between Georgia and the Creek Nation."[46]

In July one thousand dollars were placed to Hawkins's credit with Halsted, the factor, to be used for the journey. Accompanied by Timothy Barnard, as interpreter, he led six chiefs to Washington. On October 4, the deputation passed through Sparta, Georgia;[47] and, when three days later they reached Augusta, their arrival was the occasion of an editorial in the *Augusta Herald* praising Hawkins for his efforts among the Creeks. Of the Indians, the two best known of the dele-

---

43. *Georgia Republican and State Intelligencer*, Jan. 14, 1805.
44. *American State Papers, Indian Affairs*, I, 690-691.
45. Indian Office, Secretary of War Letter Book B, 41-42.
46. *Ibid.*, 88.
47. *Augusta Chronicle*, October 12, 1805.

gation were the half-breeds Alexander Cornells and William McIntosh.[48]

On November 14, 1805, Henry Dearborn, Secretary of War, signed a treaty with the six chiefs. Its terms were almost identical with those of the treaty which Hawkins had negotiated but which the Senate had refused to ratify. The principal difference was that under the treaty of 1804 payment was to have been made in stock held in trust and bearing semi-annual interest, while in Dearborn's treaty annuities were to be paid for eighteen years.[49] Hawkins signed as witness only but wrote to Governor Milledge: " . . . knowing as I do, the anxiety of my fellow citizens in Georgia on this subject I have taken upon me to make this communication to you."[50]

During the summer of 1806 Hawkins was again engaged in running boundary lines between Georgia and the Creeks. On August 30, he announced their completion to Governor Milledge and his purpose to forward maps of the survey as soon as they had been drafted.[51]

No further treaties or boundary lines engaged Hawkins's attention for several years. His duties between 1806 and 1810 were principally routine. On the whole the Indians were quiet and Georgia was comparatively acquiescent in regard to its boundaries. Thefts, illegal trading, and mutual trespasses created minor disturbances while Georgia continued to clamor for the return of stolen properties.

In 1810 David B. Mitchell was Governor of Georgia.[52] On October 8, 1810, he wrote Hawkins that he had appointed General Daniel Stewart to proceed to the Creek Agency and demand the return of Georgia property. General Stewart carried with him specifications of all the property of which

---

48. *Ibid.*, October 10, 1805.
49. *American State Papers, Indian Affairs*, I, 698-699.
50. Hawkins Papers, November 17, 1805. On reaching Raleigh on January 25, 1806, on his return to the Agency, Hawkins was in company with Aaron Burr.
51. *Farmers Gazette*, (Sparta), September 20, 1806; *Augusta Chronicle*, September 13; *Georgia Republican*, September 19.
52. Upon Hawkins's death in 1816 Mitchell was to succeed him as Agent.

he expected an accounting with the value of each item. Mitchell informed Hawkins that he was addressing his application directly to the agent "under the fullest confidence that a settlement of the just claims of the citizens of Georgia will meet immediate attention."[53]

When General Stewart arrived at the Agency with his demands Hawkins informed him that he would present them to the chiefs of the nation and then to the Secretary of War. He called the Georgian's attention to the fact that since 1797 he had tried repeatedly to get the governors of Georgia to make their settlements with the Creeks but that only in 1804 and 1810 had agents even been appointed. Hawkins maintained that many of the claims of Georgia, some going back to 1775, were neither just, accurate, nor valid under the terms of the treaties.[54] Stewart reported to Mitchell: "I am sorry that the result of my mission has not met with more speedy success; however, I flatter myself, that claims of the citizens of this state are now in a right train for complete justice though perhaps tedious."[55]

Georgia did not get all of her claims. Possibly the state fell a little short of obtaining justice because Hawkins was also interested in seeing that justice for the Creeks was considered. Where the claims of Georgia could be clearly justified he continued to demand a restoration of property on the part of the Indians. In July, 1811, he arranged for a delegation of Creeks to go to Milledgeville to discuss their difficulties with Governor Mitchell in person. As a result better relations were established which lasted until the outbreak of the War of 1812. Mitchell, however, continued to resent what he felt was overzealousness on the part of Hawkins in the interest of the Indians.

He ended a letter to Hawkins in August, 1813: "Leaving you therefore to enjoy your own opinion and to indulge the resentment to the people and want of confidence in the gov-

53. Hawkins Papers.
54. Ibid., Hawkins to Stewart, October 13, 1810.
55. Ibid., October 18, 1810.

ernment of Georgia which your insinuations evidently discover you to possess."[56] To which Hawkins replied:

> I hope you will order your Secretary to blot it out, from your letter book, and I will do the same from the letter. It is not true, and has no connexion with the subject between us. I have no resentment against the people of Georgia, and should feel degraded if I had. They have done me no injury. As to that part of them who may be called fault finders and monitors of falsehood to traduce public characters, even they have not my resentment. When I am the subject of their calumny, they have my pitty [sic] and sometimes my contempt. I know these are inconveniences all public people are liable to and I submit without repining.[57]

---

56. Hawkins Papers.
57. *Ibid.*, Hawkins to Mitchell, Sept. 18, 1813.

CHAPTER XI

Diplomacy and Commerce

AFTER the Revolution the notorious adventurer Wil-liam Augustus Bowles, Maryland native who had joined the British Army to fight against the Colonists and who later supported himself as actor, musician, portrait painter, and soldier of fortune, appeared among the Creeks and became a serious rival of Alexander McGillivray for headship among these Indians. In 1792 he was captured by McGillivray and turned over to Spanish authorities by whom he was sent to Spain and thence to Manila. He had either been freed by the Spanish, or had escaped, and made his way to England. There he was received cordially by British officials and was returned to Florida on board His Majesty's schooner *Fox*.[1] In September, 1799, the *Fox* had run aground in a storm off the mouth of the Apalachicola River. Here Bowles was visited by Andrew Ellicott after his surveying party had been driven away from the Flint by the attack of the Creeks. In October Ellicott addressed a long letter to Colonel Haw-kins informing him that Bowles was back in America and was planning to stir up the Indians to hostility against Spain.[2]

Styling himself "Chief and Director General of the Creeks," Bowles insisted that the Indians were an independent nation and subject neither to the United States nor Spain. Soon he stirred up disaffection among them and caused Hawkins additional difficulties. In December Hawkins wrote Governor Jackson of Georgia:

> Mr. Bowles he [*sic*] is near the mouth of this river from whence he continued to pour forth his threats against the affairs of the U. S. in this department. . . . I find it an ar-

---

1. *Ellicott's Journal*, 226-227.
2. *Ibid.*, 228-232.

duous undertaking with a few assistants to make the impressions I wish on the minds of my red charges who are scattered over a wild country of at least three hundred miles square and to fit them to be good neighbors, I am assisted by Bowles and other mischief makers, who are by every opportunity poisoning the minds of the Indians with their abominable lies and misrepresentations.[3]

One of the arguments of Bowles in attempting to gain control of the Creeks was that Spain and the United States had conspired to take away all of their lands. Had he not returned, he said, this would have been accomplished, but his letters to King George and President Adams would stop the running of the line. He also promised the Indians presents and "talks" from the King, and informed them that "I am now the master of all the talks of the red people."[4]

While Hawkins realized that the return of Bowles was unfortunate and would be unpleasant, he did not feel that the adventurer would succeed in his intrigue to the point where his efforts would be dangerous. He constantly played down the seriousness of Bowles' threats and thus let himself in for considerable criticism by irate Georgians.

In October, 1799, Bowles had issued a proclamation to the Indians in which he directed them to drive out of their territories all persons who held commissions under the United States. According to one newspaper correspondent:

This proclamation exceeds in insolence, impudence and bombast, anything that hath heretofore been exhibited by this well known adventurer. . . . We will soon see which of these men have the most influence among the Indians, as Hawkins must quit the ground, or drive Bowles. . . .[5]

This writer called upon the United States to take positive action and not to consider this conspiracy, as Hawkins did, "a feeble shew of opposition from a few Simonolias."

3. Hawkins Papers.
4. *Ibid.*, Emautlau Haujo to Hawkins, Dec. 16, 1799.
5. *Columbian Museum & Savannah Advertiser*, Jan. 21, 1800.

In November Bowles wrote to Chief Little Prince:

> Mr. Hawkins is the man who if he is not gone must go immediately as he is a dangerous man and will cause some mischief to you by staying, I shall seize him if I find him, for not obeying the proclamation, and proceed against him according to law.[6]

The lines were thus drawn and the contest for Creek control was on between Colonel Hawkins and General Bowles. Though Hawkins was the agent of the United States, and the Indians knew it, this fact gave him no advantage. The Indians could not understand the intricacies of international agreements, and Bowles professed to have, and probably had, the support of the British Crown. Furthermore, he could promise greater remuneration for adherence to him than could Hawkins as agent of the United States. Bowles at first confined his operations to Spanish Florida and secured most of his Indian support from the Seminoles. By April of 1800 he had collected an army of between two and three hundred Indians and was beseiging St. Marks.[7] On May 20, the fort was captured, Bowles claimed, without the loss of a single man.[8] In June, Bowles sent his forces across Florida and was threatening St. Augustine. At this time "a planter" from St. Marys wrote a letter criticizing the United States and Spain for their lethargy since the day of Bowles's landing, Spain making only a feeble attempt and the United States none at all to put him down.

> Our government, perhaps, are in some degree excusable, as they have had several powerful anodyne draughts administered to them from time to time by their superintendent of Indian affairs; who ever since Bowles' arrival has been amusing us with the peaceable good disposition of the Indians. . . . Stubborn facts now prove; that the superintendent has been egregiously mistaken, or suffered himself to be imposed on, or if not, he must have intentionally misrepresented matters.[9]

6. *Ibid.*
7. Hawkins Papers, Hawkins to James Jackson, May 14, 1800.
8. *Augusta Chronicle*, July 5, 1800.
9. *Ibid.*, July 12, 1800.

This writer asked why Hawkins, if he had any influence over the Indians, had allowed so many to join Bowles. He then answered his own question.

> But this is a well known fact, that such is the nature of the restless savages, that even without invitation they would sooner travel one thousand miles on foot to do mischief, than by earnest solicitation they would go five miles to do a good act, or even be induced to sit so long in peace.

The purpose of this letter, the writer asserted, was to spread news of frontier disturbances among the citizens. In conclusion he asked why the troops of cavalry at Fort Wilkinson had not taken the field. In answer to this question he suggested that the commander was probably also under the influence of Hawkins.

In July Governor Jackson issued a proclamation warning all citizens against accepting commissions from Bowles.

> . . . the said Wm. A. Bowles can be considered in no other light, than a common plunderer and vagabond, and a common disturber of the peace of nations, he having had the insolence, even to threaten the life of the superintendent of the United States in the Creek nation, substantiated by documents now in my hands.[10]

In June, 1801, Secretary of War Dearborn wrote Hawkins in regard to Bowles:

> I earnestly recommend to you to be strictly on your guard against the improper views of that adventurer; to counteract them as effectually as possible by all suitable means; to watch all his movements attentively, and to persevere in endeavoring to fortify the minds of the Indians against his artful schemes.
>
> Should Bowles at any time come within the limits of the United States, every exertion must be made to apprehend him taking care only not to compromise the peace of the United States.[11]

---

10. *Ibid.*, July 19, 1800.
11. Secretary of War Letter Book A, 51-52.

Bowles continued his operations but confined them mostly to Florida among the Seminoles, with only an infrequent foray across the line. Nevertheless, he made some headway with the Creeks. Particularly did he gain sympathizers in the Upper Creek towns. As a result the Indians became restless, sullen, and difficult to manage. Bowles managed to defeat a proposed treaty in 1803 and even persuaded the Upper Creeks to deny in writing the authority of Colonel Hawkins.[12] When the council was in session at Tookaubatchee, however, delegations of the Cherokees, Chickasaws, and Choctaws joined the Creeks. On May 24, 1803, Bowles arrived at the head of a band of Seminoles and was accompanied by Upper Creek chiefs who were friendly to him. Hawkins's influence won out and on May 25 Bowles was arrested, placed in chains, and delivered to Governor Folch of Florida.[13] He was confined in Morro Castle and died there in April, 1806.[14]

There had been some signs of resistance to Bowles's arrest but Hawkins and the Lower Creek chiefs had prevailed; the discontent subsided, and the council drew up a declaration that they were resolved "on eternal peace with all the world, that when they were dead and gone their children might grow up in peace, repeat and remember this talk and take it to the end of the world."[15]

As an explanation of the confidence which he had felt since the return of Bowles, Hawkins wrote to James Madison in July, 1803.

It was inconceivable to me that Bowles who understood a good deal of the Indian language, had been here formerly and routed General McGillivray, should not have been able to make the necessary distinction between the past and the present. He must have seen a material change in the manners of the Indians . . . and yet he goes on reacting his former part of the Director General, until he was apprehended

---

12. *Augusta Chronicle*, July 25, 1803.
13. Hawkins Papers, Hawkins to Milledge, May 30, 1803.
14. *Augusta Chronicle*, June 7, 1806.
15. Hawkins Papers, Hawkins to Milledge, June 8, 1803.

in the midst of his guards, and adherents and at the eve in imagination of being a king of the four nations, and quits the stage in irons.[16]

Hawkins thus demonstrated his influence upon his charges in the face of formidable opposition by a powerful adversary.

After the return in 1783 by England of Florida to Spain, William Panton, an English trader, secured the good will of Vicente Manuel de Cespedes, Spanish Governor of St. Augustine, who had interceded for him at the Spanish court. The requests of Cespedes were reinforced by similar recommendations from West Florida and Louisiana. It was argued that Panton knew the Indians and could control them, that isolated Spanish posts would be endangered if control was relaxed, and that Americans from Watauga and Cumberland settlements were coming into Indian country and were securing trade. Cespedes, and other colonial officials therefore requested that certain British merchants be allowed to remain in the Floridas "since they alone could undersell the Americans, avert Indian hostility from the exposed garrisons and exposed planters, and assure the retention of the border colonies." By royal orders of 1786, the English firms of Panton, Leslie & Company, and Mathew and Strother were authorized to continue trade with the Indians.[17]

Panton, Leslie & Company made a fortune out of the Indian trade. Beginning in 1784 with stores at St. Augustine and St. Marks for the Upper Creeks, they established another at Pensacola for Lower Creek trade, supplanted Mathew & Strother at Mobile in their trade with the Choctaws and Chickasaws in 1789, opened trade with the Cherokees in 1792, and reached the heights of expansion when a store was opened on the Mississippi River at Chickasaw Bluffs.[18]

16. Madison Papers, XXV, 93. Library of Congress.
17. Arthur Preston Whitaker, translator and editor, *Documents Relating to the Commercial Policy of Spain in the Floridas*, xxx-xxxii; see also pp 98-103, "Actas de la Suprema Junta de Estrado, 22 de Septiembre 1788"; Carolina Mays Brevard, *A History of Florida from the Treaty of 1763 to our own Times*, I, 4-5.
18. Whitaker, *Documents*, xxxiv-xxxv.

William Panton, head of the firm, seems to have been a man of integrity and ability. He had no obligations to the United States, and was not averse to political manipulations. He, no doubt for personal business reasons, encouraged the Indians in allegiance to Spain. Envious rivals charged that he "placated a critical governor with a present of 'English furniture in the latest mode.' "[19]

Alexander McGillivray was an intimate associate of Panton and is in fact generally considered to have been a silent partner of the firm. Certainly Panton used him to advance Indian trade north of the thirty-first parallel. There is no evidence that Panton actually stirred up hostilities between the Creeks and the United States, but he certainly was opposed to any alliance which would take trade away from his firm. Though the Treaty of New York was used by his enemies in Florida to convince Spanish authorities that Panton was planning to move into United States territory, it is definitely known that he opposed McGillivray's going to New York. It is also likely that his influence had caused the failure of the proposed treaty at Rock Landing in 1789.[20]

Panton, Leslie & Company were a legitimate trading firm. Their smuggling of goods across the border and other manipulations were probably of the type that any firm operating on such a frontier would have engaged in. William Panton can not be compared to William Bowles, whom he hated and described as a "mad dog, a pirate, whom any decent person should shoot down on sight." He offered one person a pension for life to kill the "freebooter."[21] The firm, nevertheless, fixed its prices to undersell competitors from Georgia and South Carolina, sent agents throughout the Indian country, and carried official Spanish communiques among the Indians.[22] These conditions obtained when Hawkins arrived in the Indian country, but he shortly thereafter inaugurated the factory system.

---

19. *Ibid.*, xxxv.
20. *Ibid.*, 236.
21. *Ibid.*, xxxv.
22. Hamilton, *Colonial Mobile*, 336.

The origin of the trading system between the United States and the Indian dates back to July 12, 1775, when a committee of Congress was appointed to "devise a plan for procuring goods and carrying on the Indian trade."[23] The next year trading posts were established, but licensed traders were allowed to continue private trade and the system was not successful. Nothing further was done until the administration of Washington.[24]

Impelled by the horrors of the Creek War then raging along the Southern frontier, Washington devoted a portion of his fourth message to Congress to the possibility of Indian control through better trade relations.

> Next to a rigorous execution of justice on the violators of peace, the establishment of a commerce with the Indian nations, in behalf of the United States, is most likely to conciliate their attachment. But it ought to be conducted without fraud, without extortion, with constant and plentiful supplies; with a ready market for the commodities of the Indians, and a stated price for what they give in payment and receive in exchange. Individuals will not pursue such traffic, unless they be allured by the hope of profit; but it will be enough for the United States to be reimbursed only. Should this recommendation accord with the opinion of Congress, they will recollect that it cannot be accomplished by any means yet in the hands of the executive.[25]

In his fifth message Washington again brought the matter to the attention of Congress, and a year later he added: " . . . I cannot refrain from again pressing upon your deliberations the plan which I recommended at the last session, for the improvement of harmony with all the Indians within our limits, by the fixing and conducting trade houses upon the principles then expressed."[26]

---

23. Edgar B. Wesley, "The Government Factory System among the Indians, 1795-1822," *Mississippi Valley Historical Review*, VI (Sept. 1919), 489.
24. *Ibid.*
25. *American State Papers, Foreign Relations*, I, 22. Washington to Congress, Dec. 3, 1792.
26. *Ibid.*, 25, Nov. 19, 1794.

As a result of these messages, the growing anxiety for more effective control of the Indians, and the increasing influence of Panton, Leslie & Company, the subject was taken up for debate in Congress on February 28, 1795. The three objects urged in favor of the trade system were protection of the frontiers, protection of the Indians through trade restraints on the frontiersmen, and the elimination of foreign influence. The bill was defeated because of the growing fear of presidential power.[27]

On March 3, an experimental bill was substituted and passed. It called for an appropriation of $50,000 and the establishment of Indian trading houses, or factories, at Coleraine and Tellico.[28] On the basis of this law the first factory among the Creeks was established in 1793 at Coleraine with Edward Price as factor. Price was on hand during the negotiations leading to the Treaty of Coleraine and formed a friendship with Benjamin Hawkins which led to cordial relations when Hawkins, as Principal Temporary Agent, was given supervision over Price's factory.

On May 18, 1796, an act was passed which assured the factory system sufficient support for two years. For purposes of destroying foreign influence among the Indians, as well as for economic and military advantages, $150,000 was appropriated in addition to the $50,000 of the year before, most of which had not been expended, plus $8,000 annually for maintenance. By subsequent acts the system was extended beyond the incumbency of Hawkins as agent.[29]

Both of the original factories, at Coleraine and at Tellico, were within the Agency to which Hawkins was appointed. It thus fell to his lot to inaugurate the system and supervise it during its early years. Coleraine, due to its location so far from the Indian towns, was not a good trade center. The Creek factory was consequently moved from there to Fort

27. Wesley, "The Government Factory System," *loc cit.*, 490-491.
28. *Ibid.*, 490-491. The purpose of this bill was to try out the factory system on a small scale before adopting a general policy.
29. *Ibid.*, 491-493.

Wilkinson in 1797, and, to keep pace with the westward movement of Georgia's frontier, it was moved to the Ocmulgee Old Fields in 1806, to Fort Hawkins in 1808, and finally to Fort Mitchell on the Chattahoochee in 1817.[30]

Though the factory system provided for a superintendent of Indian trade, contractors and depositories in the port cities, and factors in immediate charge of each trading post, Hawkins, as agent was directly over the factors in his Agency and it was from him they sought advice and direction, and, when necessary, protection. The factor, on the other hand, acted as the clearing house for the funds of the Agency. It was to the factor that annuities and salaries were transmitted to be held subject to the order of the agent. Seldom was it necessary for the funds to be used, as annuities were often paid by Hawkins in orders on the factory for goods which the Indians desired. The factory also kept ledgers of the official and private accounts of the agent, and often payments to Hawkins were offset by his indebtedness to the factor. Thus, the factories, in addition to their original purpose of regulation of the Indians by means of trade, also served as commissaries for the Indian department.

Hawkins sometimes issued detailed instructions to the factors. When a new factor took up his duties at Fort Wilkinson in 1799, it was the occasion for a five-page letter of instructions. The duties of the factor were discussed under seven headings. Under the first heading, "Credit to Indians & Indian Traders," the factor was informed that credit was injurious to both white and red men, and made the Indian reckless. "If he wants a whore he cloaths her in fine calico with rich silver ware . . . If an Indian wants anything and cannot obtain it he will pick up his gun and hunt a month for the means." Hawkins saw no objection to "Selling to traders without credit," as most of the traders were married to Indians and had Indian families and if the factor refused to trade with

---

30. *Ibid.*, 494; see also, George D. Harmon, "Benjamin Hawkins and the Federal Factory System," *North Carolina Historical Review*, IX, 138-152 passim.

them personally they would get the goods anyway by sending their Indian kinsmen for them. Other instructions were entitled "Selling for Money or Peltry only to Indians," "Trading with others at the Garrison or the neighbourhood," "Kind treatment of the Indians," "Supplying the Indian with rum," and "The Manner of Trading in the Nation." Hawkins informed the factor that the evil of selling rum could not be overcome immediately, but that he had prevailed upon the Indians to get drunk, if they would, only at home and in the public square, and not on visits.

> If we had the entire direction of Indian affairs the evil would be checked effectually, but we have not and if they are refused Rum they will go directly to a Spanish post and get a supply. The small quantity which they drink at the factory must always when furnished be accompanied with an injunction to drink it at their camps.[31]

One of the first difficulties that Hawkins encountered in his relationship to the factory system was a dispute between Edward Price and the officers and soldiers of the garrison at Fort Wilkinson, but the cause of the dispute is not clear. In April, 1798, the officers of the fort determined to remove Price from the factory. Hawkins, at the time, was at Tallahassee but he was informed of the difficulties by both Price and Colonel Gaither and expressed regret that disorder of such an alarming nature had taken place. He demanded of the commandant protection for the factor, and in response to Gaither's request for advice wrote:

> Mr. Price has been selected by the proper authority for the trust reposed in him; he has given security for the faithful discharge of that trust, and he is in the execution of it, and it is unquestionably as respectable as that of any gentleman who has only the fatigue of doing once in 4 or 5 days the honour of officer of the day.[32]

---

31. Indian Office files, Hawkins to Wright, August 2, 1799. National Archives.
32. Hawkins, *Letters*, 305-306.

On the same day Colonel Hawkins wrote to Mathew Hopkins, assistant to Price, and expressed the opinion that the removal of the factor by the military was an insult to the President of the United States.[33] Price was restored to his position by Colonel Gaither but bad blood continued and on June 4 he wrote Hawkins:

> I was sorely mauled and wounded by the guard a few days ago I wont trouble you with particulars but you may judge as is generally the case there was fault on both sides the officers seem very envious towards me and I believe are determined to make my situation untenable I attempt to keep my temper under the guidance of reason but sometimes my philosophy is overcome.[34]

On December 7, Hawkins wrote to the factor:

> It is high time the bickerings and misunderstandings in your neighborhood had subsided, and given place to that interchange of good offices which is necessary to render the society of Fort W. sociable and agreeable. I think in our progress through life, it is indispensable to our own happiness that we should by every effort in our power remove everything discordant and may tend to make us uneasy, or instrumental in making others so.[35]

Two months later Edward Price died. He was succeeded by Jonathan Halsted. Conditions at Fort Wilkinson were so bad, however, that in reporting the treaty signed there in 1802, Wilkinson, Pickens, and Hawkins suggested the removal of the garrison as appearing "indispensable to the restoration of temperance, regularity, and order, and to dissolve the sinister intrigues and connexion of a licentious soldiery, and neighbourhood, formed principally of army followers."[36]

While James Seagrove, Hawkins's predecessor, was in office he had been accustomed to give the Indians goods from

33. *Ibid.*, 306.
34. Indian Office, Factory Letter Book, 145. National Archives.
35. Indian Office files, National Archives.
36. *American State Papers, Indian Affairs*, I, 670.

the public stores as an easy means of controlling them. Hawkins felt that this policy was injurious to the Indians, as it encouraged mendicancy and was costly to the government. In October, 1797, he wrote to Price: "I shall endeavour to put an end to that system of beging [sic] which has taken such deep root among them . . . . "[37] The Secretary of War had sanctioned Seagrove's extension of credit, but Hawkins determined to permit it only until the parties already in debt could extricate themselves.[38]

Notoriously improvident, the Creeks, having spent their stipends, came to Hawkins asking for credit. When they realized that they could no longer secure supplies without effort or cost, they resented Hawkins's appointment and wished for the return of Seagrove. Hawkins wrote frequently to the factors and recommended or discountenanced trade with individual Indians.

> On the subject of credit [he wrote Price] I have one uniform answer, that you have the regulation of the trade intrusted to you, that credit may be the ruin of it and of course must be discouraged, that if you would credit him at all, you would be the judge of the amount, and they must receive your answer and be satisfied.[39]

On another occasion he wrote Price that insofar as most of the Indians were concerned he looked upon credit as so much lost.[40] Nevertheless, Hawkins sometimes departed from this general rule and recommended credit to individual Indians under certain conditions, as, for instance, when he vouched for the fact that a chief had 200 deer skins at home for which he wished credit until the skins could be delivered in the spring.[41]

Hawkins frowned upon the extension of credit to the Indians because when he reached the Indian country he found

37. Indian Office files, National Archives.
38. Hawkins, *Letters*, 307.
39. Indian Office files. Hawkins to Price, Oct. 20, 1797.
40. *Ibid.*, Hawkins to Price, Oct. 5, 1798.
41. Hawkins, *Letters*, 253.

many of them deeply in debt to independent traders, and most of the traders, as well as many chiefs, far behind in their accounts to Panton, Leslie & Company.

When the factory system was inaugurated there was a licensed resident trader in nearly every Indian town. These men were allowed to continue their trade. Occasionally Hawkins suggested that certain types of trade be carried on with a trader rather than at the factory. Licenses were secured and renewed at the factory but, because of certain abuses of the system, Hawkins instructed Price not to issue any licenses unless he had a certificate signed by Hawkins and the head men of the town in which the trader wished to locate.[42] A typical certificate issued to Hardy Reed stated that since there were no complaints as to his character, and since he was not charged with buying or trading in horses, he was to be permitted to engage in Indian trade.[43]

Even trade across the Florida border was allowed by the government. Hawkins wrote William Panton in February, 1797:

> In the course of my tour through the Creeks, I find that you have a very extensive commercial intercourse with them, and that probably your present or future prospects may be materially affected by the political state of affairs in Europe. I do not know that I can in any way contribute anything that may be of service to you, within my Agency, but if you know wherein I can, and will do me the favour to call on me, I possess the decision, and will prove to you my readiness to assist you.[44]

Again, he wrote Panton: "The plan of the U. S. . . . is intended as an instrument of peace without being a monopoly, and it will be my endeavour to make this instrument mutually beneficial to those trading under the authority of His Catholic Majesty and the United States of America."[45] The

---

42. Indian Office files. Hawkins to Price, Oct. 23, 1797.
43. *Ibid.* Hawkins to Price, no date.
44. Hawkins, *Letters*, 69.
45. *Ibid.*, 310.

sincerity of this statement is borne out by the following pass, issued by Hawkins in December, 1797:

> Henry Snell, of Pensacola, in the service of Mr. William Panton, is hereby permited [sic] to pass through the Creek country on his way to Savannah and return, and I require all the agents in the Creek Department to aid and assist him, and I recommend him to the friendly attention of my fellow citizens.[46]

In January, 1797, Hawkins wrote to Secretary of War James McHenry that "Mr. William Panton has engrossed the greatest part of the trade of this nation . . . he supplies not only the white traders, but he has set up a number of Indian factors. They are both behind-hand with him, and the Indians are indebted to them to a considerable amount . . . ."[47]

Since the purpose of the factory system was to increase the government's influence by supplying the Indians with cheap goods, there was some effort in 1802 to prevent the factories from trading with the white traders. In October, Halsted informed Hawkins from Fort Wilkinson that he had received orders from the Secretary of War to cease such trade and asked Hawkins's opinion as to the propriety of refusing the traders goods without notice.[48] This prohibition was either never enforced or obtained for only a short time, for Halsted, when the factory had been moved to the Ocmulgee Old Fields, asked for various staple supplies to be added to an order "for white trade for cash."[49]

Eventually, among the many efforts to reduce Spanish trade, duties were placed upon goods coming from Florida. The Creeks complained that such duties were in violation of a secret treaty signed along with the Treaty of New York in 1790. When Hawkins notified the War Office of this complaint, he was informed that the treaty did not cover the Creek complaints. He was further instructed that trade with

---

46. *Ibid.*, 271.
47. *Ibid.*, 57.
48. Indian Office, Factory Letter Book.
49. *Ibid.*, Halsted to Abraham Abrahams, no date, no page number.

the Spanish was not to be prohibited entirely but was to be discouraged. Duties might be reduced but were not to be removed since free trade would open too general a commerce with the Spaniards.[50]

After Panton's death in 1804, John Forbes, one of the partners, continued business as John Forbes and Company. The new firm attempted to conciliate Hawkins.[51] In October, 1812, John Innerarity, a partner in the company, left Pensacola for a collection trip among the Creeks. He announced that the traders in the Upper Creek towns alone owed the company $21,916.[52] Hawkins did not offer Innerarity any aid in collection but instructed him to "settle entirely his own business." He did not oppose collection, however, and, when the Creeks agreed to pay the amount asked in "hard silver dollars," his assistants, Barnard, Cornells, and Limbaugh signed as witnesses. Hawkins was absent because of illness.[53]

The factory ledgers show the extent of the transactions of Hawkins in both his public and private character. The credits and debits often involved large sums, and settlements were infrequent. On March 31, 1807, the Old Fields ledger showed Agency expenditures of $1,491.00 and a balance on Hawkins's private account of $304.13-1/4.[54] On January 2, 1809, Halsted at Fort Hawkins acknowledged receipt of $691.30 on his private account. Generally, all funds for the Agency and salaries of the agent were sent to the Creek factor, there to remain subject to order, and relatively little of these funds was paid to Hawkins in cash.

Perhaps one of the most important sources of business of the factories was the payment of annuities. Seldom was a treaty signed with the Creeks that did not call for annuities for the nation as a whole and for certain chiefs. Hawkins

---

50. Indian Office, Secretary of War Letter Book B, 209.
51. Whitaker, *Documents*, xxxviii note.
52. John Innerarity, "The Creek Nation, Debtor to Panton Leslie & Co., A Journal of John Innerarity," *Florida Historical Quarterly*, IX, 75.
53. *Ibid.*, 87-89.
54. Indian Office, Factory Ledger.

requisitioned these annuities and provided for their distribution, often a difficult task. After requisition, the funds were paid to the factor subject to Hawkins's order. Upon the arrival of the annuities the Creeks would proceed to the Agency where Hawkins gave them orders on the factor for as much goods as the funds due each would purchase.

The requisition for the annuities in 1812, on the basis of the treaties of New York, Fort Wilkinson, and the Washington Convention of 1805, amounted to $18,800 to be paid in part to the Upper Creeks in two tons of assorted iron and a quarter of a ton of steel for axes. The Lower Creeks wished three-quarters of a ton of assorted iron, one-quarter of a ton of iron hoops, one-quarter of a ton of steel for axes, and one-quarter of a ton of eight and tenpenny nails. The remainder of the annuity was to be paid to Halsted in cash, most of which, no doubt, would have been traded out had not the outbreak of hostilities stopped payment by the government.[55]

Among the items which the Indians wished and with which the factories were stocked were cloth, thread, looking glasses, ivory combs, wool hats, saddles, rifles, padlocks, small brass bells, brass kettles, iron spoons, scissors, Barlow penknives, and fish hooks.[56]

One purpose of the factory system was to afford the Indians a market for their goods. Trade was carried on in furs and agricultural products as well as in the money of the annuities. Hawkins wrote to Price in May, 1798, instructing him to trade Tussekiah Micco rum for ninety-seven pounds of deerskins as he was "indebt 8 kegs of rum, which he was desirous of paying."[57]

The methods of factory trading are indicated by a letter from Halsted at Fort Wilkinson in 1808 to General John Mason, superintendent of Indian trade. "The price of 25 cents to the Indians for deer skins would be as you have stated

55. Indian Office, Indian Annuities Book, 1812-1818, 11.
56. Factory Letter Books, 1795-1812, Halsted to Abraham Abrahams, no date, no page.
57. Indian Office Files.

'greatly too high for the present state of things . . . ' But as they have from long habit been accustomed to 25 cents I have thought it best to raise the price of goods to such a degree as the reduction of that for skins might have been necessary." Thus the factor made his profit, the Indian got his accustomed price, and both were satisfied.[58]

The possibilities and expectations of the factory system were expressed to Congress by President Jefferson in 1803: "The measure adopted, of establishing trading houses among them, or of furnishing them necessities in exchange for their commodities, at such prices as to leave no gain, but cover us from loss, has the most conciliatory and useful effect on them, and is that which will secure their peace and good will."[59] Again, in 1804, he expressed similar sentiments and asked for increased appropriations for the "more effectual, economical, and humane instrument for procuring peace and good neighborhood with the Indians."[60]

With the purchase of Louisiana a post road to New Orleans through the Creek country became necessary, and Colonel Hawkins was called upon by the administration for an important part in carrying out this project. In November, 1803, Dearborn asked him to suggest the location of the road which the President wished built.[61] Again, in February, 1804, the Secretary of War asked Hawkins to inform the Indians of the willingness of the government to give them presents and to make discreet inquiries as to the possibility of running the road. The Indians were to be told that the road would be paid for and that they would also benefit by being able to set up road houses.[62]

Efforts to locate the road were delayed, but in August, 1805, Hawkins was instructed to run the road without reference to expense. Little having been done by December, he was told to increase his force and run the line without de-

58. Factory Letter Book.
59. *American State Papers, Foreign Relations*, I, 62.
60. *Ibid.*, 64.
61. Secretary of War Letter Book A, 395.
62. *Ibid.*, 435; Carter, *Territorial Papers*, V, 306-307.

lay.[63] The work of constructing the road was slow in getting underway, however, and in April, 1806, Hawkins was instructed by Postmaster General Gideon Granger to lay out a horse path from Athens, Georgia, to Fort Stoddert at a cost not to exceed $6,400. The road was to be from four to six feet wide; marshy ground was to be causewayed, and "trees to be fallen across the water courses so as to enable the mail carrier to pass the waters upon them carrying the mail secure from the water and swimming his horse by his side." In the event Hawkins could not superintend the work in person he was to select "some citizen of distinguished vigilance, perseverance and integrity" to do it. Hawkins was also placed in charge of the mails as far as Fort Stoddert and was authorized to appoint postmasters.[64]

In July, 1806, Hawkins wrote Granger that illness had prevented his running the road. In August Postmaster General Granger reported to President Jefferson:

> . . . When I reflect on the occasional ill health of Colo-Hawkins, on his age, on the multiplicity and arduous nature of his other public duties, and on the great length of time we have been unsuccessfully endeavoring to establish a regular line of intelligence . . . I cannot help entertaining a fear that necessary preparations of the road will not be made. . . .[65]

Hawkins's appointee as postrider was also a disappointment to the Federal authorities as his estimate of twenty-three miles a day was far below the one hundred and twenty miles of other contractors. Jefferson, accordingly, wrote Granger: "Col. Hawkins's illness, & the feeble idea of Bloomfield . . . are sufficient grounds for our looking to other resources, & will be sufficient apology to Col. Hawkins for resorting to them."[66]

Colonel Hawkins, having completely fallen down on this

63. Carter, *op. cit.*, V, 472-476, Gideon Granger P. M. Gen. to Jefferson.
64. *Ibid.*, 459-461.
65. *Ibid.*, 472-476.
66. *Ibid.*, 476. August 9, 1806. Bloomfield was the postrider Hawkins had appointed.

official assignment, was relieved of the duty of running the road and of appointing mail carriers. His successor, however, was informed that "In order to have the stations established ... it will be necessary to act by and with the advice of Col. Hawkins, on whose judgment and fidelity great confidence is placed."[67] This letter indicates that, in spite of the seeming procrastination of Hawkins, his illness and his many duties must have been accepted as valid explanation of his failure, and he lost little in prestige and in the confidence of the administration.

Four to six feet of horse path with trees felled across the streams for bridges might have been satisfactory for post riders, but in 1811, with war clouds in the offing, military roads were needed. The citizens of Tennessee wished to open a road to Fort Stoddert so as to utilize the Tombigbee and Mobile rivers for trade outlets, but the Creeks opposed the idea. Hawkins was authorized to treat with the Upper Creeks, but was unsuccessful. Some critics felt that he failed because he approved the Indians' attitude.[68] The administration considered the Indian attitude unreasonable and in June, 1811, Hawkins was ordered to make another attempt to gain their consent and to take whatever measures he thought best to carry out the President's wishes.[69]

In July the Secretary of War wrote Hawkins again and informed him that President Madison had decided upon wagon roads from the Tennessee River to Fort Stoddert and from the Agency on the Flint to the same place. The rights of the Indians were to be respected, insofar as this was possible, and their friendship retained, but they were to be told that the roads were necessary and would be built.[70] Hawkins appeased the Creeks in such a way as to be able to inform Governor Mitchell of Georgia: "They promise to do everything which depends on them to render travelling on the road safe, and

67. *Ibid.*, V, 518-519. PMG to Meriwether, Feb. 25, 1807.
68. Isaac J. Cox, *The West Florida Controversy, 1798-1813*, 443-444.
69. Secretary of War Letter Book C, 85-86.
70. *Ibid.*, 90-91.

that people travelling on them shall be received and treated friendly as they pass and protected in their persons and property."[71]

In September a special meeting of the Creek council assembled at Tookaubatchee for the purpose of discussing the roads. Deputations from the Choctaws, Cherokees, and Shawnees were present.[72] After three days of debate permission was refused, whereupon, "Col. Hawkins, at length, told them he did not come there to ask their permission to open a road, but merely to inform them it was now cutting."[73]

Opposition among the Upper Creeks continued until it finally merged into open hostility during the War of 1812. However, Big Warrior, powerful Upper Creek chief and one of the malcontents, became the staunchest of the friendly Indians during the war.[74]

The roads were built. The one from Athens, Georgia, to Fort Stoddert was completed in November, 1811.[75] Hawkins wrote Governor Mitchell in December: "I find some difficulties in restraining our wild young men from taking toll unnecessarily and very unjustly from our travellers."

After calling the chiefs of the lower towns together Hawkins finally secured the promise of protection to all travellers. The road became popular as it became safe, and was frequently used. Hawkins reported that between October, 1811, and March, 1812, two hundred thirty-three vehicles of all kinds and 3,726 persons had passed the Agency enroute to the West.[76]

By the time the road was opened the war clouds were darker, and soon troops and artillery took the place of traders and covered wagons. The voice of commerce was drowned out by the war whoop, and dripping scalps replaced calicos and ginghams in the marts of Indian trade.

---

71. Misc. Papers, Series I, Vol. II. North Carolina Historical Commission.
72. *Republican & Savannah Evening Ledger*, Nov. 5, 1811.
73. *Ibid.*, Oct. 17, 1811.
74. Hamilton, *Colonial Mobile*, 368.
75. Hawkins Papers.
76. *Georgia Journal*, March 25, 1812.

CHAPTER XII

Prophets and Propaganda
Among the Creeks

AS the outbreak of war approached in 1811, Tecumseh, Shawnee chief and leader of the Indians of the Northwest, was persuaded by British agents to seek the alliance of the Southern tribes. He, accordingly, set out for Tookaubatchee and the meeting of the Creek council in October, 1811. The rumor that Tecumseh would be present caused an unusual attendance, and about 5,000 Indians were on hand. The day after the council convened Tecumseh with twenty-four warriors marched into the council square. He knew the esteem in which the Creeks held Colonel Hawkins and was too shrewd to attempt to influence them while the agent was near. "Each morning a Shawnee warrior announced his chief would speak at noon, and each noon the speech was put off till the next day .... "[1] Hawkins finally became impatient and left the town. Tecumseh immediately began to inflame the Indians with mysticism and impassioned speeches, but Colonel Hawkins, informed of Tecumseh's actions, attached little importance to them and declared that "Tecumseh was a sham." Hawkins was confident of his ability to control the Indians. He felt that only a few fanatics wanted war. Even after a visit to Pensacola by the Shawnee and Creeks, Hawkins maintained there was no real danger.[2]

The causes of discontent among the Creeks were numerous. The hatred engendered by the war with Georgia, the schemes of Zachariah Cox, and the wagon road "filled from one end

1. H. S. Halbert and T. H. Ball, *The Creek War of 1813-1814*, 69.
2. J. F. H. Claiborne, *Mississippi as a Province Territory and State*, I, 315-318.

to another" were enough to persuade some of them to listen attentively to Tecumseh. When he had delivered his war talk, he prepared calendars, consisting of bundles of small sticks painted red. The sticks corresponded to the number of days before the attack on the settlements was to be launched. Each morning the chiefs to whom the bundles were given were to throw away a stick. When all were gone the attack was to take place.[3]

Big Warrior, a friend of the whites and a powerful chief, aroused Tecumseh's suspicions. Tecumseh told the council that when he returned home he would stamp his foot on the ground and destroy all the houses in Tookaubatchee, the home of Big Warrior.[4] When a few weeks later a series of earthquakes actually shook the Indian country and damaged the buildings of Tookaubatchee, the Indians were convinced that Tecumseh had reached home and had carried out his threat. His prestige was heightened; prophets and witches, claiming similar miraculous powers, sprang up in every village; murder and other acts of violence were committed in their names; and restraint was impossible.[5]

Tecumseh's mission did not end with the Creeks. He made contacts with the Seminoles, Cherokees, and other Southern Indians, and at the head of six hundred picked warriors from Northwestern and Southern tribes he defied the power of the United States in the Southwest. Big Warrior and certain Lower Creek chiefs, notably William McIntosh, stood out against him but failed to counteract his influence.[6]

Colonel Hawkins was faced with a handicap similar to that he had overcome in his contest with William Bowles. He was agent of the United States and was attempting to carry out a permanent policy of Indian control. He had spent long

---

3. Edward Eggleston and Lillie Seelye Eggleston, *Tecumseh and the Shawnee Prophet*, 208-209. According to this work, the origin of the term "redsticks," applied to hostile Indians during the war, dates from this incident.
4. Meek, *Romantic Passages*. 242-243.
5. *Ibid.*, 242-243.
6. Eggleston, *op. cit.*, 208-210.

years in trying to wean the Indians from their expectation of constant and frequent gifts and favors. He was attempting to wipe out mendicancy and to develop self-reliance among his red friends. He, therefore, could not meet the offers of the British and Spanish agents when, by a system of bribery, they courted Indian support. The affection for and confidence in Hawkins held by the old chiefs, who realized from experience the insincerity and temporary nature of British and Spanish offers, kept them loyal, but the young warriors listened to the siren song of the prophets.

Georgians were naturally apprehensive. In March of 1812, Big Warrior and other chiefs, accompanied by Hawkins, called on Governor Mitchell at the capitol in Milledgeville and gave him assurances of their friendship; they also disclaimed for the chiefs any authorized participation in the hostile views of the Indians under the influence of Tecumseh and his brother, the Prophet.[7]

This attempt to relieve the anxieties of the whites was a basis of the charges of insincerity which were brought against Hawkins when hostilities actually began. Such charges, while untrue, were not completely groundless. No unbiased examination of the records could fail to reveal a sincerity of purpose and a deep desire on his part to protect both his Indians and his fellow citizens of the United States. He was, however, overconfident of his powers and guilty of wishful thinking in regard to the loyalty of the Indians. The whites were sometimes lulled into a false feeling of security with well-nigh calamitous results.

In the meantime, the hostilities had begun in Florida with many Seminoles and some Creeks involved. Hawkins was primarily interested at the time in keeping the road to New Orleans open and in demanding punishment for individual crimes. Little thought did he give, even then, to the possibility of open war. Travellers continued to pass through the Indian country, and in spite of the murder of a man named

---

7. *Georgia Journal*, April 1, 1812.

Meredith, twenty-two vehicles and ninety persons passed the Agency on April 6, 1812.[8]

On May 18, Hawkins wrote to Governor William Hawkins of North Carolina that he had just returned from a council of the Creeks, that he had persuaded the Indians once more "to lift their sticks and punish thieves; two have been cropped and whipped within four days; and forty warriors left my house this morning to apprehend a banditti of seven who have been doing mischief in my neighborhood." He stated that the chiefs were unanimously for peace, that some young warriors were for mischief, but could do nothing hostile with impunity. The remainder of the letter was devoted to an account of the progress the Indians were making and showed no apprehension of conflict.[9]

Despite Hawkins's confidence there were many indications of unrest. Murders were on the increase, and the apprehension of the murderers was uncertain. On May 23 Arthur Lott, prominent planter and former member of the Georgia legislature, was murdered within eight miles of Alexander Cornell's home, and demands for the punishment of his assailants became insistent.

When the council assembled at Tookaubatchee in June, ill health prevented Hawkins from attending. He was represented by his interpreter and assistant, Christian Limbaugh, and through him Hawkins delivered a talk addressed to all the nation. Probably no other talk Hawkins ever delivered to the Creeks was couched in such harsh language. He demanded immediate and drastic punishment for all crimes.

> Murder you cannot hide. The God of Heaven says it must be punished. I say it must be punished; and the safety and happiness of the nation requires it should be punished - I call on you to turn out yr. warriors, without delay, and punish the murderers. If you do not I shall call on the warriors of another colour to come among us, I am an enemy of thieves and murderers and a friend to honest people

8. Hawkins Papers, Hawkins to Mitchell, April 6, 1812.
9. *Raleigh Register & North Carolina Gazette*, May 29, 1812.

of every colour. If we give satisfaction we act like honest
men and shall have nothing to pay . . . If you refuse satisfaction, you are from that moment enemies—I shall be sorry to
see it . . . and lament that we have sacrificed our poor help-
less women and children for our murderers.[10]

The chiefs answered the agent's demands:

We have unanimously agreed that satisfaction shall be given
without delay for the murders committed in our land. We
have appointed three parties, one party started last evening.
The other two this morning in persuit [sic] of the murderers of Thomas Meredith and Arthur Lott. . . . The parties
have received their special orders not to stop until they have
punished these murderers.[11]

Hawkins sent copies of the Indian response to Governor
Mitchell with the request that they be published to allay the
fears of Georgians, and as evidence of the good will of the
Creeks.[12] Some of the murderers were apprehended and slain.

More alarming than the murders of individuals within the
Creek country was the massacre on the Duck River in Tennessee of several families by the Creek chief Little Warrior,
who was returning from a visit to Tecumseh. Big Warrior,
the friendly chief, took the matter in his own hands. He wrote
Hawkins that Willaubee Haujo, one of the leaders of the
Duck River massacre, had been executed and his body thrown
into the Coosa River. Two other members of Little Warrior's
party had been killed on the Black Warrior River.[13] Little
Warrior and his nephew escaped.

Not content with attempts to allay the suspicions of the
whites by means of the punishment of Creek mischief makers,
the chiefs made an additional gesture of friendship by sending, upon Hawkins's advice, a deputation to the Seminoles.
Led by Feared (Tuskeegee Tustunnugee) the party set out

---

10. Hawkins Papers, Hawkins to Chiefs, June 1812.
11. *Ibid.*, Chiefs of Creeks to Hawkins, June 17, 1812.
12. Hawkins Papers, Hawkins to Mitchell, June 22, 1812.
13. *Ibid.*, Hawkins to Mitchell, August 31, 1812.

in August, 1812, "the bearers of a strong talk of peace and neutrality."[14]

The Creek chiefs hastened the peace mission when they learned that the Seminoles had sent two scalps to the chiefs of the Upper Creek towns and had invited the Creeks to join them in an attack upon the "Virginians." As an added inducement the Seminoles informed the Creeks that there were "four British vessels at St. Augustine with a little of everything to help the poor red people."[15] Big Warrior and Old Tallassee King informed Hawkins that they had received the scalps and, upon his insistence, immediately sent runners to Aulotchewau, the Seminole town where the murders had been committed, to inform the Indians that unless the murderers were immediately punished their town would be cut off by the Creeks. Hawkins hoped that the condemnation of the Seminole hostility by the Creeks would have the effect of quieting the Florida Indians, but he was disappointed.[16]

Until the late summer of 1812, the people of Georgia demanded punishment for the perpetrators of every Indian outrage as they always had. They were lulled by Hawkins's assurances, their own wishful thinking, and a belief that the Indians would not dare oppose the United States, and there is little evidence of serious alarm. In late August, however, the newspapers disclosed evidence of jumpy nerves and began to demand action on the part of both the state and national governments. To Augusta came

". . . indications of hostility in the Creek Indians towards the citizens of this state. . . . We shall be glad if . . . their mischievous designs are confined to a few of their 'lawless young men' - but we are apprehensive, that it will become necessary to make the whole Creek nation feel the vengeance of this state, or of the United States, in order to compel them to a proper course of conduct."[17]

14. Hawkins Papers, Hawkins to Mitchell, Aug. 24, 1812.
15. *Ibid.*
16. *Ibid.*
17. *Augusta Herald*, August 27, 1812; *The Star* (Raleigh) Sept. 4, 1812.

From Augusta also came the following item:

The intelligence from our Indian frontier is truly alarming. The Creek Confederacy has long been manifesting a deadly antipathy towards the United States. . . . Although our agent has been soothing us into a belief of their peaceful & friendly intentions; their conduct on every occasion is marked with implacable enmity. Let us at once secure the peace and tranquility of our own frontier by driving them across the Mississippi; for so long as Florida is in the possession of Spain and Spain at the mercy of England, we shall never be able to secure their friendship.[18]

The same article caused additional anxiety by publishing the false rumors that Hawkins and his family were fleeing from the Agency and that Spain was offering bounties for the scalps of Georgians and friendly Creeks. On September 4, the *Augusta Chronicle* informed its readers that the Indians were supplying themselves with powder by purchase, and failing that, by force and theft.

Such newspaper agitation forced Governor Mitchell to take official notice of conditions and led him to doubt the trustworthiness of Hawkins's assurances that the murderers had been punished. He, accordingly, demanded of the agent his proof of execution. Hawkins replied that three formal reports of the council indicated eight Indians had been executed for murders in Georgia and three others for the Duck River massacre. He had demanded punishment for the Florida crimes also, but could not enforce his demands, "As the Simenolies receive no part of the annual stipend, our hold on them is by a slender thread . . . ."[19]

On September 13, Hawkins received the first news from the peace deputation to the Seminoles. He wrote Governor Mitchell as follows:

There has arisen a prophet among the Simenolies and all of them have taken his talks, this part of the deputations was not able to say any thing, and agreed to the talk too,

18. *Raleigh Register*, Sept. 11, 1812.
19. Hawkins Papers, Hawkins to Mitchell, Sept. 7, 1812.

as they were told if they did not agree to it, they would never reach home and as life was sweet they agreed to the talks. They did not see Mr. Paine the headman and Chief of the Simenolies; he did not come to this meeting, they said he was at war with the Americans somewhere near St. Augustine.[20]

When the Creeks met the Seminoles at Miccosookee they were informed that the Alligator and Aulotchewau peoples were already fighting the whites. The Seminoles of Miccosookee, however, accepted the Creek demands for peace and Feared and his deputation departed. At St. Marks they met some Spanish officials. To the demand of the Creeks for non-interference with the Indians on the part of Spain the Spanish officials replied by charging that the Americans, and particularly the Georgians, were trying to take the Creek lands and that Hawkins was cheating them of their money. The British, the Creeks were told, would soon give them many presents.[21] Neither the influence of Hawkins nor the Creek chiefs was sufficient to restrain the Seminoles, but most of the lower Creeks remained friendly to the United States.

With the Seminoles, under chiefs Paine and Billy Bowlegs, on the warpath in northern Florida, Governor Mitchell on September 23 ordered out ten companies of Georgia militia to rendezvous on the St. Marys.[22] Tennessee was also alarmed and the legislature adopted the following resolution:

Whereas murders the most horrid and inhuman, have been committed on the people inhabiting the frontier of this state, by a nation (if they can be so denominated) called Creeks: atonements for which murders the governor of this state has in the most correct and decided manner, and in strict conformity with the existing laws, demanded; and which has been [ignored?] as is believed by this General Assembly in consequence of the false representations, or Indian statements, of Ben. Hawkins, agent of the United States in the Creek nation.

---

20. *Ibid.*, Hawkins to Mitchell, September 13, 1812.
21. *Ibid.*, Feared to Hawkins, September 18, 1812.
22. *Augusta Chronicle*, October 2, 1812.

The resolution demanded that immediate steps be taken to crush the Creeks, and ended:

> Resolved also, That the senators and representatives from this state to the Congress of the United States be instructed and requested to use their best endeavors with the proper authority to have Benj. Hawkins removed from the Creek agency.[23]

The editor of the *Register* printed the resolution and added apologetically: "We have before seen some insinuations against the conduct of Col. Hawkins; but we hoped, as we yet hope, they are unfounded. The subject being now, however, brought before a Legislative Body, it becomes necessary to notice it."

Criticism of Hawkins always struck a responsive chord in certain quarters. He seemed never wanting, however, for friends to rise to his defense. "A Georgian" wrote to the *Savannah Museum*:

> I observe with some concern, the extraordinary Resolution offered by General Cocke to the House of Representatives in the State of Tennessee. If that exterminating gentleman's qualifications for the field bear any comparison with his qualifications in the cabinet I cannot compliment the state in her choice of a general.
>
> When an attack is made upon the character of a public officer of Col. Hawkins's high standing and correct conduct by the legislature of a state; strict regard ought to be paid truth. Without waiting for the issue of the governor's application to Col. Hawkins for satisfaction, for the murders and thefts committed on the frontiers of Tennessee by the Creek Indians, and within a few days of the time when eight Indian culprits were actually executed for these murders . . . a note of unqualified censure passed the house of representatives, upon the bare suspicion of Gen. Cocke . . . The President of the U. States, will, no doubt, treat these resolutions with the contempt which they justly merit.[24]

During the fall and winter of 1812-1813, Colonel Hawkins's health was very poor. He had never been free of the

23. *Raleigh Register*, Oct. 23, 1812.
24. *Ibid.*, Dec. 4, 1812.

gout or rheumatism which had plagued him for fifteen years. It had spread from his feet to his arms and hands. In September, 1812, he had an attack of influenza, and his health declined steadily from that time on.[25] Often confined to his bed and under the necessity of sending assistants to represent him at important councils, Hawkins was indeed laboring under a great handicap at the time when his influence was most needed. To add to the troubles which Creek fickleness brought about, white trespassing was constantly an additional irritant. If he was lulled into a feeling of false security, it does not necessarily follow that he was guilty of incompetence or neglect of duty. There is evidence to justify the opinion that the leaders among the Creeks were also confident of the peaceful intentions of the great majority of their warriors.

Tustunnugee Thlucco, speaker, reported at length to Hawkins the findings of the council which met in October. An unqualified and unanimous profession of friendship was made; the actions of the Seminoles of Aulotchewau and Alligator Hole were repudiated, and the whites were asked not to blame the Creeks for the crimes of the Florida Indians. The council further assured Hawkins that the promise of peace made to Governor Mitchell would be kept but that they could not assure him that some of the Florida and Alabama Indians would not take the war path.[26]

Alexander Cornells, Timothy Barnard, and Christian Limbaugh, the three assistant agents, reported to Hawkins that they had never seen a greater collection of chiefs, more evidence of friendship, or greater alarm over the situation. The chiefs were earnest in their desire "to do justice to the white people. They regretted very much that you could not attend the Council by sickness, as they never stood more in need of your advise and assistance than at present—We believe the speech is no deception."[27] When this report reached Hawkins

25. Hawkins Papers, Hawkins to Mitchell, Sept. 20, 1812; Oct. 12, 1812; Feb. 13, 1813.
26. *Ibid.*, Chiefs to Hawkins from Tookaubatchee, Oct. 29, 1812.
27. *Ibid.*, Assistant Agents to Hawkins, Oct. 29, 1812.

he was sorely stricken with a fever and could scarcely sit up in bed. He nevertheless reported the action of the council to Governor Mitchell.[28]

General John Floyd, at the head of a small force of regulars and mounted militia, was stationed near the borders of Florida. On November 3 he marched against the Florida Indians and a detachment of his command under Colonel Newman defeated the Seminoles near Aulotchewau. Paine was killed and Billy Bowlegs, his second in command, was wounded. This broke the morale of the Seminoles.[29] It was reported that some Upper Creeks were among the Seminoles and that three of them had returned home wounded. Hawkins denied this report, but on November 28 the General Assembly of Georgia passed resolutions demanding that the wounded Indians be delivered to the state.[30] Governor Mitchell disapproved the resolution and the matter was dropped.[31]

On November 13 the *Augusta Chronicle* had published an editorial designed to stir Georgia to action.

> When the tomahawk and the scalping knife are drawn in the cabins of our peaceful and unsuspecting citizens it is time, high time to prepare at least for defense. . . . The frequent and aggravated murders that are daily committing on the frontiers of Georgia and Tennessee . . . call loudly for vengeance.

A correspondent from Washington, Georgia, appealed to the patriotism of Georgians in December, 1812, when Tennessee volunteers were reported in Georgia, to defend and protect their state. He heaped shame on Georgians for relying upon the generosity of a sister state for defense against the Georgia Indians.[32]

The *Georgia Journal* of Milledgeville likewise doubted the

28. *Ibid.*, Hawkins to Mitchell, November 2, 1812.
29. *Georgia Journal*, December 2, 1812.
30. *Ibid.*
31. *Ibid.*, December 9.
32. *Raleigh Register*, January 8, 1813.

necessity of Tennessee troops, since no general hostility had as yet made itself manifest among the Creeks.[33]

The editor of the *Augusta Chronicle* exultantly boasted that "We are all tranquility on the frontiers of Georgia . . . ."[34] This feeling of security was, however, shortly to be rudely shattered.

33. *The Star* (Raleigh), January 15, 1813.
34. December 4, 1813.

Chapter XIII

The Red Sticks on the War Path

I N April, 1813, Colonel Hawkins informed Governor Mitchell that a contraband trade had developed between Pensacola and Georgia and that the British and the Indians of the Great Lakes region had sent runners among the Creeks promising arms and ammunition for use against the United States.[1] By this time there was a definite division among the Creeks—even the friendly Creeks admitted this—and civil war was imminent. Alexander Cornells learned of a plot on the part of the Alabama prophets, who were followers of Tecumseh, and informed both Hawkins and Mitchell of it. "But neither Colonel Hawkins nor Governor Mitchell could be certain that the trouble among the Upper Creeks was anything more serious than a contest for power between rival groups of chiefs."[2]

The outbreak did not come and late in May the *Augusta Chronicle* reported: "Our Indian frontier is at present tranquil . . . The nation generally are disposed to peace, and will inflict exemplary punishment on any of their people who shall attempt to interrupt it." Three days later Hawkins wrote Mitchell: "From the present disposition of the Creeks there is nothing hostile to be apprehended from them."[3]

Before the end of June, however, Hawkins was forced to report to the governor that the conflict among the Creeks had commenced and Alexander Cornells reported a crisis rapidly approaching. Captain Isaacs, who had aided William McIntosh in punishing the Duck River murderers, had been

---

1. Hawkins Papers, Hawkins to Mitchell, April 16, 1813.
2. Phillips, *Georgia and State Rights*, 50.
3. Hawkins Papers, Hawkins to Mitchell, May 31, 1813.

attacked by Upper Creek hostiles. He, his nephew, and three of his party were reported to have been killed. Though this report was untrue, hostilities had actually begun. Hawkins explained that the strength of the opposition came from the families of those Indians who had been executed at his insistence: "they have commenced their attacks on the chiefs and warriors who executed the orders of the executive council."[4] Hawkins's illness kept him at home on the Flint during most of this critical period. He was, therefore, forced to rely for information and contacts upon his half-breed assistants, Cornells and Limbaugh who lived among the Indians.

On June 16, the speaker, Tustunnugee Thlucco, met Alexander Cornells. Hearing that Peter McQueen, half-breed chief, and old Hoboheilthle Micco had given ear to the seductive voices of the prophets, they questioned McQueen and the Micco, who denied any hostile designs. A message was then dispatched to the prophets informing them that in twelve days they would be called upon by a number of the chiefs to make good on their claims to miraculous powers. Unfortunately, the messenger chosen had aided in punishing the Duck River murderers. When he arrived among the Alabama Indians he was killed and scalped. The followers of the prophets then went to the home of Captain Isaacs. Isaacs escaped, but his home was burned and two of his warriors murdered. The Alabama Indians threatened to destroy Tookaubatchee and Coweta, the council towns, and to kill Tustunnugee Thlucco, Cornells, Hawkins, and every chief who remained loyal to the agent. After they had wreaked their vengeance within the Indian country, they boasted they would be ready for the white people whom they had the power to destroy by an earthquake which would swallow them up in soft and miry ground.

The speaker appealed to the towns and sent forces to protect Tookaubatchee. The hostiles then denied that they had sent threatening messages or that they had killed any friendly

---

4. *Ibid.*, Hawkins to Mitchell, June 21, 1813.

Indians. They could not deny that some were dead, but they explained that the Indians walked without leave into circles drawn on the ground and reserved for the prophets, whereupon they had been seized with madness and had died.[5]

The hostiles were mostly Alabamans who belonged to the Creek confederation but were not Creeks. Cornells, in a report to Hawkins, expressed great surprise at the skill with which the prophets had kept their plans from the old chiefs. He was of opinion that they were under the direction of the British and Tecumseh, and that Tecumseh had worked out the plan of action in a private conference with Little Warrior.[6]

The next day Cornells reported additional information that had just reached him. Tuskeenehau of Cusseta, tired of the pusillanimous conduct of the speaker, had organized 190 warriors for the protection of Tookaubatchee and wished Hawkins to send white troops to their aid so that they might "put an end to these hatchers of war and mischief."[7]

Hawkins believed the uprising resulted from orders from Tecumseh who, fearing the Indians would disband, had ordered the attack upon the executioners of the murderers, but who insisted that travellers be not disturbed for fear the whites would be prematurely alarmed.[8]

All information received by Hawkins was transmitted to Governor Mitchell, even when the agent had a "gouty hand" and wrote with much pain. Mitchell, therefore, knew of the friendly chiefs' requests for the aid of Georgia militia and was probably ready and willing to send it. He was, however, forced to await positive authorization to send Georgia troops into Federal territory. This authorization Colonel Hawkins would not give. It is not clear whether he was inclined because of his illness, which made personal contacts impossible, to discount the seriousness of the reports and the apprehen-

---

5. *Ibid.*, Cornells to Hawkins, June 22, 1813.
6. *Ibid.*
7. *Ibid.*, June 23, 1813.
8. *American State Papers, Indian Affairs*, I, 847. Hawkins to Armstrong, June 28, 1813.

sions of the friendly chiefs, or whether he still felt that his influence was sufficient to stop the hostilities. His critics blamed his procrastination on jealousy of Governor Mitchell and his unwillingness to share the credit for subduing the hostiles. It is certain that Hawkins confined his activities in this crisis to demanding of the fanatical chiefs explanations of their hostilities. He answered the friendly chiefs' requests for aid by advising them to attack the prophets.[9]

Hawkins thought that the Indians might spend their strength in fighting one another and thus would not attack the whites. He expressed this idea to the Secretary of War on June 27, and explained his inaction on this ground.

> You see pretty plainly the source and object of this fanaticism. If it could confine itself to contest among the chiefs for power, and not interfere with the friendly relations between the Creek nation and the United States, it might be policy in us to look on, and let it be settled among themselves; but, as there seems to be another object coupled with it, and that of hostility to us eventually, we must be ready to apply a military corrective in due time.[10]

The same ideas—the desirability of peace but the possibility of eventual war—were expressed to General Pinckney:

> We know the importance of peace with these people, particularly in the present state of our affairs, and that war should be avoided, if possible; therefore, if I can prevail on them to accommodate among themselves, I will do so, and if I cannot, I recommend that a detachment of mounted infantry be sent to cooperate with the warriors of Tookaubatchee against the Alabama party.[11]

When Mitchell first received notice of the Indians' requests for aid he wrote Hawkins that he feared the friendly Creeks would be hard pressed before they could be relieved by Federal troops, and added: "Georgia can, and is willing, to afford the necessary aid, but I could have wished your

9. *Ibid.*, 848.
10. *Ibid.*, 847. Hawkins to Armstrong, June 27, 1813.
11. *Ibid.*, 848. Hawkins to Pinckney, July 9, 1813.

opinion on that point." He informed the Indians that an application to him from Colonel Hawkins "would remove every difficulty which stood in the way to a full accomplishment of their wish."[12] In comments on the Mitchell correspondence, the editors of the *Augusta Chronicle* severely criticised Hawkins for not authorizing Governor Mitchell to use the Georgia troops. The criticism, however, had no influence on Hawkins.

Early in July the friendly Creeks (under Big Warrior) at Tookaubatchee were beseiged for eight days, but beat off the attacks when they were reinforced by two hundred warriors sent by Cusseta King. Thirteen casualties were inflicted upon the attackers. When the news reached Tookaubatchee of the approach of the hostiles, the friendly chiefs sent runners with urgent messages to Colonel Hawkins for aid, offering in return for it a cession of the Alabama River lands.[13]

The only extant evidence that Hawkins had planned to aid the Indians prior to this request is the record that he had received from Governor Mitchell fifty muskets and one hundred fifty pounds of powder.[14] He had also drawn twelve muskets for use at the Agency, which he deemed sufficient unless hostilities showed a great increase in intensity in which event it would be necessary to make the Agency a military post.[15] He continued to feel that the Creeks were unduly alarmed and wrote Governor Mitchell on July 7:

> A great number of Indians seemed to be astonished exceedingly alarmed and timid at the sudden explosion of this fanaticism. Its magic powers deters them from obeying the calls of their chiefs and its denunciations has [sic] rendered the chiefs themselves opposed to it, timid, distrustful and incapable of estimating and resisting its efforts as they should

12. *Augusta Chronicle*, July 30, 1813. Mitchell to Hawkins, June 20.
13. Hawkins Papers, Talesee, a runner from Tookaubatchee to Hawkins, July 5, 1813; James Durouzeaux to Hawkins, July 7; Cusseta Micco to Hawkins, July 10.
14. *Ibid.*, Receipt signed "Farish Carter," on back of letter of Durouzeaux to Hawkins, July 7, 1813.
15. *American State Papers, Indian Affairs*, I, 848. Hawkins to Pinckney, July 9, 1813.

do. Their reports relative to it cannot be wise in all their details. I have procured eleven rifles 30 lb powder some lead and tents in this neighborhood which is ready to their order.[16]

After the siege of Tookaubatchee had been raised, Peter McQueen, half-breed leader of the Red Sticks, started with some Upper Creeks to Pensacola for supplies and munitions. En route his band stopped at the home of Joseph Cornells, the brother of Alexander, took his wife prisoner and burned his house. A company of volunteers under James Caller and a band of friendly Creeks under Dixon Baily and David Tait intercepted McQueen's party as it returned from Pensacola with its horse loads of war supplies. On July 27 at Burnt Corn, McQueen's forces were decisively defeated but the greed of the attackers for booty caused them to fail to protect their victory and a counterattack resulted in a severe defeat. This victory of the Indians over whites increased their confidence, and depredations became more common.[17]

On July 22 Hawkins had been informed by the War Office that the governors of Georgia and Tennessee had been ordered to organize 1500 men each to move separately or in cooperation into the Creek country.[18] On August 6 the *Augusta Chronicle* announced that news from Milledgeville indicated that Governor Mitchell had 3,000 men ready to march. Fifteen hundred volunteers from Tennessee would cooperate with the Georgia troops and the 3rd regiment of United States regulars. Hawkins had requested only three hundred men. "If the hostile Indians are 2,500 strong," asked the editor of the *Augusta Chronicle*, "of what avail will 300 men be as an auxiliary corps. This request is exactly in character with the whole conduct of Col. Hawkins: it shows a deadly jealousy of the people of Georgia."[19]

On July 28, the friendly chiefs, impatient at Colonel Haw-

---

16. Hawkins Papers.
17. Hamilton, *Colonial Mobile*, 369; Meek, *Romantic Passages*, 244-246.
18. Indian Office, Secretary of War Letter Book C, 161.
19. *Augusta Chronicle*, Aug. 6, 1813.

kins's delay, made a direct request of Governor Mitchell for 2,500 men, two field pieces, and plenty of ammunition.[20] When Hawkins heard of this direct approach, he wrote Governor Mitchell and insisted again that the reports had been exaggerated. He admitted that McQueen was on the warpath and that casualties had been suffered by the friendly Creeks, but he maintained that the situation was not out of hand.

> I find you have been in correspondence with the Chiefs, and that they are waiting anxiously for the aid you promised them, as they say you have done. I have no right to question the purity of your motives or the soundness of your political principles but believing as I do that the general Government has exclusively the right to manage all affairs with the Indians, I am of opinion that the communication to them should be through this Agency of Indian affairs.[21]

Even stronger was the language and the protest of the agent when he reported to the Secretary of War.

> This department has long been assailed by calumny and misrepresentation; but it has been left to the Governor of Georgia to usurp all authority of the General Government, except what relates to commerce. . . . As he is a man of legal knowledge, he must be operated on by a policy of his own.[22]

Hawkins, from his home on the Flint, attempted to assume command of the Creeks. On August 14 he ordered them into the field in strong parties on the assumption that when "the madness of the prophets begins to cool, their friends have found out they are liars and will run off from them and put them to death."[23]

Governor Mitchell had at last assumed that the emergency had arisen which would authorize his calling out the militia

---

20. *Georgia Journal*, July 29, 1813.
21. Hawkins Papers, Hawkins to Mitchell, August 9, 1813.
22. *American State Papers, Indian Affairs*, I, 851, Hawkins to Armstrong, August 23, 1813.
23. Hawkins Papers.

for the protection of the state, regardless of Hawkins's attitude. He had, therefore, assembled 2,500 men, 500 of them
cavalry, at various points on the frontier.[24] Although Hawkins continued to argue with the governor the exclusive right
of the United States to regulate Indian affairs, he did not
protest further Georgia's threat to invade Indian country under the stress of circumstances.

What was probably the most horrible event of the war
took place on August 30, 1813, when Peter McQueen massa-
cred the inhabitants of Fort Mims on the Tensaw River.
" . . . Hardly two dozen escaped of the five hundred and fifty
men, women and children in that stockaded acre of ground."[25]

General James Wilkinson, in command of the United States
troops, had been transferred from the Southwest and General
Fluornoy was left in command at Mobile.

> He was likewise early misled by the representations of
> Colonel Hawkins of the 'advanced civilization' and 'pacific
> disposition' of the Creeks. Even after the massacre of Fort
> Mims, Colonel Hawkins reiterated these assurances, laid
> the blame for the affair on the Tombigbee people, and de-
> clared that the war would be a 'civil war among the Creeks
> and not on the whites,' if let alone. Unfortunately General
> Flournoy adopted these views, and forbid any aggressive
> movement on the savages.[26]

By September, Hawkins was willing to cooperate with the
Georgia troops. After General John Floyd took command
of the militia, Hawkins kept in frequent communication with
him and gave him all the information at his command as to the
activities and hostile movements of the Indians. On September
30 he wrote General Floyd:

> The boasted power of the prophets to take American forts
> with bows and arrows, to know the secrets of their enemies,
> and determination to put to death every red man who does
> not join them has given to many such terrour [sic] which

24. *Augusta Chronicle*, August 27, 1813.
25. Hamilton, *Colonial Mobile*, 370.
26. Claiborne, *Mississippi*, I, 319 note.

nothing but the presence of our army will remove. They say they want now to see us with our waggons well loaded, that they may enrich themselves with plunder. The master of breath has permitted a conquering spirit to arise among them like a storm and it shall ravage like a storm. - Their number is 2,500 without the new converts. A grand movement is in operation among them. I request you to communicate this to the Governor and everything else I may send you interesting to him to know.[27]

By October Hawkins had become so impressed with the strength of the Red Sticks that he feared the fighting would come to Georgia instead of staying west of the Chattahoochee as he at first hoped.[28] Following the attack on Tookaubatchee the friendly Creeks had retired to Coweta, where they established their headquarters, and had fortified the town as their main defense. On October 5 Hawkins informed General Floyd that "we ought to be without delay at Cowetau, the patience of our friendly Indians has experienced a severe trial."[29] Three days later he wrote: "If we were at Cowetau we would check their hostile movements but as we are your frontier is much exposed."[30]

Now that Hawkins was willing to push the offensive, he found it was difficult to get it underway. Tennessee troops were entering Creek country from that state under Generals Jackson and Cocke and were offering to cooperate with General Floyd who was powerless to move beyond the Flint. On November 8 Floyd's Georgia command was no farther west than Fort Lawrence (on the Flint opposite the Agency). On that day he wrote to Governor Peter Early, who had succeeded Mitchell, that the lack of supplies and funds from the quartermaster department had delayed him. "The contractor has been a dead weight to the army and is truly the cause of the tardiness of the movements."[31]

27. Hawkins Papers.
28. *Ibid.*, Hawkins to Floyd, October 4.
29. *Ibid.*, Hawkins to Floyd, October 5.
30. *Ibid.*, Hawkins to Floyd, October 8.
31. *Augusta Chronicle*, November 19, 1813.

In spite of the delay of its troops, Georgia was anxious to fight. The honor and safety of the state were at stake and probably more important than that, many of its citizens saw in the war an opportunity of ridding themselves of Creek occupancy of choice lands without the necessity of negotiating treaties of purchase. One citizen of Milledgeville expressed this attitude clearly. He anticipated that if the expedition ended as it should, it would open up the Alabama River lands which offered advantages second to none. Health, he said, fertile soil, and abundant commerce awaited the conquest. New markets would be opened for sugar and shipments could be made to within 140 miles of Milledgeville. This would be greatly to the advantage of both Georgia and the Carolinas, as sugar was then selling in New Orleans at $8.00 to $10.00 per hundred, and in Savannah at from $20.00 to $25.00. If the Creeks were defeated he anticipated that sugar could be shipped to Fort Stoddert for $1.00 per hundred, and all the way to Milledgeville for $4.00.[32] Such pleasing prospect was not conducive to pacifism.

Hawkins had anticipated this attitude on the part of some Georgians and wished to keep Georgia troops out of the Indian lands until he was sure there was no other method of stopping the war. He could not condone such ambitions, as they were directed at driving out friendly Creeks along with the hostiles.

When General Floyd finally moved out toward Coweta Hawkins ordered John Ward, public interpreter, and Alexander Cornells to consider themselves under Floyd's command. Christian Limbaugh was sent ahead of the column to prepare the way for its arrival. Hawkins also gave detailed information to Floyd as to the terrain over which he was to march and advice as to how best to secure the Indians' confidence. He also promised his own services in a military capacity.

---

32. *Raleigh Register*, October 22, 1813.

As soon as I know that the friendly Indians are to cooperate with your command, or who is the commander in chief of the expedition I will be ready to take charge of them. And if you should deem my cooperation with you necessary immediately and without delay I shall be with you.[33]

Late in November, Major General Thomas Pinckney arrived at Fort Hawkins to take command of the army operating against the Creeks. Hawkins naturally was willing to cooperate with an officer of the United States army and from his knowledge of the Indians he was able to give valuable aid. On December 2 General Pinckney wrote General Jackson that he was using Hawkins for sending communications by means of the friendly Indians, and that Hawkins had worked out a method by which the red runners could enter the outposts without being fired upon. Runners, upon approaching an army post, were to give two whoops and immediately run into the lines. General Pinckney's order was that any "sentinel who hears the signal will immediately give notice to the guard to stand to their arms, but strict instructions must be given not to fire unless they see more than two Indians running in."[34]

Hawkins ordered Alexander Cornells to instruct the friendly chiefs to send a detachment of Indians, including an interpreter, familiar with the Tallapoosa country to act as scouts and runners for the Tennessee troops operating there. On December 12 a mounted detachment of twenty warriors and four runners under William McIntosh left in obedience to these instructions.

After relieving Coweta, General Floyd continued west into the Upper Creek lands. Here on January 27, 1814, he met and defeated the Red Sticks at Camp Defiance. In his official report he cited Timpochee Barnard, son of Hawkins's assistant, Timothy Barnard, who was at the head of a band

---

33. Hawkins Papers, Hawkins to Floyd, Nov. 19, 1813.
34. John Spencer Bassett, editor, *The Correspondence of Andrew Jackson*, 364-365.

of friendly Uchees, for gallantry under fire.[35] At the same time he stated that Alexander Cornells was "playing a deep game" and was giving traitorous information to the hostiles.[36] As there seems to be no repetition of the charge against Cornells it was probably unfounded. On the other hand, if it were true, this may be a clue to many of Hawkins's troubles, for he had depended more on Cornells than on any other of his assistants.

With the armies converging on the Indians from the north, south, and east, an early victory was anticipated. On March 17, 1814, John Armstrong, Secretary of War, appointed General Pinckney and Colonel Hawkins to conclude a peace as soon as the Indians showed any desire to end the war.[37] Three days later, however, Armstrong decided the treaty should take the form of a military capitulation and so instructed Pinckney that he alone was to make it. He added that Colonel Hawkins could be "usefully employed" in the negotiations.[38]

When the news of the appointments of Pinckney and Hawkins reached Tennessee, Brigadier General George Doherty and eight other Tennessee officers addressed a violent protest to George W. Campbell, member of Congress, on the ground that Tennessee's interests were vitally affected and yet the state was not to be represented on the commission. General Pinckney they described as "an amiable man, and a man of talents." But, they asked:

> . . . Who is his colleague? A man, whose interests and feelings, it is believed, are too much identified with those of the enemy, and in whom the people of the West as well as many in the East, have long since ceased to retain any confidence - A man who, - they believe has on some memorable

35. *Raleigh Register*, Feb. 11, 1814. Floyd to Pinckney, Jan. 27.
36. *Georgia Journal*, Feb. 2, 1814. Christian Limbaugh, another assistant, was accused by Hawkins of stealing 90 barrels of flour and 20 head of cattle and his arrest was requested. Hawkins to Lt. Kendal ewis, Coweta, 4 Sept. 1815. Original in Alabama Dept. Archives c History, copy in Georgia Dept. Archives & History.
37. *American State Papers, Indian Affairs*, I, 836-837. Armstrong to Pinckney, March 17, 1814.
38. *Ibid.*, March 20.

occasions shown himself unworthy any national trust, and to whom more than to any other, they would be unwilling to confide the adjustment of what so deeply concerns them.[39]

Again Tennesseans, never friendly to Hawkins, became his most severe critics. Governor Sevier, William Blount and Willie Blount, General Cocke and the Tennessee legislature had all condemned him, and now General Doherty and others added their voices in disapproval of him. Georgians, who knew him best, criticised him also, but never with equal severity. The agent could generally count on some voice of defense being raised in Georgia but seldom did he find a defender in Tennessee. One is led to wonder to what extent the influence of William Blount had tempered the Tennessee attitude toward the man. Or could it be that the hatred of Tennessee for the Indians was so great that the citizens of the state naturally suspected the motives of any man who was willing to give them a helping hand.

On March 27, 1814, General Andrew Jackson defeated the Red Sticks at Horseshoe Bend on the Tallapoosa River. Of 900 Indians engaged in this fight scarcely 300 escaped. Jackson continued his campaign down the Tallapoosa to its junction with the Coosa and there built Fort Jackson.[40]

On April 23 General Pinckney conveyed to Hawkins the terms upon which peace would be granted to the hostile Creeks with the request that he communicate them to the Indians.[41] These terms were by no means extremely severe on the hostiles and were made very specific in their guarantee of protection and indemnities for the fidelity of the friendly Indians. Hawkins immediately made the conditions known to the friendly chiefs. He was told by them that the hostiles were not ready for peace in spite of the recent defeats, and until they were punished more severely would not likely abide

---

39. Bassett, *Correspondence of Andrew Jackson*, I, 497-498 note.
40. Henry Adams, *History of the United States of America During the Jefferson and Madison Administrations*, VII, 254-256.
41. *American State Papers, Indian Affairs*, I, 857-858.

by any promise they might make.[42] While the hostiles had been reduced to dire suffering and the war was apparently at an end, the friendly chiefs showed themselves the true prophets. With the promise of munitions and supplies at Pensacola, the Red Sticks were not yet subdued. In the meantime, Hawkins, as a preliminary to peace, had allowed those who professed a desire for it to return to their homes. This was the occasion of a complaint from Andrew Jackson to General Pinckney:

> I am truly astonished that Colo. Hawkins is permitting the Indians to settle down on their former habitations. I did tell him the territory I had assigned them. I did tell him that no Indians should settle west of the Cosee or north of the allabama. At this point is the strength of the frontier of the union to be established by . . . wealthy inhabitants, unmixed by Indians.[43]

To the demands of the friendly chiefs that they seek peace the Red Sticks replied in the negative. One of the hostile Indians notified Big Warrior and Little Prince: "I have now friends and arms, you compelled me to fly and if you attempt to track me up I will spill your blood."[44]

On July 11 General Jackson informed Hawkins that he had succeeded Pinckney as the commissioner to sign the treaty and that he had set August 1 as the date for the Creeks desiring peace to meet him at Fort Jackson. Hawkins was ordered to report to the same place without loss of time, but was first to notify all chiefs of the conference.[45]

On August 9, 1814, the Treaty of Fort Jackson was signed, with General Jackson the sole commissioner for the United States. He experienced "considerable difficulty" in getting the Indians to sign because of the generous terms which Hawkins, upon General Pinckney's instructions, had offered the Creeks in the spring.[46] Nevertheless, Jackson in his official

---

42. *Ibid.*, 858, Hawkins to Pinckney, April 25, 1814.
43. Bassett, *Correspondence of Andrew Jackson*, II, 3.
44. Cuyler Collection, Hawkins report, June 14, 1814.
45. Bassett, *Correspondence of Andrew Jackson*, II, 14-15.
46. *Ibid.*, 24. Jackson to Blount.

report acknowledged himself under "great obligations to Col. Hawkins for his aid."[47]

As late as August 7 the Indians appealed to Hawkins: "We are again in trouble and have need of your advise [sic]." Jackson, they complained, had disregarded the terms offered by Pinckney and had punished the friendly Indians more than the hostiles. He had not consulted them but had drawn the lines to suit himself.[48] Hawkins, unquestionably, was sympathetic with the complaints of the friendly chiefs. If he took any action on the request it is not revealed, but from that time on he had little regard for General Jackson.

Frederick L. Paxson says of the treaty:

> In August, the Creeks were punished for their sins by a treaty which the victor dictated at Fort Jackson. . . . The braves who needed the punishment were dead or in flight; the quiet Creek warriors, many of whom had fought with Jackson, were the only ones who could be collected in the Council. The injustice involved in punishing the good for the excesses of the bad was an ordinary part of the practice of handling the tribes.[49]

Before the articles of peace were signed, Big Warrior addressed General Jackson and Colonel Hawkins and tendered each of them a reservation of three miles square, "to be chosen from what we are going to give, as near as you can to us, for we want you to live by us and give us your advice." To this generous and complimentary offer Colonel Hawkins replied graciously for both, accepting the gift, and expressing friendship to the givers. The granting of land to individuals from the lands to be conveyed to the government by treaty was most unusual. In his message to Congress on January 18, 1816, President James Madison said:

> The accompanying extract from the occurrences at Fort Jackson in August 1814, during the negotiation of a treaty

47. *Ibid.*, 26. Jackson to Armstrong.
48. Indian Office files. Chiefs to Hawkins.
49. *History of the American Frontier*, 176.

with the Indians, shows that the friendly Creeks, wishing to give General Jackson and Benjamin Hawkins . . . a national mark of their gratitude and regard, conveyed to them respectively a donation of land, with the request that the grant might be duly confirmed by the government of the United States. . . . I recommend to Congress that provision be made for carrying into effect the wishes and request of the Indians as expressed by them.[50]

Most of the hostile Creek chiefs were not parties to the treaty; in fact, there is evidence that only one such chief was on hand. The hostilities, therefore, did not cease immediately. The British continued to promise the Red Sticks aid and invited them to Pensacola for supplies. Disorders and threats continued throughout the summer. Jackson advanced into Florida and in November captured Pensacola. Hawkins, under orders from Jackson, began to enroll the friendly Creeks for service.[51] He eventually got together a force of about 800 Indians, of which he took personal command. Though he and his command saw little fighting, they were able to protect the frontier against hostile attacks and in January, 1815, they marched to and floated down the Flint in a campaign against Apalachicola.[52] A month later Hawkins was at 115 Mile Camp and was preparing to attack a white, red, and black force entrenched there behind artillery support, when the news of the Treaty of Ghent arrived.

England and the United States were at peace but the hostile Creeks even then did not cease their enmity. When Hawkins was appointed one of the commissioners to run the line of the Fort Jackson treaty, his Creeks accompanied him. At the confluence of the Flint and the Chattahoochee rivers a threatened attack by the hostiles was given up when they found the commissioners defended by a friendly Indian force nearly 800 strong.[53] General John Sevier and Hawkins started the

50. *American State Papers, Indian Affairs*, II, 26.
51. Cuyler Collection, Hawkins to Early, November 1, 1814.
52. *Ibid.*, Hawkins to Early, January 22, 1815.
53. Bassett, *Correspondence of Andrew Jackson*, II, 222 note. Hawkins to Jackson, December 1, 1815.

line. On September 24, 1815, Sevier died and Hawkins was forced by illness to quit the survey on the same day. Generals John Coffee and E. P. Gaines completed it.

After the Treaty of Ghent, Colonel Hawkins, as the representative of the United States and the person most fitted to deal with the Indians in their new relationship, was practically the sole agent between his government and the British, Spanish, and Indian forces in Florida. The British did not evacuate Florida according to agreement. In the spring of 1815, Colonel Nicholls, who commanded the British forces at Apalachicola, addressed an insolent letter to Colonel Hawkins in which he stated that according to the provisions of the Treaty of Ghent he considered the territories of the Creeks to be as they were before the war. He took this position in spite of the fact that General Jackson had negotiated the Treaty of Fort Jackson in 1814. Colonel Nicholls further arrogated to himself the entire control of the Creeks, and warned citizens of the United States neither to enter Creek territory nor to attempt to communicate with the Indians. He appended to the letter a paper signed by three chiefs agreeing to the 9th article of the treaty of peace on which he based his assertion that the boundaries were the same as in 1811. This was evidently an attempt on his part to deter the commissioners of the United States who were about to run the boundary line agreed upon by Jackson's treaty. Hawkins replied to Nicholls as follows:

> . . . the documents you enclosed signed by three chiefs, purporting to be the agreement to the 9th article of the treaty of peace, I shall lay before the chiefs of the nation at a convention soon to be held at Coweta, and send you the result of their deliberations on it. The result of my reflections with due deference I give you, as on the envelope it purports to be on his Britannic majesty's service. It is within my knowledge one of the chiefs is a Seminole of East-Florida and has never resided in the United States; and that neither of the three has ever attended the national councils of the Creeks, or are in any way a part of their

executive government. If the four witnesses had signed as principals, and the three chiefs as witnesses, it would have been entitled to equal respect from me.[54]

Governor Early of Georgia had previously protested to the Spanish Governor of East Florida against the English remaining in Spanish territory, assuming a protectorate over the Indians, and encouraging them to hostility against the United States. In his protest he enclosed the complete correspondence between Colonel Hawkins and Colonel Nicholls. He considered that Hawkins had handled the matter in a diplomatic way and had clearly stated the position of the United States.

In due time the British troops were removed from Florida and quiet again settled on the frontier. Benjamin Hawkins was to spend the latter days of his life on his farm at the Agency, surrounded by his family and his Indian friends. The harsh treatment of the Creeks by General Jackson was a bitter disappointment to him and his declining days were not happy. He got what solace he could from the certainty that he had been a faithful servant of his country and a valuable friend to the Indians.[55]

---

54. *Niles' Weekly Register*, VIII (June 10, 1815), 285. As the witnesses referred to were Colonel Nicholls, Captain Woodbine, Lieutenant Hamby, and Captain Henry, the commandant and three of his officers, this statement was bitter sarcasm.
55. Several paragraphs in this chapter are based upon "Benjamin Hawkins, Indian Agent," by Merritt B. Pound, published in the Georgia Historical Quarterly, Vol. XIII, No. 4, 392-409.

CHAPTER XIV

Conclusion

COLONEL Hawkins did not long outlive the Creek War. The closing months of his life were filled with suffering, and his illness was aggravated by heartsickness over the condition of his beloved Creeks. Discouraged, he tried on several occasions to resign. Seldom do his letters show any inclination on his part to defend himself against his critics until near the end of his life. He had previously been confident that he was doing his duty to the Indians and his country and, sustained by this confidence, he paid slight attention to personal criticism. Ill health and the effects of the war destroyed his equanimity and he showed signs of impatience in contrast to his calmness of former years. Criticism piled up on him and finally made its impression. When the *Augusta Chronicle* accused him of treason and deceit,[1] he wrote General Armstrong a long letter in his own defense.

As I hear nothing from you relative to the communications I have made you on Indian affairs, I have judged it advisable to have an understanding with myself on my situation here. I have not been concerned directly or indirectly, in commerce, or speculations of any kind to accumulate money. From all savings arising from my appointment, I have not made three thousand dollars. I have considered my public standing with the Indians as public property, and to be used as such, under the orders of Government, and for no other purpose; and I believe the period is arrived, when it is essential to that interest. Yet, if the President can find a man, who can fill this office, in his Judgment, more for the public interest or convenience than I have done, he owes it to his high standing, and to me to send him on; in doing so, he will do me no injury, or excite the least resentment. . . . This de-

---

1. July 30, 1813.

partment has always been strewed with thorns. It was first assailed by the late Governor Blount and associates, in Tennessee, and the recoil on himself destroyed his public character. It was then assailed by the British through their agent General Bowles. . . . Under an authority vested in me by the chiefs, I sent him down in irons . . . to answer for his crimes. The calumny which hovered around, and assailed the Indians and their Agent, I disregarded, as it originated from base sources, filled by dishonest motives.[2]

President Madison did not accept this offer of resignation at the time, but in February, 1815, Hawkins, while in the field at the head of his Indian warriors, wrote Governor Early that his resignation had been accepted and Christian Limbaugh was to succeed him as soon as the emergency was over.[3] The emergency, for him, ended with his death and only then was his successor appointed. As fate would have it, the next appointee was not Hawkins's assistant Christian Limbaugh, who, in the meantime, had been accused of misappropriation of funds,[4] but ex-Governor Mitchell of Georgia with whom Hawkins had had some of his most bitter strife.

Colonel Hawkins was, on occasion, referred to as a man of science. Much evidence has survived to prove that, in the sight of contemporaries at least, he was a thorough student of the Indian and his customs. A prolific letter writer, he had a wide range of correspondence and exchanged personal letters with at least five men who were, or were destined to become, president of the United States. Hundreds of his letters are extant. They are usually serious in tone and give evidence of a character devoted to the public interest. Seldom boastful, often humble, they reveal an honorable career and a broad interest in public affairs.

General Thomas S. Woodward, writing in 1857, extravagantly praised Hawkins as a student of Indian life.

He knew more about Indians and Indian history and early settlements and expeditions of the several European nations

---

2. *American State Papers, Indian Affairs*, I, 852-853.
3. Cuyler Collection, Hawkins to Early, February 15, 1815.
4. See Chapter XIII, footnote 36.

that undertook to settle colonies in the South and South-west, than all the men that ever have or will make a scrape of the pen upon the subject.[5]

Such extravagance can, at best, be taken only as indicative of partisan opinion. Hawkins, unquestionably, was studious, and applied himself seriously to a mastery of the Indian dialects, a thing perfectly natural in one who had shown proficiency in languages while a college student. Thomas Jefferson, himself a linquist of no mean ability, called on Hawkins on several occasions for instruction in the Indian tongues. When the Empress of Russia wished to make a comparison of the languages of the American Indians and the Siberian tribes, she asked General Washington for Indian vocabularies. James Madison heard of this request and sent Washington Cherokee and Choctaw vocabularies prepared and presented to him by Hawkins.[6]

Hawkins was also a keen observer and put on paper much of what he had seen. Though he published nothing of great importance he had a large collection of letters and manuscripts when he died. After his home burned the rumor was widely circulated by eye witnesses to the fire that all of his papers were destroyed. One witness vouched for the statement attributed to Hawkins that he had a trunk full of manuscripts ready for the press. "I was at Col. Hawkins when the fire took place and everything was consumed worth any note; his wife and children escaped with their lives and that was all, even their wearing clothes were burnt &c."[7]

On July 3, 1816, the *Georgia Journal* lamented:

The dwelling house at the Creek Agency, occupied by the family of the late Col. Hawkins, we understand has been consumed by fire, together with the furniture and papers,

5. *Publications of the Alabama Historical Society*, I, 175. Woodward to Edward Hamrick, May 12, 1857.
6. *Correspondence of the American Revolution*, IV, 165. Madison to Washington, March 18, 1787.
7. *Alabama Historical Society Publications*, I, 175. Thomas M. Ellis to A. J. Pickett, August 26, 1847.

including his valuable manuscripts. Much of Colonel's leisure from official duties had been devoted to Science and Literature, and his friends had consoled themselves at his death with the reflection, that his works had not perished, but would survive him, to enlighten his countrymen and immortalize their author. By this accident the public have lost more than his family. No man living was conversant with the character of the North American Indians, or better knew the habits, customs and traditions of the aborigines.

No doubt great quantities of valuable historical material were destroyed. Nevertheless, much was saved. How, and in what way it was preserved, is something of a mystery. In the library of the Georgia Historical Society are eight manuscript volumes of letters and journals in Hawkins's handwriting. These volumes cover much of his activities from 1797 to 1806 and were published in 1916 as Volume IX, *Collections of the Georgia Historical Society* under the title *Letters of Benjamin Hawkins.*

In addition to the manuscripts preserved, a magnificent library of more than five hundred volumes was sold at a small fraction of its cost at an inventory sale of Hawkins's property in October, 1816. Among the titles listed were: Gibbon's *Rome*, Blackstone's *Commentaries*, Jefferson's *Notes on the State of Virginia*, Adam Smith's *Wealth of Nations*, Chesterfield's *Letters*, Bartram's *Travels*, Ramsey's *Washington*, Pain's *Architecture*, Pike's *Arithmetic*, *Sinclair on Revenue*, *Laws of the United States*, the works of Horace, Xenophon, and Cicero, the *New Testament* in Latin, French and Spanish grammars, medical books and dispensatories, and volumes on agriculture, bee culture, and midwifery. Quite a distinguished library for one living deep in the Indian country and indicative of the versatility and diversity of interests of its owner.[8]

Hawkins's chief claim to fame as an author is due to the

---

8. Record of the sale at the Creek Agency of Hawkins' property at the plantation on the Agency, 3rd week in October, 1816, in Ordinary's Office, Jones County, Georgia. Copy in Georgia Department of Archives and History.

publication in 1848 of his *Sketch of the Creek Country 1798-1799*, as Volume III, Part I, of the *Collections of the Georgia Historical Society*. This brochure on the Creeks was written originally in a bound notebook. Because of the natural interest in its subject matter, the desire for information about the country on the part of land owners, military leaders, and speculators, and the generosity of the author, many handwritten copies were made of this manuscript. The Georgia Historical Society has three copies—one complete, and one nearly so, in Hawkins's handwriting, and a beautiful copy made by General John Floyd while he was campaigning during the War of 1812. There is another copy in the Library of Congress, and one made by John Howard Payne from the original manuscript in 1835 is in the Edward Ayer Collection in the Newberry Library in Chicago.

A Sketch on the Creek Country, as published, contains an introduction by William B. Hodgson, the editor, explaining how the manuscript volumes upon which it is based were presumably preserved. "The present manuscripts, it is supposed, have been preserved by their having been submitted to the Governor of the State at Milledgeville for his perusal."[9] If this supposition is based on the same type of inaccurate research as are other statements in the introduction, it is of little value. The statement is made that Colonel Hawkins was living in 1825. The fact that a letter to Governor Troup of Georgia signed Benjamin Hawkins and complaining of affairs in the Agency was written in 1825 confused Hodgson. As a matter of fact, many of the Indians took the name Hawkins out of respect for the agent and the letter to Troup was written by one of these.[10] Following the introduction there is an inadequate sketch of the author and a few of his selected letters; then follows a brief description of the Creek Confederacy by the editor.

The work itself contains about forty-eight printed pages descriptive of the country through which Hawkins travelled

---

9. Hawkins, *A Sketch of the Creek Country*, 4.
10. *American State Papers, Indian Affairs*, II, 766.

in 1797 and 1798, with frequent discussions of individuals and their agricultural and domestic surroundings, and an eighteen page description of the government, laws, and customs of the Creeks. It is of great value for a study of the Southern Indians of the period.

Hawkins occasionally wrote articles for publication in the newspapers. One such, under the caption "Parch-corn Flour," written on August 23, 1814, ended with the following request:

> The period is at hand for using [parch-corn] flour . . . and it being probable my fellow citizens will have occasion for much of it in all parts of the United States, I hope the printers in every state will give it [the article] a place in their papers.[11]

Another article, "*Strawberry Culture*," was sent to the *Georgia Journal* on August 17, 1812. "I send the enclosed for your paper, hoping by its promulgation your neighbors will be induced to make an effort to supply themselves with strawberries."[12]

In addition to studying books from the shelves of his well stocked library, Hawkins also kept abreast of the times as well as one could in the Indian country by reading several newspapers constantly. In 1811 he desired more news from the Southwest and requested Governor W. C. C. Claiborne to subscribe to the best New Orleans paper for him. Claiborne replied that he had taken out a subscription to the *Louisiana Courier* in his name and had paid the editor five dollars in advance. Books mentioned in letters are Ramsey's *History of South Carolina*, which he borrowed from Jefferson,[13] and Adair's *History of the American Indians*, and Bartram's *Travels*, which were requested, along with an order of sup-

---

11. *Georgia Journal*, August 31, 1814.
12. August 26, 1812.
13. McPherson, "Letters from North Carolinians to Jefferson," in *North Carolina Historical Review*, XII, 259. Hawkins to Jefferson, March 26, 1792.

plies, from Edward Price, the factor.[14] At the time he made the request of Price for these special titles, he also asked him to send him all of the other books on Indians he could locate.

Although Hawkins asserted in 1814 that he had saved less than three thousand dollars out of his salary, his inheritance and holdings acquired before 1796 must have been considerable and his farming operations lucrative. Hating credit and debt as he did, he naturally attended his personal affairs carefully. Wheeler estimated Hawkins's personal fortune at his death to be $160,000, and this was probably only slightly exaggerated.[15] Unlike many Southern planters, even at a later period, all of his holdings were not in land and farm equipment. In the *Daily Georgian* on January 21, 1819, one hundred shares of the Planter's Bank of the State of Georgia, upon each of which $80 had been paid, was offered for sale as a part of his estate. In a suit respecting his will in the Crawford County court in 1830 the estate, "consisting of lands negroes money" was estimated at more than $100,000, despite the fact that much loss had been sustained in the destruction of his home by fire shortly after his death. Jeffersonia Bacon, the defendant, Hawkins's only child born after the will had been drawn, was placed under $10,000 bond for having received a child's share.[16]

Seventy-two Negro slaves comprised a considerable portion of Hawkins's personal estate. Of these slaves four were superannuates and were inventoried as of no value. The others were estimated as being worth $28,800 and were divided on this basis among his wife, his nephew, Governor William Hawkins of North Carolina, and the six children living at the time his will was drawn. Each of these heirs received not less than seven nor more than eleven slaves. In an attempt to liquidate the estate a few months after Hawkins's death, a sale of his remaining personal property, which was inventoried at $37,190, was held at the Agency. It is quite evi-

---

14. Indian Office files. Hawkins to Price, December 7, 1798.
15. Hawkins, *Sketches*, 430.
16. Hawkins Papers.

dent this inventory did not represent true value as expensive books were sold for only a small fraction of their replacement cost and household furniture and farm equipment were similarly marked down.[17]

As evidence of the magnitude of Hawkins's farming operations, the inventory listed on the Agency plantation 20 horses, 58 sheep, 59 goats, 81 pigs, and 291 cattle. In addition, he owned another plantation in the vicinity of Fort Hawkins but here his operations were much smaller. The household effects were of little value and the farm stock consisted of one horse, one steer, and 20 cows.[18]

Hawkins left a widow, six daughters, and one son. Lavinia, his widow, entered business partnership with John Buchanan and lost her share of the estate. Georgia, the oldest daughter, died without marrying, as did also Carolina. Both were intestate, and their shares were divided among the other heirs, including Jeffersonia who had not been born when the will was drawn. She was a very small child when her father died and had not participated in the original settlement. Muscogee married Bagnell B. Tiller, who "separated himself from her." Cherokee married Lewis Lawshe. Virginia became Mrs. William Carr, and Jeffersonia married Francis Bacon. The fortune was dissipated, and there resulted many bitter disputes and law suits among the heirs.

On June 6, 1816, Hawkins, still among his Indians, died, and was buried on the Agency. In 1931 a monument to his memory was erected by Congressional appropriation in Roberta, Georgia, about six miles from his grave. At the time of his death many extravagant eulogies were written and uttered by his contemporaries. On June 29, 1816, the following brief notice appeared in Niles Weekly Register:

Colonel Benjamin Hawkins-the good, the benevolent and venerable Hawkins, agent for Indian affairs, died at his

---

17. Inventory October 17, 1816. Ordinary's Office, Jones, County, Georgia. File No. 65, Annual Return Book B, 140-144. Copies in Georgia Department of Archives and History.
18. *Ibid.*

post among the Indians on the 6th inst. The Indians have indeed lost a 'father,' and the United States one of their most faithful and respectful agents. It appears he died as he lived—with complacency and firmness.

Reputable historians of recent years have found his career praiseworthy. Marquis James speaks of Hawkins as agent as "an anomaly among such officials, being both honest and able."[19]

It would be easy to enter into the spirit of the partisans of Hawkins and close this volume with a eulogy, but the record of his family Bible seems essentially just.

Colonel Benjamin Hawkins Agent for the Creek Indians departed this life on the 6th of June at 8 o'clock in the evening in 1816, in the 62nd year of his age he has served as a Publick Character in various departments and always discharged the Trust faithfully for 36 years—a worthy honest man.[20]

19. James, *Andrew Jackson, Border Captain*, 166.
20. Recorded in the Family Bible of the Hawkins family. Copies of the entries from which this quotation was taken are in the archives of the North Carolina Historical Collection. This tribute was written by his brother Philemon.

Bibliography

I. Manuscript Collections

(a) Georgia Department of Archives and History.

Manuscript Collection of Hawkins's papers. About 125 MS letters and reports.

Executive Letter Books of Governors of Georgia, 1786-1789, 1798-1802.

Hays, Louise Frederick, "Unpublished Letters of Benjamin Hawkins, 1797-1815," bound volume, typed.

———————, "Unpublished Letters of Timothy Barnard, 1784-1820," bound volume, typed.

(b) Georgia Historical Society.

Hawkins, Benjamin, "A Sketch of the Creek Country, 1798-1799." Two manuscript copies of this work in the handwriting of Hawkins. One, evidently the first draft, is incomplete. A third manuscript copy beautifully written in the handwriting of General John Floyd and copied from "the journal of Col. Hawkins in the Creek War in 1813-1814" is also a part of this collection.

Hawkins, Benjamin, eight manuscript volumes of letters and journals in Hawkins's handwriting. These plus one other volume with caption on the fly leaf, "R. Thomas, His Book," published as *The Letters of Benjamin Hawkins.*

Thomas, R., "His Book," manuscript volume.

(c) Library of Congress.

Washington Papers

Jefferson Papers

Madison Papers

(d) National Archives, War Department, Indian Office Records.

Creek Factory Day Books, Miscellaneous dates.

Creek Factory Ledger, 1808-1814.

Factory Letter Book, 1795-1812.

Indian Annuities Book, Miscellaneous items, 1812-1818.

Invoices of Furs, Creek Factory, November 30, 1812.

Ledger of Hawkins's Accounts with the Factory at Ocmulgee Old Fields, November 1808, and at Fort Hawkins 1809-1814.

Original Incoming Letters and Reports 1767-1816. Unbound in folders. Contains many letters from Hawkins.

Outgoing Letter Books of the Secretary of War 1800-1816, in 4 volumes.

(e) North Carolina Historical Commission.

Governors' Papers, State Series, papers of Governors Caswell, Nash, Martin, and William Hawkins.

Copy of entries in the Hawkins family Bible.

(f) The University of Georgia.

The Telamon Cuyler Collection contains about thirty original autographed letters to and from Benjamin Hawkins and two journals of boundary line commissions.

II. NEWSPAPERS.

(a) Georgia Historical Society.

Columbian Museum and Savannah Advertiser, 1796-1798, 1800-1801, 1804, 1807-1808.

Columbian Museum and Savannah Daily Gazette, 1818.

Columbian Museum and Savannah Gazette, 1817.

Daily Georgian, (Savannah), 1818-1819.

Gazette of the State of Georgia (Savannah), 1783-1784, 1787-1788.

Georgia Gazette (Savannah), 1788-1789, 1794-1796.

Georgia Republican (Savannah), 1806-1807.

Georgia Republican and State Intelligencer (Savannah), 1803-1806.

Public Intelligencer (Savannah), 1803-1806.

Republican and Savannah Evening Ledger, 1808, 1810-1812.

(b) Library of Congress.

Christian Advocate, The, conducted by Ashbell Green, D.D., Vol. II, for the year 1824. Bound Volume.

New York Journal and Weekly Register, July 19, 1787.

(c) The University of Georgia.

Augusta Chronicle, 1796-1815.

Augusta Herald, miscellaneous files from 1802 to 1806.

Columbian Sentinel (Augusta), 1806-1809.

Columbian Museum and Savannah Advertiser, 1802-1803.

Farmers' Gazette (Sparta), August 1806-July 1807.

Georgia Journal (Milledgeville), 1810-1817.

National Intelligencer (Washington), 1813-1821.

Niles' Weekly Register, 1814-1816.
  (d) The University of North Carolina.
Hall's Wilmington Gazette, 1797-1799. Photostats.
Minerva (Raleigh), 1807-1808.
Newbern Gazette, 1798-1800. Miscellaneous numbers. Photostats.
North Carolina Centinel and Fayetteville Gazette, July 25 to August 29, 1795. Photostats.
North Carolina Gazette (Newbern), 1787-1797.
North Carolina Journal (Halifax), 1792, 1794, 1799, 1805-1807.
Raleigh Register and North Carolina Gazette, 1812-1814.
The Star (Raleigh), 1810-1814.
State Gazette, 1789-1799.
Wilmington Centinel and General Advertiser, June 18, 1788.
Wilmington Chronicle, 1795-1796. Photostat.
Wilmington Gazette, 1797-1799, 1813-1818.

III. PRINTED RECORDS, DOCUMENTS, AND CORRESPONDENCE

Abridgement of the Debates of Congress from 1789 to 1856. 16 vols. New York: D. Appleton & Co., 1857.

American State Papers. 38 vols. Washington: Gales and Seaton, 1832-1861.

Annals of Congress 1789-1824. 42 vols. Washington: Gales and Seaton, 1834-1856.

Bassett, John Spencer, editor, *Correspondence of Andrew Jackson.* 5 vols. Washington: The Carnegie Institution of Washington, 1926.

Burnett, Edmund C., editor, *Letters of Members of the Continental Congress.* 8 vols. Washington: The Carnegie Institution of Washington, 1921-1936.

Calendar of the Correspondence of James Madison. Bulletin of Bureau of Rolls and Library of the Department of State, no. 4. Washington, 1894.

Carter, Clarence Edwin, editor, *The Territorial Papers of the United States.* 5 vols. Washington: Government Printing Office, 1934-1937.

Clark, Walter P., editor, *The State Records of North Carolina.* 20 vols. Winston, N. C.: M. I. and J. C. Stewart, 1896.

Dexter, Franklin B., editor, *The Literary Diary of Ezra Stiles.* 3 vols. New York: Charles Scribner's Sons, 1901.

Documentary History of the Constitution of the United States of America. 5 vols. Washington: Department of State, 1905.

Fitzpatrick, John C., editor, *The Diaries of George Washington.* 4 vols. Boston: Houghton Mifflin Co., 1925.

Forbes, John, "A Journal of John Forbes, May 1803, The Seizure of William Augustus Bowles," *Florida Historical Quarterly,* IX, 4, (April 1931).

Ford, Worthington C., editor, *Journals of Continental Congress, Edited from Original Records in Library of Congress.* 32 vols. Washington: Government Printing Office, 1904.

Hamilton, Stanislau M., *The Writings of James Monroe.* 7 vols. New York: G. P. Putnam's Sons, 1898.

Hawkins, Benjamin, *A Sketch of the Creek Country in the Years 1798 and 1799,* Vol. I, part 1, Collections of the Georgia Historical Society. Savannah, 1848.

———————————, *Letters of Benjamin Hawkins,* IX. Collections of the Georgia Historical Society. Savannah, 1918.

Ker, Henry, *Travels Through the Western Interior of the United States.* Elizabethtown, New Jersey: Privately printed, 1816.

Lipscomb, Andrew A., editor, *The Writings of Thomas Jefferson.* 20 vols. Washington: The Thomas Jefferson Memorial Association, 1904.

Maclay, Edgar S., *The Journal of William Maclay, United United States Senator from Pennsylvania, 1789-1791.* New York: Albert and Charles Boni, 1929.

Martin, Francois Xavier; Haywood, John; and Battle, William M., editors, *North Carolina Reports.* I, second edition. Winston, N. C.: M. I. and J. C. Stewart, 1898.

McPherson, Elizabeth G., editor, "Unpublished Letters from North Carolinians to Jefferson," *North Carolina Historical Review,* XII, 1, (January 1935).

———————————, editor, "Unpublished Letters from North Carolinians to James Madison and James Monroe," *North Carolina Historical Review,* XIV, 2 (April 1937).

———————————, editor, "Unpublished Letters from North Carolinians to Washington," *North Carolina Historical Review,* XII, 2 (April 1935).

McRee, G. J., *Life and Correspondence of James Iredell, One of the Associate Justices of the Supreme Court of the United States.* 2 vols. New York: D. Appleton & Co., 1868.

Owen, Thomas M., editor, *Publications of the Alabama Historical Society, Miscellaneous Collections.* I. Montgomery, 1901.

Rowland, Dunbar, editor, *Executive Journals of Governor Winthrop Sargent and Governor William Charles Cole Claiborne.* I. The Mississippi Territorial Archives 1798-1803. Nashville, 1905.

------------------------------------, editor, *Official Letter Books of W.C.C. Claiborne, 1801-1816.* 6 vols. Jackson: Printed for the Department of Archives and History, 1917.

Senate Documents. Vol. 33, 60th Congress, 1st Session. Washington: Government Printing Office, 1908.

Sparks, Jared, editor, *Correspondence of the American Revolution; Being the Letters of Eminent Men to George Washington from the Time of His Taking Command of the Army to the End of His Presidency.* 4 vols. Boston: Little, Brown & Co., 1853.

------------------------------------, editor, *The Writings of George Washington.* Boston: J. B. Russell, 1835.

Wagstaff, H. M., editor, *Papers of John Steele.* 2 vols. Raleigh: The North Carolina Historical Commission, 1924.

Watkins, Robert and George, *A Digest of the Laws of the State of Georgia from its First Establishment Down to the Year 1798.* Philadelphia: R. Aitken, 1800.

Watson, Winslow C., editor, *Men and Times of the Revolution, or Memoirs of Elkanah Watson, Including Journals of Travels in Europe and America, from 1777 to 1842.* New York: Dana & Co., 1856.

Whitaker, Arthur Preston, translator and editor, *Documents Relating to the Commercial Policy of Spain in the Floridas.* Deland: The Florida State Historical Society, 1931.

IV. ARTICLES IN JOURNALS AND PERIODICALS

Berry, Jane M., "The Indian Policy of Spain in the Southwest 1783-1795," *Mississippi Valley Historical Review*, III, 4 (March 1917).

Cotterill, R. S., "Federal Indian Management in the South 1789-1825," *Mississippi Valley Historical Review*, XX, 3 (December 1933).

Farrand, Max, "The Indian Boundary Line," *American Historical Review*, X, 4 (July 1905).

Foreman, Carolyn Thomas, "Alexander McGillivray, Emperor of the Creeks," *Chronicles of Oklahoma*, VII, 2 (March 1929).

Harmon, George D., "Benjamin Hawkins and the Federal Factory System," *North Carolina Historical Review*, IX, 2 (April 1932).

Innerarity, John, "The Creek Nation, Debtor to Panton, Leslie & Co., A Journal of John Innerarity," *Florida Historical Quarterly*, IX, 2 (October 1930).

Kinnaird, Lawrence, "The Significance of William Augustus Bowles's Seizure of Panton's Apalachee Store in 1792," *Florida Historical Quarterly*, IX, 3 (January 1931).

Kinnaird, Lucia Burk, "The Rock Landing Conference of 1789," *North Carolina Historical Review*, IX, 4 (October 1932).

Morton, Ohland, "The Government of the Creek Indians," *Chronicles of Oklahoma*, VIII, 1 (March 1930).

McMurray, Donald L., "The Indian Policy of the Federal Government and the Economic Development of the Southwest, 1789-1801," *Tennessee Historical Magazine*, I, 1 and 2 (March and June 1915).

Pound, Merritt B., "Benjamin Hawkins, Indian Agent," *Georgia Historical Quarterly*, XIII, 4 (December 1929).

————————————————, "Colonel Benjamin Hawkins—North Carolinian—Benefactor of the Southern Indians," *North Carolina Historical Review*, XIX, 1 and 2 (January and April 1942).

Wagstaff, H. M., "Federalism in North Carolina," *James Sprunt Historical Publications*, University of North Carolina, IX, 2 (1910).

Way, Royal B., "The United States Factory System for Trading with the Indians," *Mississippi Valley Historical Review*, VI, 2 (September 1919).

Wesley, Edgar B., "The Government Factory System among the Indians, 1795-1822," *Journal of Economic and Business History*, IV, 3 (1932).

Whitaker, Arthur Preston, "Alexander McGillivray, 1783-1789," *North Carolina Historical Review*, V, 2 (April 1928).

————————————————, "Alexander McGillivray, 1789-1793," *North Carolina Historical Review*, V, 3 (July 1928).

V. General Works

Abernethy, Thomas Perkins, *From Frontier to Plantation in Tennessee, A Study in Frontier Democracy*. Chapel Hill: University of North Carolina Press, 1932.

Adams, Henry, *History of the United States of America During the Jefferson and Madison Administrations*. 9 vols. New York: Charles Scribner's Sons, 1921.

Arthur, T. S. and Carpenter, W. H. *The History of Georgia, from its Earliest Settlement to the Present Time*. Philadelphia: Remsen & Hoffelfinger, 1869.

Beard, Charles Austin, *Economic Origins of Jeffersonian Democracy*. New York: The Macmillan Co., 1915.

Brevard, Caroline Mays, *A History of Florida From the Treaty of 1763 to Our Own Times*, edited by James Alexander Robertson and published posthumously in 2 vols. Deland: Florida State Historical Society, 1924.

Caughey, John Walton, *McGillivray of the Creeks*. Norman: University of Oklahoma Press, 1938.

Chappell, Absolom H., *Miscellanies of Georgia, Historical, Biographical, Descriptive, Etc.* Atlanta: James F. Meegan, 1874.

Cheshire, Joseph Blount, *Skecthes of Church History in North Carolina*. Wilmington: William L. De Rosset, 1892. (Sometimes cited as DeRosset's Church History.)

Claiborne, J. F. H., *Life and Times of General Sam Dale*. New York: Harper & Brothers Co., 1860.

——————————, *Mississippi as a Province, Territory and State with Biographical Notices of Eminent Citizens*. Jackson: Power and Barksdale, 1880.

Collins, V. L., *President Witherspoon*. 2 vols. Princeton: Princeton University Press, 1925.

Connor, R. D. W., *History of North Carolina*, Vol. 1, *The Colonial and Revolutionary Periods*. Chicago and New York: The Lewis Publishing Co., 1919.

——————————, *North Carolina, Rebuilding an Ancient Commonwealth, 1584-1925*. 4 vols. Chicago and New York: The American Historical Society, 1929.

Coulter, E. Merton, *A Short History of Georgia*. Chapel Hill: University of North Carolina Press, 1933.

Cox, Isaac Joslin, *The West Florida Controversy, 1798-1813. A Study in American Diplomacy*. Baltimore: Johns Hopkins University Press, 1918.

Cushman, H. B., *A History of the Choctaw, Chickasaw, and Natchez Indians*. Greenville, Texas: Privately printed, 1899.

Dodd, William E., *The Life of Nathaniel Macon*. Raleigh, N. C.: Edwards and Broughton Printers, 1903.

Eggleston, Edward and Seelye, Lillie Eggleston, *Tecumseh and the Shawnee Prophet*. New York: Dodd, Mead & Co., 1878.

Gilmore, James R., *John Sevier as a Commonwealth Builder*. New York: D. Appleton & Co., 1898.

Gilpatrick, Delbert Harold, *Jeffersonian Democracy in North Carolina, 1789-1818*. New York: Columbia University Press, 1931.

Greene, George Washington, *The Life of Nathanael Greene*. 3 vols. Boston and New York: Houghton Mifflin Co., 1890.

Halbert, H. S. and Ball, T. H., *The Creek War of 1813-1814*. Chicago: Donohue & Henneberg, 1895.

Hamilton, Peter J., *Colonial Mobile*. Boston & New York: Houghton Mifflin Co., 1898.

Hays, Louise Frederick, *Hero of Hornet's Nest, A Biography of Elijah Clark*. New York: Hobson Book Press, 1946.

Haywood, John, *The Civil and Political History of the State of Tennessee*. Nashville: W. H. Haywood, 1891.

Historical Collections of the Joseph Habersham Chapter, Daughters of the American Revolution. 3 vols. Savannah: Published privately, 1902.

Humphreys, Frank Landon, *Life and Times of David Humphreys*. 2 vols. New York & London: G. P. Putnam's Sons, 1917.

James, Marquis, *Andrew Jackson, Border Captain*. New York: The Literary-Guild, 1933.

Knight, Lucian Lamar, *Georgia and Georgians*. 6 vols. Chicago & New York: The Lewis Publishing Co., 1917.

Livermore, Shaw, *Early American Land Companies, Their Influence on Corporate Development*. New York: Oxford University Press, 1939.

Meek, A. B., *Romantic Passages in Southwestern History: Including Orations, Sketches and Essays*, 2nd edition. Mobile: S. H. Goetzel and Co., 1857.

Mohr, Walter H., *Federal Indian Relations 1774-1788*. Philadelphia: University of Pennsylvania Press, 1933.

Moore, J. W., *A History of North Carolina*. 2 vols. Raleigh: Alfred Williams & Co., 1880.

McLendon, S. G., *History of the Public Domain of Georgia*. Atlanta: Privately printed, 1924.

Nevins, Allan, *The American States During and After the Revolution, 1775-1789*. New York: The Macmillan Co., 1924.

Phelan, James, *History of Tennessee, The Making of a State*. Boston: Houghton Mifflin & Co., 1889.

Phillips, Uhlrich Bonnell, *Georgia and States Rights*, American Historical Association Annual Report, 1901.

Pickett, Albert James, *History of Alabama and Incidentally of Georgia and Mississippi from the Earliest Period*. Birmingham: Webb Book Co., Republished 1900. Originally published 1851.

Pratt, Julius W., *Expansionists of 1812*. New York: The Macmillan Co., 1925.

Rabun, James, "Georgia and the Creek Indians," unpublished Master's Thesis in History, The University of North Carolina, 1937.

Ramsey, J. G .M., *The Annals of Tennessee to the End of the Eighteenth Century*. Kingsport, Tennessee: Kingsport Press, reprinted by Judge David Campbell Chapter, Daughters of the American Revolution, 1926. Original edition, 1853.

Royce, Charles C., *Indian Land Cessions in the United States*, 18th *Annual Report* of the Bureau of American Ethnology, 1896-97. Washington: Government Printing Office, 1899.

Schmeckebier, Laurence F., *The Office of Indian Affairs, Its History, Activities, and Organization*, Institute for Government Research, Service Monographs of the United States Government, no. 48. Baltimore: Johns Hopkins University Press, 1927.

Stevens, William B., *A History of Georgia from its First Discovery by Europeans to the Adoption of the Present Constitution*. 2 vols. New York: D. Appleton & Co., 1847.

Swanton, J. R., *Early History of the Creek Indians*, Smithsonian Institution, Bureau of Ethnology Reports no. 73. Washington: Government Printing Office, 1922.

Thomas, Cyrus, *Indian Land Cessions in the United States*, 18th Annual Report, Bureau of American Ethnology. Washington: Government Printing Office, 1899. (Land cessions compiled by C. C. Royce; "Introduction" written by Thomas.)

Trenholme, Louis Irby, *The Ratification of the Federal Constitution in North Carolina*. New York: Columbia University Press, 1932.

Wheeler, John H., *Historical Sketches of North Carolina from 1584-1851*. 2 vols. Philadelphia: Lippincott, Grambo & Co., 1851.

------------------, *Reminiscences and Memoirs of North Carolina and Eminent North Carolinians*. Columbus, Ohio: Columbus Printing Works, 1884.

Whitaker, A. P., *The Spanish American Frontier, 1783-1795*. Boston: Houghton Mifflin Co., 1927.

White, George, *Historical Collections of Georgia*. New York: Putney & Russell, 1854.

Willett, William M., *A Narrative of the Military Actions of Col. Marinus Willett, Taken Chiefly from his own Manuscript*. New York: G. C. and H. Carvill, 1831.

Williamson, Hugh, *The History of North Carolina*. 2 vols. Philadelphia: Thomas Dobson, 1812.

Woods, David Walker, *John Witherspoon*. New York: Fleming H. Revell Co., 1906.

Index

Abbecoos, a district of the Upper Creeks, 108

Adams, Major David, 180-181, 182, 183

Adams, John, commissioner for Treaty of Paris, 1783, 22; Vice President, 65, 69; President, 97, 99, 131, 138

Alabama River, 110, 227, 232

Allison, Ensign Samuel, at Coleraine, 85

Amis, Thomas, goods seized by Spanish at Natchez, 32

Anderson, General David, defends Hawkins, 179-180

Apalachee River, 160, 178, 181, 184

Apalachicola, 238, 239

Armstrong, John, Secretary of War, 226, 227, 228, 229, 234

Articles of Confederation, 23, 27, 38, 53, 54

Ashe, John B., Congressman from North Carolina, 23, 28, 29, 49

Athens, Georgia, 208, 210

Augusta, Georgia, 186, 216, 217; Treaty of with Creeks, 37, 38, 42, 45, 55, 88

Aulotchewau, Seminole town, 216, 218, 221

Bailey, Richard, white man among the Creeks, 110

Baily, Dixon, at battle of Burnt Corn Creek, 228

Baldwin, Dr. William, 145-146, 151

Barnard, Timothy, interpreter at Coleraine, 90; assistant to Hawkins, 116, 118, 186, 205, 233

Barnard, Timpochee, son of Timothy, 233-234

Big Lieutenant, Creek chief, 135

Bignall, Robert, trade commissioner for North Carolina, 8

Big Warrior, Creek chief, 86, 89, 210, 212, 213, 215, 216, 227, 236, 237

Billy Bowlegs, Seminole chief, 218

Bloodworth, Timothy, elected to Congress, 23; in Congress, 49; succeeded Hawkins in Senate, 79

Blount, Willie, Governor of Tennessee, 235

Blount, William, in Congress, 15, 16, 26, 27, 28, 29, 31, 33; pleasure at Hawkins's election to Congress, 23-24; letter from John Sitgreaves, 37; at Hopewell, 38, 46-49, 51; at Galphinton, 41, 45; Governor of the Territory south of the River Ohio, 60, 67, 82, 235, 242; in Constitutional Convention, 61; for ratification in North Carolina, 62; at Fayetteville Convention, 64; nominated for U. S. Senate, 64; negotiated Treaty of Holston, 118; expelled from Senate, 126-129

Boos-ke-tah, Creek festival, 135

Boudinot, Elias, letter from Sir Guy Carleton to, 19

Bowdoin, James, Governor of Massachusetts, papers to Congress on Shays' Rebellion, 24

Bowles, William Augustus, adventurer among the Creeks, 81-82, 190, 191, 192, 193, 194, 196, 212, 242

Bradford, William, Senator from Rhode Island, 75

Bradley, Stephen R., Senator from Vermont, 75

Brevard, Ephraim, delegate to Congress, dies, 13

British in Florida, 239-240

Brown, John, Senator from Kentucky, 75

Bryant, Langley, interpreter at Coleraine, 90
Buchanon, John, 248
Burges, James, interpreter at Coleraine, 90, 134
Burke, Thomas, letter to, 10
Burns, Colonel Andrew, Georgia boundary line commissioner, 130-131
Burnt Corn Creek, battle of, 228
Burton, North Carolina delegate to Congress, 27, 28, 29
Burr, Aaron, in Senate, 69-70, 75
Bute County, North Carolina, birthplace of Benjamin Hawkins (later a part of Bute became Warren County), 1, 3, 4
Butler, Pierce, Senator from South Carolina, 72, 75
Byers, James, U. S. factor at Tellico, 124, 127

Cabot, George, Senator from Massachusetts, 75
Caller, James, at battle of Burnt Corn Creek, 228
Campbell, David, from Tennessee, 122-123
Campbell, George W., member of Congress from Tennessee, 234
Camp Defiance, Creeks defeated at, 233-234
Carey, James, interpreter among the Cherokees, 127, 128, 129
Carleton, Sir Guy, 19, 22
Carnes, Thomas P., Congressman from Georgia, 83
Carroll, Charles, in Congress, 35
Carroll, Daniel, delegate to Congress, 37, 38, 40
Caswell, Richard, Governor of North Carolina, 7, 8, 24, 27, 28, 39, 40, 41, 48
Cespedes, Vicente Manuel, Governor of St. Augustine, 195
Charles City County, Virginia, 1
Charleston, Hawkins in, 39, 40
Chattahoochee River, 102, 103, 113, 114, 133, 134, 135, 141, 177, 199, 231, 238
Chattooga River, 102
Cheehaw King, Creek Indian, 170-171

Cherokee Indians, Treaty of Hopewell with, 27, 45-52, 59, 60; Treaty of Holston with, 60; Treaty of Dumplin Creek with, 47; complain of violation of treaties by North Carolina, 53-54
Chicahominy River, 1
Chickasaw Indians, Treaty of Hopewell with, 46, 50, 51, 52; Treaty of 1801 with, 176
Chisholm, Captain John, 127
Choctaw Indians, Treaty of Hopewell with, 46, 50, 51, 52; Treaty of Fort Adams with, 176
Cincinnati, Society of, 30
Claiborne, W. C. C., Governor of Mississippi Territory, 159, 160, 246
Clarke, General Elijah, 43, 44, 45
Clark, General John, 180, 182
Claypole, David C., printer of the Philadelphia Packet, 19
Clements, Colonel J., Georgia boundary line commissioner, 130-131
Clinch River, 127, 129
Clymer, George, commissioner to treaty with Creeks, 83; at Coleraine, 83-98, passim.
Cocke, General John, in Tennessee militia, 219, 231, 235
Coffee, General John, 239
Coleraine, Treaty of with Creeks, 81-98; 140, 174, 182; factory at, 198
Conecuh River, 132, 133, 135
Continental Congress, 13-34
Constitutional Convention, 26, 27, 28, 61
Coosa River, 108, 110, 215, 235
Cormorant, British ship seizes the Endeavour, 22
Cornells, Alexander, interpreter at Coleraine, 86, 90, 108, 109, 110, 111; assistant to Hawkins, 118, 143, 187, 205, 214, 223, 224, 232, 233, 234
Cornells, Joseph, brother to Alexander, 228
Corn Tassel, Cherokee chief, 54

Coweta, Creek town, 114, 115, 138, 183, 224, 231, 232, 233, 239

Coweta Tallahassee, Creek town, 114, 134, 143, 156

Cox, Zachariah, land speculator, 125-126, 211

Crawford County, Georgia, 140

Creek Agency on the Flint River, 138-154, 175, 184-185, 187, 188, 199, 206, 209, 217, 227, 231, 240, 241-249

Creek Indians, 35 ff. *passim;* called Blount the "Dirt King," 26; Treaty of Augusta with Georgia, 37, 38, 42, 45, 55, 88; Treaty of Galphinton with Georgia, 39, 40, 42, 43, 44, 45, 50, 55, 58, 81, 88, 91, 176; Treaty of New York with U. S., 57-60, 81, 82, 83, 89, 91, 98, 177, 182, 196, 206; Rock Landing Conference, 56, 196; Treaty of Coleraine with U. S., 81-98, 140, 174, 182; Treaty of Shoulderbone with Georgia, 54, 55, 81, 83, 89, 94; Treaty of Fort Wilkinson, 177-179, 206; Treaty at Agency, 1804, 184-185; Treaty at Washington, 1805, 187, 206; in War of 1812 (see also Red Sticks), 223-240; Treaty of Fort Jackson, 236-237

Currahee Mountain, 131

Cusseta, Creek town, 113, 138, 149, 225

Cusseta King, Creek chief, 227

Cutler, Manassah, 69

Darouzeaux, James, interpreter, 113

Davie, William R., delegate to Constitutional Convention, 61; works for ratification in North Carolina, 62-63; at Fayetteville Constitution, 64; 139

Dearborn, Henry, Secretary of War, 147-148, 159, 160, 178, 180, 183, 184, 186, 187, 193, 207

Dinsmoor, Silas, Cherokee agent, 104, 118, 119, 123, 124, 127, 159, 160

Dodd, William E., quoted, 2, 13, 139

Doherty, General George, 234-235

Downs, Lavinia (Mrs. Benjamin Hawkins), 149-150, 151, 248

Duane, James, in Congress from New York, 17, 35

Duck River, murders on, 120, 176, 215, 217, 223, 224

Dumplin Creek, Treaty of with Cherokees, 47

Durant, Mrs., sister of McGillivray, 110-111, 112

Early, Peter, Governor of Georgia, 231, 240, 242

Edenton, North Carolina, 8

Edwards, John, senator from Kentucky, 75

Elbert, Samuel, Governor of Georgia, 43, 44

Ellery, William, in Congress from Rhode Island, 22

Ellicott, Andrew, U. S. surveyor, 101, 131, 132, 133, 134, 135, 136, 190

Ellsworth, Oliver, senator from Connecticut, 75

Emautlau, Haujo, Creek chief, 166

Emautle Hutke (White Chief), Creek chief, 113

Endeavour, American ship seized by *Cormorant*, 22

Etowah, Cherokee town, 104

Factory system a m o n g the Creeks, 198-207

Faulkener, William, 153-154

Fayetteville, North Carolina, convention in ratifies Constitution, 63; mass meeting in 1794, 78

Federalism in North Carolina, 63-64, 78, 138-139

Few, William, delegate to Congress from Georgia, 44

Fisk, Ichabod E., dies at Agency, 151

Flint River, 115, 116, 134, 135, 140, 141, 190, 209, 224, 229, 231, 238

Florida, British in, 239-240; Spanish in, 82, 131-136, 190-196, 205, 217-218, 239-240; see also Seminoles
Flournoy, General, 230
Floyd, General John, 221, 230, 231, 232, 233-234, 245
Folch, Governor of Spanish East Florida, 131, 132, 133, 134, 135, 194
Forbes, John, successor to Panton, Leslie & Co., 205
Fort Fidius, 116, 118
Fort Hawkins, 140, 199, 205, 233
Fort Jackson, 235; Treaty of, 236-237, 238, 239
Fort Lawrence, 140, 231
Fort McIntosh, Treaty of, 41
Fort Mims, massacre at, 230
Fort Mitchell, 199
Fort Stanwix, Treaty of, 41
Fort Stoddert, 208, 209, 210
Fort Wilkinson, 124, 130, 138, 159, 175, 206; Treaty of with Creeks, 177-179, 206; factory at, 198-199, 200, 201, 204
Foster, Theodore, Senator from Rhode Island, 75
Franklin, Benjamin, 22
Freeman, William, boundary line surveyor, 180-181
Frelinghuysen, Frederick, Senator from New Jersey, 75
Fusatchee Micco (White-bird King), Creek spokesman at Coleraine, 90, 91, 114

Gaines, General E. P., 239
Gaither, Lieutenant Colonel Henry, at Coleraine, 84, 86, 89, 113, 116; at Fort Fidius, 118; at Fort Wilkinson, 200-201
Galphinton, Treaty of, 39, 40, 42, 43, 44, 45, 50, 55, 58, 81, 88, 91, 176
Gallatin, Albert, in Senate from Pennsylvania, 75; seat declared vacant, 76, 80
Gayoso, Spanish Governor of Florida, 101
Georgia, passim; aggrieved over Indian affairs, 38, 43, 45, 48,

50-52, 55, 60; criticized by McGillivray, 42; named agents to treat with Indians, 42-44; Treaty of Shoulderbone with Creeks, 54; sells western lands to speculation companies, 83; cedes western lands, 177
Gerry, Elbridge, in Congress from Massachusetts, 22
Ghent, Treaty of, 238, 239
Glascock, Thomas, Georgia treaty commissioner, 44, 45, 50
Graham, John, student at Princeton, 5
Granger, Gideon, Postmaster General, 208
Gray, John, 33
Greene, Griffin, 69
Greene, General Nathanael, 39
Greensboro, Georgia, burned by Creeks, 55
Grierson, Robert, trader among the Creeks, 107, 108, 109, 144
Griffin, Cyrus, commissioner at Rock Landing, 56, 89, 94
Grove, William B., in Congress from North Carolina, 70, 78
Gunn, James, Senator from Georgia, 72; speculator, 83

Halsted, Jonathan, U. S. factor at Fort Wilkinson, 175, 181, 186, 201, 204, 205, 206
Hamilton, Alexander, in Congress, 19, 21; Secretary of the Treasury, 78, 80
Handley, George, Governor of Georgia, 55
Hanging Maw of Chota, Cherokee chief, 53-54
Hawkins, Ann (Mrs. Macajah Thomas), sister of Benjamin, 3
Hawkins, Benjamin, passim; birth, 4; at Princeton, 5; on Washington's staff, 5; commercial agent, 6-8; commissioner of Board of Trade, 9-10; trustee of University of North Carolina, 12; in Continental Congress, 13-34; commissioner for Indian affairs, 35-60; U. S. Senate, 61-80; for ratifica-

tion in North Carolina, 61-63; at Fayetteville Convention, 64; Treaty of Coleraine, 81-98; among the Creeks, 99-249, *passim;* tracing boundary lines, 118-137; life on the Agency, 138-154; Indian control, 155-173; War of 1812, 223-240; final days, 241-249

Hawkins, Cherokee (m. Lewis Lawshe), daughter of Benjamin, 248

Hawkins, Delia, mother of Benjamin, 1, 2, 3

Hawkins, Delia (m. L. Bullock), sister of Benjamin, 3

Hawkins, Georgia, daughter of Benjamin, 248

Hawkins, James Madison, son of Benjamin, 248

Hawkins, Jeffersonia (m. Francis Bacon), daughter of Benjamin, 248

Hawkins, Colonel John, brother of Benjamin, 3

Hawkins, Colonel John D., nephew of Benjamin, 3

Hawkins, Colonel Joseph, brother of Benjamin, 3, 5

Hawkins, Muscogee (m. Bagnell B. Tiller), daughter of Benjamin, 248

Hawkins, Philemon, father of Benjamin, 1, 2, 3, 4

Hawkins, Colonel Phileman, Jr., brother of Benjamin, 3; elected to House of Commons, 64

Hawkins, Stephen, trader among the Cherokees, 107

Hawkins, Virginia (m. William Carr), daughter of Benjamin, 248

Hawkins, William, nephew of Benjamin, 151; Governor of North Carolina, 247

Hawkins, Wyat, nephew of Benjamin, elected to House of Commons, 64

Hay, David, trader among the Cherokees, 106

Hendricks, James, Georgia commissioner at Coleraine, 86, 87, 89, 93, 94, 95, 96

Henley, Colonel David, 121, 122

Hickory Ground, McGillivray's home, 58, 111

Hill, William, assistant Creek agent, 159-160

Hillabees, Creek town, 107

Hillsborough, convention at, 61

Hilton, Mrs. Elizabeth, attacked by Indians, 166

Hoboheilthle Micco, Creek chief, 224

Hodgson, William B., 245

Holston, Treaty of with Cherokees, 60, 68, 118

Hopewell on Keowee River, home of General Andrew Pickens, 118; Treaty of with Cherokees, 27, 45, 46, 47, 48, 49, 50, 51, 52, 59, 60, 68; Treaty of with Choctaws, 46, 50, 51, 52; Treaty of with Chickasaws, 46, 50, 51, 52

Hopkins, Mathew, 201

Hopoie Micco, Creek chief, 182, 183, 185

Horseshoe Bend, battle of, 235

Humphreys, David, at Rock Landing, 56, 89, 94

Indians, *passim;* Congress passes ordinance for regulation of, 53; see also Cherokees, Chickasaws, Choctaws, Creeks, and Northwest Indians

Indian Willy, Creek, 134

Innerarity, John, partner of John Forbes, 205

Iredell, James, for ratification in North Carolina, 62, 73

Irwin, Jared, Governor of Georgia, 92, 145, 172, 173

Isaacs, Captain, 223-224

Istehoce, Creek chief, 147

Izard, Ralph, Senator from South Carolina, 72, 75

Jackson, General Andrew, in command Tennessee troops, 231, 233, 235, 236, 237, 238, 239

Jackson County, Georgia, 166

Jackson, James, 44; in Senate, 75, 76, 80; Georgia Commissioner at Coleraine, 86, 87, 89, 90-91, 93, 94, 95, 96; Gov-

ernor of Georgia, 130, 156, 164-165, 167, 170-171, 174, 175-176, 177, 190-191, 193
James, Marquis, quoted, 249
Jay, John, 22, 34, 70, 80
Jefferson, Thomas, President, 22, 25, 29, 34, 52, 61, 64, 70, 79, 138, 139, 140, 141, 142, 143, 146, 152, 162, 165, 166, 176, 186, 207, 208, 243; Secretary of State, 77, 80
Johns, Kensey, Senator from New Jersey, 77
Johnson, Dr. William, Senator from Connecticut, 72
Johnston, Samuel, resigns from Congress, 13; elected U. S. Senator, 64; in Senate, 65, 67, 69, 72, 73, 77

Kean, John, delegate from South Carolina in Congress, 26
Keowee River, 45, 118
Ker, Henry, visits Agency, 151
King, John, Georgia commissioner at Galphinton, 44, 45, 50
King, Rufus, Senator from New York, 72, 75
Knox, Henry, Secretary of War, 22, 57, 58, 59, 60, 68

Land speculations, William Blount involved in, 26, 60; Ohio Company, 69; Yazoo companies, 82, 83, 125; Cox, 125-126
Langdon, John, Senator from New Hampshire, 75
Leach, Colonel Joseph, 10
Lee, Arthur, in Congress, 35
Lee, Henry, 70, 71
Lee, Richard Henry, opposes ratification of the Constitution, 62
Lenoir, William, nominated for the Senate, 64
Limbaugh, Christian, assistant to Hawkins, 205, 214, 224, 232, 242
Lincoln, General Benjamin, at Rock Landing, 56, 89, 94
Little Prince, Creek chief, 192, 236

Little Warrior, Creek chief, 215, 225
Livermore, Samuel, Senator from New Hampshire, 75
Lott, Arthur, 214, 215
Louisville, Georgia, 177

McCall, Major Jesse, 180-181, 182
McGillivray, Alexander, 36, 37, 41, 42, 55, 56, 57, 58, 59, 81, 82, 91, 163, 190, 194, 196
McHenry, James, Secretary of War, 119, 120, 122, 126, 128, 131
McIntosh, Lachlan, 40, 43, 48, 50, 51
McIntosh, William, Creek chief, 187, 212, 223, 233
McKee, John, Cherokee and Choctaw agent, 157, 159
McNeil, James, criticizes commissioners at Coleraine, 94-95
McQueen, Peter, halfbreed Creek chief, 224, 228, 229, 230

Maclay, William, Senator from Pennsylvania, 68, 72
Macon, Gideon, father of Nathaniel, 4
Macon, John, brother of Nathaniel, 4, 5, 6; elected to North Carolina Senate, 64
Macon, Nathaniel, 4, 5, 12; in Congress, 70, 77, 138-139
Mad Dog, Creek chief, 132, 133
Madison, James, 18, 22, 24, 29, 30, 32, 61-62, 63, 64; in Congress, 74, 75, 80; President, 79, 146, 152, 160, 194, 209, 237-238, 242, 243
Martin, Alexander, Governor of North Carolina, 13, 16, 20, 22; in Congress, 23; in Constitutional Convention, 61; in Senate, 65, 75
Martin, Joseph, 37, 39, 41, 45, 48, 50, 51, 53
Martin, Zachariah, father of Delia Hawkins, 1
Mason, General John, superintendent of Indian trade, 206
Mathew and Strother, trading house in Mobile, 195

Mathews, George, Governor of Georgia, 55, 79

Maxant, Colonel, Spanish officer, 133

Meigs, Return J., Cherokee agent, 159, 160

Meredith, Thomas, 215

Meriwether, General David, 181, 182, 184

Methology, Creek chief, 101

Miccosookee, Seminole town, 218

Milledge, John, Governor of Georgia, 169, 172, 180, 183, 185, 187

Milledgeville, Georgia, 188, 213, 232, 245

Minor, Captain, Spanish line commissioner, 133, 134, 135

Mississippi River, navigation on, 30-34; 131, 171, 195, 217

Mississippi Territory, created, 157

Mitchell, David B., Governor of Georgia, 187, 188, 189, 209, 210, 213, 215, 217, 218, 221, 223, 225, 226, 227, 228, 229, 230, 231, 242

Mitchell, Samuel, agent to Choctaws, 157, 158, 160

Mitchell, Stephen, Senator from Connecticut, 75

Mobile, Alabama, 230

Mobile River, 209

Monroe, James, in Senate, 70, 75, 76

Moreau, General, visits Creek Agency, 151

Morris, Robert, Superintendent of Finance, 15; Senator from Pennsylvania, 75

Nash, Abner, Governor of North Carolina, 9, 10, 11, 15, 16, 23

Newman, Colonel, 221

New Orleans, 34, 131, 213, 214

New Yaucau, Creek village, 106-107

New York, Treaty of, 57-60, 81, 82, 83, 89, 91, 98, 177, 182, 196, 206

Nicholls, Colonel, British commander at Apalachicola, 239, 240

North Carolina, passim; protest Jay's Treaty, 34; protests treaties with Indians, 38, 48, 49, 50, 52; violation of treaties by, 53; refuses to ratify Constitution, 63; Federalism in, 63-64; ceded western lands, 67; Republicanism in, 79

Northwest Indians, 35, 36, 41, 70, 223

Northwest Ordinance, 25

Ocmulgee Old Fields, 199, 204

Ocmulgee River, 140, 172, 175, 178, 179, 183, 184, 185, 186

Oconee River, 114, 116, 124, 130, 131, 138, 177, 179, 184

Ohio River, 131

Old Tallassee King, Creek chief, 216

Oliver, Robert, 69

Oneill, Spanish Governor of Florida, 37

Osborne, Henry, at Rock Landing, 56

Paine, Chief of Seminoles, 218

Paine, Thomas, 17

Panton, Leslie & Company, 85, 101, 108, 111, 195, 196, 198, 203, 204

Paris, Treaty of, 1783, 21, 22, 30, 35

Parsons, Samuel, 26

Paxson, Frederick L., quoted, 237

Payne, John Howard, 245

Pensacola, 131, 132, 133, 134, 135, 136, 228, 236, 238

Perry, William, treaty commissioner, 37, 38, 40

Peters, Richard, 35

Petersburg, Virginia, 4

Pettigrew, Charles, 4, 5

Philadelphia, mutiny of soldiers in, 20; Convention in, 27, 28

Pickens, General Andrew, 37, 39, 41, 45, 48, 50, 102, 130, 139, 176, 177, 179, 201; at Coleraine, 83-98, passim; Cherokee boundary commissioner, 118, 119, 120, 121, 122, 126

Pickering, Timothy, Secretary of War, 83, 101; Secretary of State, 157, 158

Pierce, William, Congressman from Georgia, 27

Pinckney, General Thomas, 226, 233, 234, 235, 236, 237

Pleasant Hill, homeplace of Hawkins, 3, 4

Polk, Thomas, elected to Congress, 23

Price, Edward, U. S. factor, 115, 118, 124, 150, 198, 200, 201, 202, 206, 247

Princeton, Hawkins enters college, 5; 6, 20, 21

Prophet, brother of Tecumseh, 213

Putnam, Rufus, 69

Queen of Tookaubatchee, 149

Read, George, Senator from New Jersey, 77

Read, Jacob, in Congress from South Carolina, 19, 22

Red Sticks, hostile Creeks, 223-240

Richardson, James, ferryman on the Clinch River, 129

Roberta, Georgia, 248

Robertson, William, 181

Robinson, Moses, Senator from Vermont, 75

Rock Landing, conference with Creeks, 56

Rogers, John, ferryman on the Clinch River, 127, 128, 129

Russell, Christian, trader among the Cherokees, 104

St. Augustine, threatened by Bowles, 192, 195, 216, 218

St. Eustatius, 7, 8

St. Marks, captured by Bowles, 192; 195, 218

St. Marys, 84, 135

St. Marys River, 134, 135, 218

Sargent, Winthrop, Governor of the Mississippi Territory, 101, 157, 158, 159

Savannah, Hawkins in, 40

Schuyler, Philip, Senator from New York, 72

Scott, Philip, interpreter at Coleraine, 90

Seagrove, James, Creek agent, 82, 84, 85, 93, 95, 96, 100, 101, 201, 202,

Seminole Indians, 131, 132, 191, 192, 194, 212, 213, 215, 216, 217, 218, 221, 239-240

Sevier, John, Governor of Tennessee, 47, 120, 121, 235; line commissioner, 238; dies, 239

Sharpe, William, in Congress from North Carolina, 13

Shoulderbone, Treaty of, 54, 55, 81, 83, 89, 94

Simms, James, Georgia commissioner at Coleraine, 86, 87, 89, 93, 94, 95, 96

Sitgreaves, John, in Congress from North Carolina, 37

Six Pound Creek, 1

Smith, Daniel, secretary to William Blount, 67, 142

Snell, Henry, agent for Panton, Leslie & Co., 204

Spaight, Richard Dobbs, in Congress, 16, 37; in Constitutional Convention, 61; for ratification in North Carolina, 62-64

Spain, negotiations with regarding navigation of the Mississippi River, 30-34

Spanish in Florida, 82, 131, 132, 133, 134, 135, 136, 190, 191, 192, 193, 194, 195, 196, 205, 217, 218, 239-240

Sparks, Captain Richard, 120-121, 122

Sparta, Georgia, 186

Speed, James, 10

Steele, John, in Congress from North Carolina, 70, 71, 78

Stewart, General Daniel, 187, 188

Strong, Caleb, Senator from Massachusetts, 75

Strother, George, commandant at Tellico, 122

Sullivan, James, trader among Cherokees, 106

Sweet Springs, Virginia, 152
Symmes, John Cleve, 70

Tait, David, at battle of Burnt
Corn Creek, 228
Taliaferro, Benjamin, Georgia
judge, quoted, 96-97
Tallapoosa River (Aquonausete),
106, 108, 109, 110, 163, 235
Tallahassee, 200
Tallassee, Creek town, 132, 135
Tallulah River, 103
Tame King, Creek chief, 132,
135
Tassell of Chota, Cherokee chief,
47
Tatnall, Josiah, Governor of
Georgia, 171, 177
Taylor County, Georgia, 140
Taylor, John, of Caroline Coun-
ty, Virginia, 74, 75
Tecumseh, Shawnee chief, 211-
213, 215, 223, 225
Telfair, Edward, Governor of
Georgia, 44, 45, 50
Tellico Blockhouse, 117, 118,
119, 122, 123, 124, 125, 128,
198
Tennessee, admitted as state,
99; displeased with Cherokee
line, 118-123, 171, 218; sends
volunteers against Creeks, 221,
222, 228, 231, 233, 234; citi-
zens critical of Hawkins, 234-
235
Tennessee River, 209
Tensaw River, 230
Territory south of the River
Ohio, 60, 67
Thomas, Richard, clerk in Indian
department, 100
Tombigbee River, 171, 209, 230
Tookaubatchee, council town of
the Creeks, 107, 109, 136,
138, 163, 181, 182, 194, 210,
211, 212, 214, 224, 225, 226,
227, 228, 231
Trist, Mrs. Eliza, 154
Troup, George M., Governor of
Georgia, 245
Tugalo River, 131
Tuskegee Tustunnugee, Creek
chief, jailed in Oglethorpe

County, 166-167; 172, 173,
215, 218
Tuskeenehau, Creek chief, 225
Tuskena Patki (White Lieuten-
ant), Creek chief, 107
Tussekiah Micco, Creek chief,
206
Tustunnugee Haujo, Creek chief,
136
Tustunnugee Hopoie, Creek
chief, 172
Tustunnugee Thlucco, Creek
chief, 224
Twiggs, John, 43, 44, 45

Upaulike, Creek Indian, 147-148
Uchee Indians, at battle of Camp
Defiance, 234

Vining, John, Senator from Delaware, 75

Wagstaff, H. M., quoted, 138-
139
Ward, John, interpreter, 232
Warrenton, home of the Hawkins
family, 1, 2, 3
War-Woman of Chota, Cherokee
chief, 47
Washington, D. C., treaty with
Creeks, 187, 206
Washington, George, President,
29, 30, 57, 58, 59, 60, 62, 65,
66, 67, 71, 79, 82, 97, 99-100,
143, 160-161, 197, 243
Watson, Elkanah, quoted, 2, 3-4
Weatherford, Charles, brother-
in-law of McGillivray, 110
Western lands, North Carolina's
cession of, 30-31, 60; Geor-
gia's, 83, 125
White Chief, Creek chief, 113
White, James, in Congress, 23,
48-49; superintendent of Indians, 53, 55
White, Nicholas, trader among
the Creeks, 111
White Lieutenant, Creek chief,
107
Wilkinson, General James, 176,
177, 178, 180, 201, 230
Willaubee Haujo, Creek, 215

Willett, Colonel Marinus, at Rock Landing, 57, 58

Williamson, Hugh, in Congress, 13, 15, 16, 18, 19, 20, 22, 29, 33, 67, 72; in Constitutional Convention, 61; for ratification in North Carolina, 62

Wilson, James, in Congress from Pennsylvania, 19

Winchester, James, on Cherokee boundary commission, 118, 119, 120

Winn, Richard, 55

Wissoetaw, Indian parched corn meal, 106

Witherspoon, Dr. James, President of Princeton, 5, 6

Woodward, General Thomas S., quoted, 242-243

Yates, Robert, in Congress from New York, 25

Yazoo fraud, 83, 125

Young, Henry, 10

Zespedes, Don Vincent Emanuel de, Governor of East Florida. 39